A Very Queer Family Indeed

A VERY Queer FAMILY *Indeed*

SEX, RELIGION,

and

THE BENSONS

in

VICTORIAN BRITAIN

Simon Goldhill

The University of Chicago Press

Chicago and London

The University of Chicago Press, Chicago 60637
The University of Chicago Press, Ltd., London
© 2016 by The University of Chicago
All rights reserved. Published 2016.
Printed in the United States of America

25 24 23 22 21 20 19 18 17 16   1 2 3 4 5

ISBN-13: 978-0-226-39378-0 (cloth)
ISBN-13: 978-0-226-39381-0 (e-book)
DOI: 10.7208/chicago/9780226393810.001.0001

Library of Congress Cataloging-in-Publication Data

Names: Goldhill, Simon, author.
Title: A very queer family indeed: sex, religion, and the Bensons in
    Victorian Britain / Simon Goldhill.
Description: Chicago; London: The University of Chicago Press,
    2016 | Includes bibliographical references.
Identifiers: LCCN: 2016007240 | ISBN 9780226393780 (cloth: alk.
    paper) | ISBN 9780226393810 (e-book)
Subjects: LCSH: Benson family. | Benson, Edward White,
1829–1896. | Benson, Mary, 1842–1918. | Benson, Arthur Christopher,
1862–1925. | England—Intellectual life—19th century. | Homo-
    sexuality—England. | England—Biography.
Classification: LCC DA562 .G65 2016 | DDC 929.20942—dc23
LC record available at http://lccn.loc.gov/2016007240

Contents

PART

I

THE
FAMILY
THAT
WROTE
ITSELF

1

Sensation!

WE CAN BEGIN WITH A KISS, THOUGH THIS WILL NOT TURN out to be a love story, at least not a love story of anything like the usual kind.

One afternoon in 1853 in Cambridge, an intense, evangelical twenty-three-year-old student sat on the sofa with a plumpish, earnest twelve-year-old girl on his knee, as he had so often that year, and now carefully proposed marriage. She burst into tears, but, as he wrote later with un-self-aware pride, she said nothing girly or foolish. Instead, she tied the ends of his handkerchief together in a knot and gave it to him. He kissed her, and, to the unabating anxiety of her widowed mother, the engagement was official.

Six years later, as soon as she was eighteen, after a courtship that was as much a schooling as an affair, they married. He went on to become the Archbishop of Canterbury at the height of Victoria's reign. She went on to discover that her passion was directed toward women. She spent months in Germany, leaving her baby and five other children, in desperate longing for a Miss Hall. After the archbishop's early death, she spent her last twenty years sleeping in the same bed with the daughter of the previous Archbishop of Canterbury. This is not a trendy Bloomsbury Group story, where such affairs might be passed off in the name of love and art, but a tale from the heart of the British establishment. She was comforted after the archbishop's death by Queen Victoria herself, who knew a thing or two about public bereavement.

The archbishop and his wife had six children, none of whom ever had heterosexual intercourse, as far as we can tell; certainly none of them ever married.

The oldest boy, Martin, died as an adolescent from "brain disease" at school, almost certainly meningitis; Nellie, one of the sisters, died not long after, picking up an infection while working among the poor. Arthur, tall, luxuriantly mustachioed, taught at Eton, edited Queen Victoria's letters from Windsor Castle, became a celebrated writer and eventually Master of Magdalene College at Cambridge, holding the position till his death, despite long periods in hospital for severe, crippling depression. His writings, including a huge diary, offer a rich portrait of the male world of Victorian and Edwardian Cambridge college life—and he wrote the words for Edward Elgar's nationalist hymn, "Land of Hope and Glory." Fred—fair and slight, who loved ice-skating, golf, and a high social life—became a celebrated novelist, famous for writing flippant society fiction, which finally was made into a successful retro-chic comedy series, *Mapp and Lucia*, in the 1980s by Channel 4 in Britain, with a remake screened by the BBC in 2015. He ended up living with his collie dog and butler in Rye in Kent, a pillar of the bourgeois society he lampooned, in a house once owned by his and Arthur's good friend Henry James, more serious anatomist of bourgeois society. Maggie, educated at Oxford, was the first published female Egyptologist; she found a passionate relationship with the quiet and persistent Nettie Gourlay. When Maggie, the archbishop's daughter, and Nettie lived with Maggie's mother and *her* companion, the previous archbishop's daughter, there were stormy rows and an atmosphere the boys found it hard to come back home to. There are not many such households—then or now—of a mother and daughter, both with an intimate female friend, all living together. Maggie, however, also had a severe mental breakdown and was hospitalized for some years before her death in early middle age: one of the symptoms of her mental disease was a violent, suspicious hatred of her mother. Hugh, the baby of the family, found his own route to rebellion, by becoming—shockingly for the son of the archbishop—a Roman

Catholic priest. He also became a widely successful novelist and distinguished preacher, before his early death from heart disease. He specified that his veins should be opened after his death, like a stake through the heart, because he was terrified of being buried alive.

This, then, was the Benson family: Archbishop Edward White Benson, his girl bride, Minnie Sidgwick, and their renowned children. It could make for a sensational story.

CERTAINLY THE NARRATIVE PIECES ARE ALL IN PLACE FOR a sensational picture of Victorian family life. The archbishop was, as a young man, flamboyantly handsome. His father, a somewhat feckless inventor, had died young, leaving the family impoverished. Edward, with a fierce sense of duty, struggled to succeed against his poverty and to make his way to Cambridge, with the help of his scattered relatives; but his mother died while he was still a student, leaving the immediate family penniless. He was sufficiently pious, sufficiently stubborn, and sufficiently authoritative not to allow his young brother and sister to be brought up by a wealthy uncle, because of strongly held religious scruples—the uncle was a Unitarian, unacceptable to the Anglican Edward. Consequently, he arranged for his two siblings to live with his cousin, Mary Sidgwick, who, in the way of such narratives, would turn out to be his future mother-in-law. He made it through Cambridge (and beyond) thanks to the help of a Mr. Martin, the bursar of Trinity College, an elderly fellow, rich, evangelical, unmarried, who in best Dickensian tradition offered the handsome young man all the financial and moral support he needed and "treated him with a half lover-like, half paternal adoration." They read together, and Mr. Martin stroked Edward's hair. Edward's firstborn was duly called Martin. Edward won a fellowship at Trinity, became a schoolmaster, rising to be the first, pioneering headmaster of Prince Albert's new school, Wellington College, where he first lived with his new wife, who was the same age as his sixth-formers. He ruled the school and his family in the manner of Thomas Arnold: terrifying, religious, strict, violent, fair . . . From Wellington, like so many schoolmasters, he turned to the church, and from his first position at Lincoln, became the founding Bishop of Truro, a new see and the first new cathedral in England since the Middle Ages. From Truro to Lambeth Palace and the leadership of the Anglican communion, all with the same spirit of hard work and total commitment to a mission: "I mean to rule," he declared privately on his appointment—"a supreme piece of self-revelation," as his son sardonically commented. . . . This is a classic Victorian success story: a passionately driven man, charismatic, full of energy and ambition and desire to make the world a better place, working up from misfortune through the great institutions of university, the public schools, and the church, rising to a position at the heart of the empire's power. He died from a heart attack while praying in Prime Minister Gladstone's private chapel. His portrait, symbolically enough, is set next to Queen Victoria's in the stained glass at Canterbury Cathedral.

Yet Benson was tormented by depression, the "black dog" that haunted the family's whole life. He was, in the manner of a Victorian patriarch, fearsome, angry, and constantly critical of his children—in a way that his fits of depression exacerbated. He needed to educate, to direct, to correct. As an undergraduate, when a black student, one Crummel of Queen's College, was graduating, someone in the gallery tauntingly yelled out, "Three groans for the Queen's Nigger"; Benson, then a pale undergraduate, immediately shouted back, "Shame! Shame! Three groans for you sir!" and led the whole audience in an impromptu three cheers for Mr. Crummel, to the total humiliation of the racist bully. Yet he constantly bullied his own children about not wasting time, about being serious, about doing their duty, as he chastised his wife for smoking, for not keeping proper household accounts, not reading the right books. Desperate for affection, he had no idea how it might be fostered. His children remembered long walks, when he would read aloud to them improving books, awkward and anxious mealtimes, judgments of morbid solemnity, and how in comparison to their father's little head shake of disapproval, "no gesture in the world has ever seemed so formidable." Typically, when he and Minnie had not conceived a child in the first year of marriage, he wondered to her what sin they might have committed to be barred from the joy of parenthood. It would be easy to tell Edward White Benson's story as a deeply upsetting tension between remarkable public success and constant private torments and familial psychological violence.

Minnie Sidgwick's story, too, seems destined for an overexcited narrative arc. Wooed from the age of eleven, married at eighteen, her diaries reveal a brittle desperation to appear happy through making her husband happy. Her brothers became educational and intellectual luminaries, and the Cambridge University humanities campus, the Sidgwick Site, is named for her brother Henry Sidgwick, the great moral philosopher. As the wife first of a headmaster and then a bishop, and finally of an archbishop, she was required to be a hostess in an equivalently glittering milieu. William Gladstone wondered if she was the cleverest woman in England or in Europe, a pleasantry that has been taken far too seriously by her admirers—her education was spotty at best. But she was renowned for the fascination and attractiveness of her conversation, not as a wit firing off glittering *bon mots*, but as an attentive, engagingly personal fabricator of a tent of intimacy through talk.

Yet her private anxieties, too, were in stark contrast with her public life. She fell in love with women and indulged her passion, leaving her young family for months and months. She whiled away long hours with her female friends—"we spent the month in the most complete fusing," she wrote of her time with Emily Edwardes. "She did not often walk with us or play with us," remembered Arthur, with characteristic melancholy: "The truth is she had a life of her own, apart from my father's life, apart from ours"—an idea that goes against all the expected stereotyping of a Victorian wife and mother. At some point in her mid-thirties, however, she also became deeply religious—not with the fierce evangelical and institutional commitment of her husband, but with an intense, personal faith. It allowed her to treat the death of her oldest child with an equanimity her husband could not match. Martin had truly and simply, for her, gone to heaven, and she quietly rejoiced at the journey, while Edward, the bishop, was crushed with "a nightmare of grief and dismay." Her religion never left her, even and especially after Edward's death, even as four of her children died before her. "Her married life, though she would not have purchased her freedom at any price, had been a constant and urgent strain," throughout which she struggled with the physicality of her desire, the powerful feelings of her intimate relations with women, and the spirituality and restraint her Christianity demanded. Love, she knew, was a gift from God, but the extreme pleasures and pains—along with insistent carnal longings—were hard for her to regulate within her powerful Christian conviction, a turmoil her children barely recognized as she lived out her life quietly, sharing her bed with Lucy Tait, as a Victorian matriarch, in a grand house, supported financially by her successful sons. So Minnie Sidgwick's life is twisted between selfishness and duty—between duty to others and care for herself—and between religious propriety and fleshly feelings, doubly tormenting, doubly transgressive, both as desire itself and as desire for women, not her husband. Could she have a life apart? And at what cost? There is a psychodrama waiting to be written—of the Christian lover of women, trapped in a psychologically violent marriage at the center of the empire's church and state apparatus, struggling with her conflicting and all but overwhelming feelings.

All six children disappointed their father. Martin, the eldest, was a paragon: brilliant at school, quiet, pious—his father's dream. He stuttered, which may reflect the strain of such perfection under such parents. His death at age seventeen tore a hole in his father that never healed. Nellie tried to be the perfect daughter—working with the poor, caring for her parents, gentle, but always willing to go for a hard gallop with her father for morning exercise. Her death at a young age, unmarried, was for the whole family an afterthought to the awfulness of Martin's loss. Arthur, Fred, and Hugh all found the Anglican religion of their father impossible. Arthur went to church, appreciated the music, the ceremony and its role in social order, but struggled with belief, even when he called out to God in the despair of his blackest depression. Fred was flippant and disengaged, and his first novel, *Dodo*, the hit of the season in 1893, outraged his father's sense of seriousness. Fred represented Britain at figure skating—a hobby that was as far as he could get from his father's ideals of social and religious commitment, the epitome of a "waste of time." Hugh's turn to the Roman Catholic Church was after his father's death— but like all the children, the fight with paternal authority never ceased. While his father was alive, Hugh muffed exams, wanted to go into the Indian Civil Service against his father's wishes— he failed those exams too—and argued with everyone in the family petulantly. Maggie, too, was "difficult": "her friendships were seldom leisurely or refreshing things," commented Arthur; Nellie, more acerbic, added, "If Maggie would only have an intimate relationship even with a *cat*, it would be a relief." Her Oxford tutors found her "remorseless." At age twenty-five, still single, she did not know the facts of life. Over the years, her jealousy of her mother's companion Lucy Tait became more and more pronounced, as did her adoption of her father's expressions of strict disapproval. Her depressions turned to madness and violence, leading to her eventual hospitalization.

There is another dramatic narrative, then, of the six children, all differently and profoundly scarred by their home life, which they wrote about and thought about repeatedly. Cross-currents of competition between the children, marked by a desperate need for intimacy, in tension with a restraint born of fear of violent emotion and a profound distrust (at best) of sexual feeling, produced a fervid and damaging family dynamic. There is a story here of what it is like to grow up with a hugely successful, domineering, morally certain father, a mother who embodied the joys of intimacy but with other women—and of what the costs of public success from such a complex background are.

This looks like a family ripe for sensational biographical exploration. The interwoven tapestry of life histories, rich with sexual innuendo, madness, creativity, and power, together with the backdrop of beautiful houses, famous friends, and the corridors of imperial and ecclesiastical authority, make for a heady and worryingly voyeuristic brew. Add an unparalleled richness of sources—diaries, letters, reminiscences, biographies, novels, essays—and it will come as no surprise that indeed Minnie Sidgwick has found a small but significant place in modern studies of lesbian life and been treated to a recent, somewhat luridly told biography. Arthur Benson, too, has his modern biography, based on his voluminous diaries, which, in the modern way, dwells at length on his troubled sexuality. There are also less insightful and rather dully hagiographic versions of E. F. Benson, born out of a love for his comic novels and their untroubled world; and even the occasional attempt to tell the history of the whole family, though without the necessary research in the family papers or understanding of the Victorian cultural context. The movie or TV series would be a blockbuster.

BUT THIS BOOK WILL NOT BE A BIOGRAPHY, NOR EVEN A family history, even though it started with a kiss and will traverse in detail some extraordinary scenes of a family that does offer a remarkable window on to Victorian and Edwardian society.

This book is not a biography partly because, like Adam Philips—who ventriloquizes Freud while writing a Freudian biography of Freud—I find biography a ludicrous genre. There are, for sure, more and less sophisticated biographies, and there will be plenty of biographical moments in this book, but the attempt to summon up a life in neatly chronological prose is bound to be an expression of its own failure. From what perspective is such a life to be constructed? From the self-deceptions of autobiography? From a fantasy of the omniscient narrator, from the dutiful child looking upwards and backwards to a parent, from a competitive or loving brother, a partner, locked in a self-defining embrace? What events, what feelings, what external or internal dynamics are to make up a life story? No life can be lived without narrating itself, but how can a biographical narrative not distort, change, or restructure the experiences of the passage of time, hourly, monthly, yearly?

Such questions are insistent and inescapable with the Benson family in particular. Edward White Benson, Minnie Benson, and

Arthur Benson all wrote diaries. The children read their parents'
diaries after their deaths (and much material, called "too sacred"—
that is, tellingly intimate and potentially scandalous for public
eyes—was destroyed by Fred); the siblings, and others, read parts of
Arthur's diary while he was alive, and published admiring comments
on the privately circulated diary. Arthur wrote the official biography
of his father; the life and letters of Maggie; a biography of Hugh; an
autobiography or two; and a memoir of his mother, left unfinished
at his death. Fred wrote a biography of his mother and three volumes of autobiographical reminiscences, and left two hundred pages
of notes for an unfinished biography of his father, to supplement
Arthur's official account. Edward White Benson wrote a memoir of
his daughter Nellie after she died, in which, to her brother Arthur at
least, she was "wholly unrecognisable." Arthur wrote essays and fiction, which dramatized the life of a Cambridge don and author, and
thus produced a vivid public persona of a secluded writer; he also
wrote essayistic reminiscences of himself and his friends, a different carapace; an account, too, of his depression. Fred wrote novels,
which appear to stage scenes of his parents' and his own relationship, more bitterly than his witty and sunny memoirs. Hugh also
wrote an autobiography—only one, but he died young. Hugh read
aloud all his books, as he wrote them, to his mother, who criticized
them, a practice wickedly fictionalized in a novel by Fred. They all
worried in print and in private about how memory distorted the
past and how after death hagiography set in, as a corruption of intimate and complex recollection. They all struggled with unforgivable
hatred and regret, which they performed and masked across the different genres of literary production. The family published over 200
books. This extraordinary public output of self-representation and
family stories is fenced by the circulation of letters between them
all and corrective marginalia added to the drafts of their biographical narratives. Arthur left 180 volumes of handwritten diary; there
are thousands of official papers, letters, journals, notes that remain
unpublished. This is *a family that wrote itself.*

These fragmentary portrayals, conflicting voices, multiple perspectives, concealed and paraded portraits—all veined by the recognition of how a person can fall into "a sudden mistrust as to the stability of her own character"—should make any would-be biographer extremely cautious of any single, consistent narrative. The threat in drawing any character, wrote Fred, is always that "the bright, clever, superficial self" takes over, and "it turns out something quite neat and readable, but machine-made and unreal." The dynamics of intricate family life, coupled with the multiple and shifting perspectives of (self-)representation, create a mass of variables rather than a position from which to take a view. The self-distortion of depression and madness is a repeated, damaging vector in the rewriting of the family's personal life. For the Benson family, there is a constant redrafting of the self, in conversation, in narrative, in writing—and in the eyes—the writing—of each other. This is a family that repeatedly and continually (re)wrote itself.

This book, then, is not a biography but will be about how this family of graphomaniacs constantly used their writing to tell and retell the stories of their lives, to themselves, to one another, and to a broader public. The era of their lives covers a sudden and whole-scale change in the circulation and dissemination of the written word. The postal service, along with the telegraph system, guaranteed rapid and multiple written exchanges across the country (and from abroad) in a way that transformed the networks of knowledge and family ties: hours a day were spent by them all on their correspondence; the standard Victorian biography is a "Life and Letters"—or a life in letters: Arthur complained that he wrote over 3,000 letters a year. The cheapness of paper, and the railway's ability to transport it swiftly, altered the number, type, and the reach of publications, with journals, periodicals, and serial novels, as well as newspapers, becoming hugely influential. The education system extended the reading classes greatly, and the public libraries also increased the availability and reach of novels and other forms of prose. This was a new era of writing and reading, and the scope and scale of the written production of the Benson family reflects this change. They have left a record of type and volume that would be unthinkable for any previous century and is unlikely to be paralleled in the equally revolutionary world of digital networking. One question, then, that this book asks is: How do the technologies of writing that are so pervasive in the Bensons' experience play a role in the family dynamics through which their lives are lived? How do their writings and their lives mutually inform and structure each other? How does writing play a role in self-formation?

Sex, of course, sells books, and the Benson family history comes replete with its particular mix of thwarted desires, transgressive longings, and a marriage where the combination of misplaced passions, psychological violence, and public propriety seems to confirm Tolstoy's declaration that every unhappy family is unhappy in its own way. But much as the technologies of writing are changing in this era, so, too, are the lineaments—the technologies—of sexuality. Although I recognized Minnie Sidgwick's current place in lesbian history, lesbianism was not a vocabulary open to her, any more than homosexuality was to her sons, all of whom could be reclaimed for gay historiography. Pathologizing and medicalizing same-sex desire was a process *taking place* in the late nineteenth and early twentieth century. Arthur Benson was given a lecture by his father, the headmaster, before he went to Eton, "to set me on my guard against impure temptation." But he "spoke so guardedly that I had not the least idea what he was alluding to, having passed through my private school in complete and virginal innocence." Arthur grew up in his time at school, as a pupil and as a teacher; he wrote publicly—with supreme guardedness—about the most scandalous case of Charles Vaughan, the headmaster of Harrow who was compromised by his letters to a boy. He describes in his diary a range of male desire for undergraduates, choirboys, teachers. But he does not use the word "homosexual" until the last year of his life, 1925, more than thirty years after Richard Krafft-Ebing or Henry Havelock Ellis began to make the term familiar, and then only twice in his diary. None of the other members of the family used such terminology at all, even when discussing Oscar Wilde, their own remembered desires, their mother, their relationships or fears.

Arthur Benson—or rather his persona—was mocked by *Punch* for his continually passive, bourgeois, comfortable inability to engage with the grittiness of things: their brilliantly funny title for his next book was *At a Safe Distance*. Fred Benson's novels, especially as he grew older, seemed to embody, like P. G. Wodehouse's fictions of Bertie Wooster, an imaginary comic world that prided itself on its lack of engagement with any politics of consequence. His schoolboy and undergraduate stories were lapped up by soldiers in the First World War precisely as an escapist flight to a sunnier and gentler place. Hugh Benson's fictions were transparently Roman Catholic apologetics and promoted the most conservative values of religious marriage: marrying outside the faith guarantees a character's demise. Nonetheless, despite such postures of disengagement, it is easy to be surprised today both by the forms of explicitness and the forms of reticence with which male desire for men appears in their writing. The category of homosexuality was emerging out of medicine, the new sciences of sexology and psychiatry; and male desire for males was the cause of highly publicized trials, changes in the law, and, inevitably, of much discussion within the public school system and universities, then all-male societies. Within this changing climate, Arthur was reading John Addington Symonds's privately circulated and explicit autobiography, alongside the much more restrained and much-loved memoir of William Cory—and forming intense, chaste, erotic friendships with undergraduates at Cambridge; Fred was writing how a man might love a man, or imagining youths swimming naked together and promising to go to Greece—and he himself holidayed often on Capri, chosen destination of a group of actively gay upper-class Englishmen; Hugh had a close and passionate relationship for two years with Frederick Rolfe, "Baron Corvo," whose sexual interest in male adolescents was a scandalous open secret. So, while there is not much sex, it must be confessed, to be found in the pages that follow, there is a fascinating story of how what we would call homosexual desire is formulated, discussed, regulated, and explored across the time of the invention of the language, pathology, and medical morality of homosexuality as a category. Through the reticence demanded by religion, law, and personal propriety, a language of sexuality was being formed, whose consequences we are still living with, and whose differences can still shock us into the self-recognition of our own cultural specificity.

So between Edward's pure, evangelical love for an eleven-year-old girl; Minnie's marriage, with its repeated dramas of passion and "fusing" with other women, while living stressfully with her own daughter and her companion; and the intricate narratives of repressed desire lived out by the teacher Arthur, the man about town Fred, and the Catholic priest Hugh—we have not merely a very queer family indeed, but also a family whose sexual history takes place in and through the invention of modern sexuality. Yet this is not the self-consciously shocking, modernizing, self-dramatizing life of a Carpenter, a Whitman, or a Strachey: it takes place at Eton, Windsor Castle, in the church—in the middle of a community bound by and to respectability. How this particular family lets us see the discourse of modern sexuality taking shape is the second big question of this book.

Edward White Benson may stand as an icon of the importance of religion to the public life of Britain in the nineteenth century. His easy move between university, school-teaching, the church, and a platform in politics articulates the institutional structures that support the establishment as a coherent system of power—much as the often bitter arguments about the relation between church and state—disestablishment or the emancipation of Jews and Catholics, or Erastianism—expose the potent tensions within such a system. Huge amounts of money from the state and from private benefaction transformed the landscape of religion in these years: fully 70 percent of English churches were rebuilt in the nineteenth century, and many new churches founded, including Benson's cathedral at Truro. Religious groups outside the Anglican Church and divisions within it competed for allegiance and struggled over doctrine—and Benson prided himself on his success at working with the Methodist majority at Truro. Missionary and Bible societies marched with the imperial expansion of British interests, and, in the inner cities of increasingly industrialized Britain, young Christians worked to alleviate the political, moral, and social consequences of poverty (as Nellie Benson did, at the cost of her life), while Christian Socialists campaigned for change (Charles Kingsley, icon of Christian Socialism, was a close friend of Edward White Benson). Benson was passionate about his religion from his earliest upbringing, as were his friends from early days such as Joseph Lightfoot, Brooke Foss Westcott, or Christopher Wordsworth, bishops all; and their shared sense that a relationship with God was fundamental to a notion of the self was formed by the evangelical movement of the early part of the century, and tested personally and theologically by the great series of religious debates that ran through the century. After the Oxford Movement's convulsions and John Henry Newman's conversion (and Benson as archbishop was later crucial in developing the church's position on ritualism), the Gorham Trial, the Colenso Case, the *Essays and Reviews* scandal, all helped set religious conflict front and center of public debate, with especial fervor through the middle decades of the century from 1840 to 1880. For young men and women, religion was the topic that fueled idealism, dissent, rebellion, and social conscience. Sermons could cause riots on the street; great preachers became public celebrities; writers of critical biblical history, religious novels, religious poetry became the arbiters of inner life, guides to the soul's journey, and were lionized or despised with equal fury. Edward White Benson became a public figure of major significance and recognized charisma, and no doubt his children's success fed off his celebrity.

Yet by 1940, when Fred Benson died of cancer in a London hospital, British society may well have seemed to be on a journey elsewhere. Although the commonplace narrative of scientific discovery, headed by Darwin and leading to an increasingly dominant secularization, is a self-serving and misleading oversimplification of a yet-unfinished history, nonetheless the public role both of the church as an institution and of religion in the cultural imagination undoubtedly weakened between 1850 and 2000, especially after the Second World War. As the celebrated judge Lord Denning declared ringingly in 1949, "It was thought that a denial of Christianity was liable to shake the fabric of society, which was itself founded upon Christian religion. There is no such danger to society now." To look back from 1949 to 1849 was to see a gulf of change in the relation between religion and society.

The children of Edward White Benson and Minnie Sidgwick offer a particular and evocative perspective on this historical process. The religious attitudes of both mother and father produced a certain confusion and distance in the boys at least—and between the boys. So, although he found his own faith precarious and struggled with his notions of social form and religious truth constantly, Arthur also thought Fred's rejection of religion simply ignorant and silly. Yet he also was deeply uncomfortable with Hugh's Catholicism, partly because he never really stopped thinking of Hugh as petulant and inconstant. Both Arthur and Fred saw the comfort their mother took in religion at the time of Martin's death and found it incomprehensible and disturbing; all three sons were alienated from their father's assured belief by his behavior. Arthur and Hugh both greatly enjoyed ritual, though neither seem to have struggled with ritualism as an idea, as their father had. Hugh made it the mainstay of his religion and had a little prayer room with an altar consecrated in the family house, licensed to take Catholic Mass (bringing home his conversion, in all senses). The servants grumbled about the painted plaster statue of the Virgin and the ringing of bells as he celebrated Mass in the morning. Arthur, for his part, participated lovingly in the grandest of state occasions at Westminster Abbey and writes lengthily about it. Typically, the heroes of Hugh's novels fight bravely for the Catholic Church; Arthur's heroes stare out of the window and worry about their inner lives.

For Mrs. Humphry Ward in her best-selling novel *Robert Elsmere*, her eponymous hero, a clergyman, loses his faith painfully though contact with critical history and its exposure of the dubious status of the texts of the early church; for James Anthony Froude in his scandalous book *The Nemesis of Faith*—burned before the students in Oxford—it is sexual opportunity that leads to his hero's corruption; for Samuel Butler in *The Way of All Flesh*, too polemical to publish during his own lifetime, religious doubt is tied up with the hero's growing hatred of his parents. The loss-of-faith genre was big business in Victorian Britain. But Arthur, Fred, and Hugh Benson had more complex and layered responses to the religious experiences they grew up with. On the one hand, family dynamics constantly framed inner feelings of any sort. On the other hand, religion was not easily separable from other political and social networks. Anglicanism was a national religion in a time of intense nationalism; a historical sense of the present as a unique era, defined by its loss of the past, was typical of Victorian historical self-consciousness and closely embroiled with an investment in religion as a tradition and a sign of continuity of culture. For Arthur, institutional norms of school and college were dutiful expectations; for Hugh, the celebrity of his conversion was itself a thrilling endorsement; Fred seems to have maintained a certain insouciance toward religious practice and belief, which threatened to border on contempt. The third question with which this book is concerned, then, is how the Benson family may help us see a culture's shifting religious engagements, over the fundamental period from 1840 to 1940.

So this will not be a family biography because it is focused not on telling the sensational story of the Bensons' family life, but rather on the interrelated questions of how the culture of writing, the discourse of sexuality, and the public and private space of religion developed from the time of Edward White Benson in his pomp through his children's lives, and how the dynamics of this very particular family enable us to see such transitions from the high Victorian period into modernity. To construct such a story—for we have never been modern, as Bruno Latour announces—is also about how contemporary self-definition conceptualizes its distance and difference from the nineteenth century, and what its inheritance might be. There is a necessary self-interest in such a narrative of change (as if the self-interest in stories of sexuality, religion, and writing were not enough). The archbishop and his three sons were all famous and celebrated in their day, and why the family has in general slipped out of public consciousness as figures of the past and why they can again become figures that are good to think with are questions that go to the heart of why history matters for the present. It cannot be by chance that it seems good now to remember and worry about the thoroughly respectable and pious man who fell in love with an eleven-year-old girl; the loving mother who left her family in pursuit of another woman and came back to her authoritarian clergyman husband; the teacher who was erotically involved with his students; the Catholic priest terrified of being buried alive; the daughter whose madness was hating her mother. . . .

This story of nineteenth-century transgressive family desires— interlocked with religion, a father's authority, and the dense interplays of revelation and concealment in the language of self-description— cannot avoid evoking Freud (and why should it want to?). Between the sons' compulsion to write and to keep rewriting the lives of the family (Arthur did not start his massive daily diary until the death of his father) and the desire for intimacy repeated throughout their writing stands the lure of knowing—knowing oneself as much as another person, a lure that hovers at the heart of the Freudian project. Freud liked to see himself as an archaeologist, digging down into the sediment and stratigraphy of the self. But he also had to tell stories about people and their lives, for all his rejection of the genre of biography. So, as I follow the tracks of my three questions—the technologies of writing, the discourse of sexuality, the challenge of religion—perhaps the best way to categorize what follows is, in best Freudian sense, as *case histories*. Fragments hewn from the ludicrous promise of biography. To show again why escaping the past is a never-ending project.

2

Wooing Mother

SO LET US GO BACK TO THE KISS.

In 1930, when his parents and brothers and sisters were all dead, E. F. (Fred) Benson wrote *As We Were: A Victorian Peep Show*, the second of his three volumes of autobiographical reminiscences. The book is ringed by a nostalgic longing for "the old order of secure prosperity," which "England will know . . . no more," an evocative sense of loss; but it also revels with an amused wonderment in the "real gulf, vastly sundering," that "lies between the two eras" of present habit and Victorian proprieties. For Fred Benson, although he is writing at the start of the Great Depression and finishes his narrative with the assassination of Archduke Ferdinand in 1914 as the incendiary start of the destruction of the world he lovingly reconstructs, the really big difference between the 1870s and the 1930s lies not in the superficial changes of transport, dress, or literary fashion—let alone the seismic political shifts of the interwar period—but in the openness of discourse practiced by contemporary society in comparison with the norms of his youth: "Men and women now discuss together everything that they could only have spoken of before with the members of their own sex." He is less sure what to think about such "frankness and freedom." It is good to sweep away "the cobwebs of Victorian conventionalism" that kept women ignorant, but he also suggests that "these Victorian reticences and secrecies may also have been profitable as well as prudish." He reverts again and again to the "smiling oasis of public respectability," the "outward form of dignity and politeness," "the true spirit of Victorian reticence and unconsciousness of anything disagreeable"—this last on the producer who covered over the name of Oscar Wilde on posters advertising *The Importance of Being Earnest*, so that polite company could attend the play without thinking of the recently convicted author. Reticence is an ironically highlighted theme of these reminiscences, as the book's subtitle suggests. It is a peep show, promising through its small opening a larger and titillating view, destined, however, all too often to disappoint the prurient.

Fred Benson's proclamation of the strategies of reticence provides a necessary introduction to the decorous account he offers of his mother's wooing. He had already told the story in brief summary in the biography *Mother*, five years earlier, where, he claims, *her* version "reads like some extraordinary and imaginary romance of a child." But, he assures us, "it was the actual story of her life, which she recorded, the faithful prelude to the forty years which followed." He tells it just as a romance. Enter the hero: "There was he, twenty-three years old, masterful and convincing and convinced, writing his first love-poem to his cousin of eleven, sure in his own soul that Minnie was to be his wife as soon as she was old enough, and carrying that conviction through both to her mother and to her." There are the obstacles to his love, surmounted. Mary Sidgwick's demand that he stop courting her daughter, still so young, "seemed to have been a very ineffectual bar to his ardency," because there was "soon another interview when he held her hand and kissed her, and embarked again on the forbidden topic." Minnie, notes her son, blamed herself for the transgression, and, he concludes, it is "delightful to linger over this picture of herself, these compromising confessions." The calm with which Fred Benson imagines—lingers over—the passion of a man, his father, for a girl of only eleven, and the insouciance with which he notes the ignoring of her mother's ban, and the child's misplaced guilty sense of complicity for the transgressive kiss, open a "real gulf, vastly sundering" between *his* now-dated story of a lost past and *our* contemporary Western expectations. It would be all too easy for us to recast this story as an archetypal case of nasty familial child abuse, not least in the poignant detail that the child thought it was her fault. It is hard to read this story without a certain bewildered disgust.

Five years later, in *As We Were*, Fred Benson tells the story again, now primarily through his father's eyes—relying on his diary. His father is "an earnest, young Victorian wooer"—and each of these adjectives sets a tone of misty-eyed retrospective. There is nothing flippant or casual about Edward White Benson, even as the son undertakes the telling psychological process of imagining his own father as a young man ("earnest," we should remember, had already had its treatment by Oscar Wilde, and could never again be a simply positive term, except in a remembered past); but he is Victorian—not a man of instantly comprehensible contemporary style. Each adjective, differently, frames the portrait at a certain distance. Fred tells the story through four long extracts from his father's journals, the wooer's own words, carefully selected. In the first, Edward reflects that because "I have always been very fond of her and she of me with the love of a little sister," and because he is unlikely to marry soon because of "the circumstances of my family," and because he has, he recognizes, a worrying "weakness for falling suddenly in love," which might have dire consequences, therefore "it is not strange that I should have thought first of the possibility that some day dear little Minnie might become my wife." The careful logic of reasoned and allowable passion "perhaps rather chills us," comments Fred, before explaining that his father was obviously being led by the elevated inspiration of Tennyson's *The Princess*, a thoroughly "Victorian poem," which he was reading with Minnie at the time. Indeed, Edward's feelings become less calculating. When Minnie wonders one day whether, when she is twenty, she will still look "so little compared to you," he finds himself blushing and, he writes, "the palms of my hands grew hot." Then he observes, "She is remarkable for great beauty and changefulness of expression: one of the sweetest things I ever saw is her look of affection or of tenderness." Finally, we get to the scene of the proposal, the tears, the handkerchief. He asks if she had not had thoughts of marriage when reading *The Princess* together, and she is amazed that she should not have seen the point of "this passage or that till today." The romantic scene ends, with just the right note of romantic closure, as "she repeated the words [from the poem], 'Love, children, happiness.' 'Two of those are mine now,' she said." Slow fade-out . . .

The plot goes happily on, however, with Fred's summary: "And then this little authentic Victorian love story, so precise and fabulous with its readings out of Tennyson's 'Princess,' and its adorable heroine of twelve years old, tenderly and exquisitely plighting herself, and striving to 'set herself to man,' without as yet the slightest notion what it all meant, becomes a very real affair." And finally, despite proper hesitations and misgivings through the next seven years, all duly triumphed over, the celebration of marriage is reached: "From that time onwards she was the staff on which he leaned and the wings that gave him flight."

Even granted the awkward edginess of describing one's own parents' courtship and growing love, and even granted the knowledge he needs to repress after reading his mother's diaries and papers, this is a remarkably idealized portrait, which uses its Victorian distance to move from reticence to "adorable," "exquisite," "tender" idealization. But before we can start to see the work that has gone into Fred Benson's two accounts of his parents' love, it is worth looking at one of the most extraordinary documents to have come down to us from the Victorian archive.

After Edward White Benson's death, his wife was completely distraught. "She looked out on to an inconceivable emptiness. . . ." "It was as if some earthquake had occurred, some elemental upheaval and tearing, that separated her from an entity that had once been hers." Fred Benson, in *Mother*, quotes from a long prayer she wrote for herself at this time: "All the beauty of our past life together, the home we made, the dignity and glory of it, the fellowship, the humour, the conspiracies, the discussions, the beating, fervent, keen, pulsating life, the splendid web which Thou gavest us to weave— all this is over. . . ." "There is nothing within, no power, no love, no desire, no initiative: he had it all, and his life utterly dominated mine." In the course of this sense of desolation, she set herself the task of writing a daily spiritual diary, in which she looked back over her life. Each meditation is timed and interspersed with prayers on the opposing page. This brief document gives a quite different sense of her wooing. I know of no other example of women's writing like this, certainly from the nineteenth century—a private reflective account forty years later of what it was like to be a young girl in such a situation. Her remarks are lapidary and fragmented reminders to herself, and all the more moving for the dark silences between the expressivity.

"Mother rather feared than loved." "Ed. coming. Fear of him. Love? Always a strain. Never the love that 'casteth out fear.'" (Arthur placidly noted of his father's need to express his love, "I remember my mother saying it all caused great strain"—the word "strain" seems to be Minnie's careful word for her terror and its consequences.) Even the proposal and her tears prompt retrospective distance: "E's disclosure—tears and emotion—why? No real thought about it after." She sums it all up brutally: "A terrible time. Dreary, helpless. From the first the most fatal thing was the strain on my conscience of the position toward Edward and mama. He had been allowed to tell me, and was not allowed to speak. but he <u>did</u>. and more. Hand. Embrace. & all weight on my conscience — & which did I love best/ it was <u>not</u> love that growing for him—." She knows he has not been given permission to speak to her, but does, and she feels the burden of this guilt. But he did not only talk ("and more"). The single words "Hand," "Embrace" are grimly evocative of her discomfort at his physicality. Even as she is devastated by her husband's loss, she is emphatic that she did not when wooed love him—though, needless to say, her childish letters of the time are full of expressions of love and romance. So she compares the awful schooling he insisted on—"Lesson with Ed.—so dreaded— architecture and physical geography"—with a sudden recognition of the direction of her real erotic desires: "first friendship—now, how far was I right—I fell in love with her, and spent a great deal of time with her—and loved her über alle Mädchen." Minnie was, she laments bluntly about herself, "Oh how unfit for marriage." Yet she could also recall these moments with a laugh amongst friends. Arthur remembers her giggling with her chums, "Edward Benson's child-bride. Oh, how silly I was." A sunnier recollection, a smiling mask.

The intense pain and conflicting emotions are captured with vivid bitterness in her long description of their wedding night and honeymoon:

> misery—knowing that I felt nothing of what I knew people ought to feel. Knowing how disappointing this must be to Ed, how evidently disappointed he was—trying to be rapturous—not succeeding feeling so inexpressibly lonely. & young. But how hard for him! Full of all religious and emotional thoughts and yearnings. They had never woken in me—I have learnt what love is through friendship. How I cried in Paris! Poor lonely child, having lived in the present only—living in the present still—The nights!—I cant think how I lived. I cdnt have thought so much about myself as I do now. We prayed, but didn't come near to God. I mean I didn't.

She was made desperately sad by her own ignorance—her sexual, emotional, spiritual numbness. She knew that she was unfulfilling to him, and how she was faking, unsuccessfully, the rapture she wanted to feel. Even as she recalls how young and lonely and sad she was, she still with emphatic underlining recognizes the intense strain on *him.* As she writes on the same day, "He restrained his passionate nature for 7 years, and then got me! This unloving, childish, weak, unstable child! Ah God, pity him!" She sees herself, at a distance, through his disappointed eyes and her self-dismay and retrospective pity. Yet she reverts to her own overwhelming sense of misery, loneliness, and inability to pray. Throughout, it is the gap between her current sense of God and her former self that haunts her. And her current sense of love, discovered only through friendship with other women, in those days still inarticulate. There is a profoundly complex sense of loss—of potential, of the past, of her husband

and their life, of her own earlier fantasies—coupled with pity that swerves into recalled misery, with a clarity that allows her to see that she could not yet pray to God adequately and that her misery was imbricated with his disappointment. There is no sense here of the "adorable," "exquisite," "tender" romance.

Yet her letters and diaries from these early days of courtship and marriage fit exactly such romantic stereotypes. Hence Fred writes with calm patriarchal assurance in *Mother* that these first weeks of marriage were "a triumph of surrender to my father": in her diary "she obliterates herself completely"—and, he adds, for clarity in parentheses "(her own private self, now hermetically bottled)." The parentheses bottle up any lingering doubts, a re-performance of a muffling. Arthur comments more acerbically that her early diaries were written "no doubt at the behest of my father. There is not a particle of her in them." So, before her marriage, in a still childish hand, matching the sentiments and grammar, she writes to Edward, "You must not measure my love by the length of my letter, for my love is much bigger than my letter." Or, "Ah mine own love. God bless you. My best beloved my prayers are with you for ever. When my desire to see you is so great that I scarcely know what to do, I press my ring and that makes me better." As she recalled of her early married life, forty years later, "I wd have died rather than anyone shd have thought for a moment I wasn't happy." To her later self, and even to her son Arthur, the intimacy and revelation of diaries and personal letters now seem like acts of self-deception and conceal-ment.

I have juxtaposed Fred's "delightful" romance with his mother's own bitterest recollections. But this is not to demonstrate the sim-ple truth of one account over the other. Minnie's sense of loss was as profoundly expressed as the bitterness of her memory. On Feb-ruary 14, 1897, she writes in her diary: "I dont feel that I can do anything. I cant pray. I havent, at all. I cant offer anything. I cant live. I don't care. All is quite far off. I havent kept for one moment a single thing I promised and vowed." Nine days later she writes only, "Feb 23. worse and worse. all has gone," and the rest of the page is

FIGURE I: Minnie Benson, already pregnant with Hugh—the summer before her trip to Germany and meeting Miss Hall.

heavily scored out with a large X, and the next entries are scribbled over violently. Yet Minnie did find prayer and comfort in remembering "all the beauty of our past life together." The prayer Fred quotes at length is a heartfelt and desperate search for self-recognition, raising herself up from blackness: "Good Lord, give me a personality," she prays. "I feel exactly like a string of beads, always in one string, worn, carried about till they seemed as if they had some real coherence. In a moment the string was cut; they rolled to all the corners of the room, a necklace for glory and beauty no more, but just scattered beads. Who will string my life back together again?" She needs, she writes, to find herself: "But united as I was with so dominant a personality as Edward, and being, especially of late, so often in such anxiety about him, combined with the tremendous claims of the position, how was I to find myself?" She struggles to express her sense of fragmentation: "I have fallen to pieces since Edward left me. I seem to have been only a service of respondings, and no core. But there must be a core, and it is in God."

In these private, intense strugglings, she moves from a sense of fragmentation expressed in the homely imagery of the necklace of beads, through a sense of passive interaction in the world through the religious image of a "service of respondings," finally to seek a core for her self in God—the turn to her private certainty in religion, which her children knew to be central to her. This is a juncture: her prayer goes on to anticipate not merely her own growth back into the role of matriarch of the family but also a moving discourse of self-fulfillment, a woman who will learn to live without a man, which finds echoes in inspiring feminist literature of a much later date: "I have never had time to be responsible for my own life. In a way, I feel more grown up now than I have ever felt before. Strange, when for the first time in my fifty-five years I am answerable to nobody. No one has a right to question my actions, and I can do what I like. What a tremendous choice!" This potential for a new life sets in motion more than a spark of resistance to fragmentation—and to her previous life, where her actions were always open to question, by her mother and, above all, by her husband.

For Fred—and, according to Fred, for all those who looked at her with "eyes most scrutinizing and loving"—there were no outward signs of such a struggle during this period. His brother Arthur had a similar reaction: "She always seemed so secure, so ready to talk, so willing to do anything for anyone, that it is very pathetic to think what was going on behind. In fact, the whole record seems a

<u>tragic</u> one." Fred is amazed that his mother in her desperate prayer reveals "not one touch of self-pity or hint of resignation, that most deadly of Christian virtues"; and the discovery in her papers of this prayer makes him understand in retrospect the "brave face" she put on before "nothingness." We have, then, a rather more complex, emotionally layered scene than it might at first have seemed. Fred is writing in the years after the First World War, not just reminiscing with nostalgic and ironic humor about a lost world of Victorian propriety, but also engaging in the wary act of reimagining his parents' courtship and marriage: if social reticence is a theme of his memoirs, we should expect a special internal silencing, especially in the exposing act of publishing, when it comes to such reimagining. How can a child imagine his mother's passion, his father's desire— without excruciating and self-implicating prurience and embarrassment? He remembered how his mother in her mourning "appeared to suffer no loss of humour, of pleasure, of entranced interest in life," and is now trying through his writing to express his new sense of what she was actually feeling and what the tension between her outward show and internal anguish betokens, and he discusses it as he writes with his brother, comparing memories. *Mother* begins with the death of the father and is structured around this loss and the life that followed in response to it. It is a book about restructuring, rewriting the course of things. So he focuses on expressing his changing sense of how his mother was rewriting her reaction to loss. In this framework, however, his narrative stretches in a smooth line from courtship to marriage to loss to rediscovery of a core, and he consequently omits his mother's absence in Germany, his parents' experience of depression, the bitterest recollections that his mother writes. The question to which we will return, is what—beyond a sense of social reticence—prompts Fred both to write this story and to write it like this? What internal drives made him want to write the story of his mother's life, wooing and all, and then to write it with such brittle romanticization?

As for Minnie, she looked back in very different registers. For different audiences (including God and her private meditation), and at different points in her life, before and after her religious change, before and after her relationship with particular women, especially Lucy Tait, before and after Edward's death, she could tell the story of her past in strikingly varied colors. She could laugh off her status as a child bride; she could from the darkness lament it as "a terrible time." She could recall in the same month both that "terrible time" and the "beauty" of their life together. How Minnie allowed her memories to be expressed, (re)constructed, revealed, and concealed is not just a problem for biographers in pursuit of a straight-line story, but part of her own ongoing and reflective discovery and performance of her self: "Good Lord, give me a personality." On March 16, 1876, aged thirty-five—the year when she found her religious belief—she tried to plot out her whole life so far on a piece of rather scrappy paper. She writes under "72.73," "4th period Absence in Germany. Greatest Change. E.H. return. To Lincoln." In this schematic biographical plan, it is not being wooed, getting married, having six children that get underlined. The "Greatest Change" is set between her absence in Germany and Miss Hall (E.H.) and her return "to Lincoln." (Arthur, with a psychological if not a physical truth, bizarrely appears to state in the unpublished memoir that his mother never came to Lincoln.) Twenty years later in her retrospective meditation, she remembers her "complete fascination" with Miss Hall, but the emphasis on where the great changes of her life were are quite different.

Arthur does not read his mother quite as Fred does. He would encourage us not to dwell on the "morbid and self-scrutinizing mood" of her writing after his father's death, where "one only sees . . . the pits and morasses of character in which she seemed to herself to have been engulfed from time to time." "It is a strange and sad document." Her bitter memories are, for him, not the true mother's feelings, but the distortions of grief and despair. Arthur's own depressions were overwhelming and suicidal. He knew not to trust the self-representations of a mind under severe strain.

In his official biography of his father, the archbishop, he had offered for his part the briefest and most anodyne account of the courtship and long engagement: "From the time when he was at the University, and played with her as a little child, he desired some day to make her his wife." When "at Rugby . . . he found time to teach her, this desire was formulated not only to himself but to others"; "when she was just eighteen they were married." In contrast with his brother's "delightful" "little authentic Victorian love story" written long afterward in 1930, Arthur, back in the Victorian dress of 1899, in a biography read and checked by his mother, knows starkly how to observe the proprieties of reticence. No kissing for Arthur. As he wrote in his diary of the biography: "I need not define the strains: this book is not a confessional." Minnie herself wrote to Hugh (as usual writing to one son about how another son is writing about their shared past, inadequately): "At present he has said nothing about his family life, but he will. Of course the earlier part of his life . . . Arthur only knew them as a child knows." Later, when Minnie had died and he had read all her papers, Arthur, still stiff-collared and firmly buttoned up, left this summary and unpublished sentence, an understatement both strikingly telling and painfully inadequate in its multiple reticences: "My mother, I gather from some manuscript notes written long years after, began to experience a certain fear as to whether she could give my father exactly the quality of affection which he claimed." The strain in restraint here is horribly palpable. In his diary he wrote, "It must have been terrible to be so near him and his constant displeasure." In a personal letter to Fred in the year Fred was writing *Mother*, Arthur could write more unguardedly, "But her diary is very painful to me because it shows how little in common they had and how cruel he was"; the boys agree that "it was a case of real, natural incompatibility." "We wondered if they had ever really loved," Arthur recalls. "Certainly I never remember their seeking each other's company or wanting to be alone together." Over the years and for different audiences, Arthur struggles for the right words, the right story; but it was never for him just a delightful little love story.

Neither son, in their own and different ways, can, publicly at least, countenance the darker story, because both prefer—and prefer to

circulate—what they saw in their mother's calm behavior, the sunnier tales she told them, her memories of the beauty of a life lived
together. And both see in her prayers a noble grief, and, in her even
harsher meditations, not a truth finally uttered but a falsehood produced by the desperation of her misery. Yet both struggled painfully
with their father's frightening personality and idealized what they
saw as their mother's ability to deal with him with generosity and
loving care. As Minnie writes and rewrites her own autobiographical narratives, so, too, her children write and rewrite the primal
scene of courtship, especially after their father's death and their later
access to their mother's papers. Such complicity and such strong
emotions, as the story of a wooing and a marriage are told and retold
over the changes of time, from different perspectives, through competing memories, and with different reticences and exaggerations,
produce a dynamic, shifting picture of what we might mean by a
family history.

SO, HOW SHOCKING *WAS* EDWARD'S LOVE FOR AN ELEVEN-
year-old girl? Edward was a good, evangelical Christian of fierce
moral probity. Minnie's family, Edward's cousins, at this time
matched his religious zeal—though Henry Sidgwick would go on
to become a famous agnostic, and Arthur Sidgwick was extremely
liberal in his religious views. The legal age of consent in this period
was thirteen and only raised to sixteen in 1885 after a campaign
that dwelt luridly on the drugging and raping of thirteen-year-old
girls in London. The legal age for a girl's marriage had been lower
throughout Europe in the eighteenth century, and even Juliet in
Shakespeare's romantic play was only thirteen years old. The age difference was not remarkable, and many intellectual women—Eliza
Lynn Linton or Sarah Grand, say—married very young to older
men (and repented their marriages at length). In later life, nobody
seems to have worried about Edward's desire. When his feelings for
the twelve-year-old Minnie were raised with her aunt Henrietta,
"she said it was rather romantic—then that there was something
very pure and unworldly about such an affection." When in the later

decades of the century, the campaign for social purity and the attack on the sordid worldliness of child prostitution combined to raise the age of consent, this judgment on Edward as "pure and unworldly" would take on its full weight of approval. It is, again, a phrasing that radically separates our contemporary expectations from this nineteenth-century past.

Nor was it especially surprising that Edward conceived of marrying Minnie and then was prepared both to wait and to see her educated. Sabine Baring-Gould, five years younger than Edward White Benson, was a clergyman with Tractarian leanings. He wrote the hymn "Onward Christian Soldiers," collected folk songs from his native Devon, and was a keen amateur antiquarian and writer of saints' lives. At the age of thirty-five, the emotionally constipated vicar fell surprisingly in love with a sixteen-year-old working girl from a local village. He sent her away for two years to get "civilized," that is, to become sufficiently educated to marry and to play out her social role in his circle. They duly had fourteen children (one of whom Baring-Gould failed to recognize at one of his own parties, to her dismay). The oddest parallel is perhaps John Ruskin—though nobody would take Ruskin as a solid model for a happy marriage. After the disastrous failed marriage with Effie Gray, later, at age forty-four, he fell in love with the eleven-year-old Rose La Touche and proposed to her when she was seventeen. She died young, mentally ill in a sanatorium, and he suffered from fits of mental disease also, perhaps precipitated by her death. Marriage to a ward, brought up from childhood in the same house as her guardian, is a staple trope of the fiction of the era—mocked knowingly in *The Importance of Being Earnest*. The nineteenth century is a great period for "systems," for schemes of education designed to produce the perfect young adult (of which eugenics is only the most biologically developed and eventually most lethal example). The oppressive failure of such systems also becomes a staple of literature by the end of the century.

So in terms of a cultural history specific to England in the 1850s, one could perhaps make a case that the desire of a young man for an eleven-year-old girl and his schooling of her for marriage are not in themselves shocking occurrences, even if it is not common to have such detailed accounts of the drama, and even if the evangelical and educational context provides a specific frame for such an enterprise. Such a romance, publicly acknowledged, was certainly no bar to Edward White Benson rising as a schoolmaster and clergyman to the greatest positions. But before we could reach such a bland conclusion, much as the versions of the courtship provided by Fred and Arthur would also seem keenly to encourage us to do, there is another unparalleled archive, which offers a further extraordinary perspective on the primal scene of this marriage. For where was Minnie's mother in this story?

3

Bringing Up the Subject

MARY SIDGWICK HAD BEEN MARRIED TO THE REVEREND
William Sidgwick for only eight years when he died in 1841. She
was then just thirty and had four surviving children to bring up (two
had died shortly before, aged three and five). She was a dignified and
attractive woman, whose strong sense of religious and familial duty
enabled her to go beyond these three shattering deaths in a year with
some directedness and strength. Her unmarried sister, Henrietta,
lived with her, and when Edward White Benson's mother died, leaving his family impoverished, she took in two of his sisters, Eleanor
and Ada—the families were cousins. In this way, Edward became
closely linked with the Sidgwicks.

As a youth, Minnie's brother Henry Sidgwick idolized Edward—
nine years older than him—for his brilliance, religious intensity, and
charisma. They remained close throughout their lives, even when
Henry drifted away from religion in his student days and became
a distinguished and controversial moral philosopher. Arthur Sidgwick, born the year before Minnie, became an educationalist who
contributed significantly to the politically motivated workingmen's
education movement, and whose textbook on Greek prose composition was still being used at the close of the twentieth century: Uncle
Arthur floats affectionately through the letters and reminiscences
of all the Benson family. William, the oldest and least distinguished
son, taught at Merton College, Oxford. This was a family growing
into outstanding public, intellectual distinction.

Mary Sidgwick was close to Edward, who visited often. They talked with intimacy. She could write how much she enjoyed seeing him in Cambridge: "I wish I could just come and take tea with you and stir your fire and stroke your face and have a nice chat with you this windy rainy evening." The openness of physical contact—remember Mr. Martin stroking Edward's hair—is a normal part of Victorian interaction between certain categories presumed to have a non-sexualized relationship; between women, for example, who often are described to embrace, kiss, and stroke one another, and here between an older female cousin and younger male relative. In 1852 she was only forty-one, when Edward, aged twenty-three, broached the subject of his growing desire for Minnie, aged eleven. This prompted an extraordinary, often anguished correspondence as well as heated conversations between mother and wooer. Although only her side of the exchange still exists, there are fully 320 pages of letters from her in the eight months from May. Arthur Benson, it will be recalled, with characteristically laconic reticence, described these months with the single sentence "this desire was formulated not only to himself but to others." For the participants, it was an all-consuming drama in which Edward cajoled, bullied, persuaded the sensible Mary Sidgwick to accept the idea of him telling Minnie, and then an even longer process of complicit "training" in which Minnie was prepared by her mother and by him for marriage.

The exchanges between Mary and Edward are intricate and swirl with competing emotions. To begin with, Mary is intent on three points that she repeats again and again. First, she insists that her own affection for him is constant. So one Monday in May at midnight, alone in her room (as she tells him) she writes, "I earnestly hope that you will not the less feel, that under all circumstances, my affectionate interest in you will <u>never</u> cease." As they argue, she appeals, like a lover, to their feelings for each other: "It <u>cannot be that</u> the love and confidence which you have so freely given me are thus to be clouded." Her admiration for Edward—his future suitability—underlies her writing. But, secondly, she is clear that however good a man Edward now is, he is too young to be regarded as having made a stable choice, a choice that could survive seven years of engagement. So, alone again, she writes, with typically emphatic underlining, "a few more midnight words with you. . . . I shall think my child singularly blessed to be <u>the</u> one whom your <u>mature</u> judgment and <u>older</u> affection would choose above <u>every other</u>—and be satisfied with the choice. <u>Plus</u>, my dear Edward (please forgive me) my faith is not sufficiently strong in the constancy of <u>any</u> man's affection, who has not yet reached the age of 23—especially when feelings are so warm as yours, I am sure, are." The nervousness and attempted tact with which she broaches the issue of how any young man could survive seven such years of enforced emotional more than physical chastity in the face of all other temptations—especially a man of such strong feelings as he—is well-placed, since he later appears to respond to her with strident anger, which deeply upsets and cows her. She imagines indeed that he cannot now feel the sort of love on which a marriage depends, and may find it elsewhere: "Still it cannot be said that <u>now</u> your deepest affections are engaged, and it is quite possible that you may some day soon see <u>full grown much more than your beau ideal</u> of what it must take years—ever to become." This is because, thirdly, Minnie is just too young and will be so even at eighteen. "I do not wish you to suppose," she writes in her first letter of May, "that her love is anything but the childish affection of little sister <u>yet</u>—and long <u>tho</u> I wish it to be none other—only how difficult will it be—to know when it is becoming of a deeper character?" Indeed: "only 18 <u>is very</u> young & I cannot think of it quite comfortably." A year later: "I am quite sure she thinks of you as much and as warmly as her childish nature is capable of." Edward has Mr. Martin, as an older adviser, plead his cause, but Mary seems firm: "I cannot <u>for a moment</u> agree with Mr Martin in thinking that any such communication should be made to dear Minnie <u>so</u> early," she declares. "I really think it would be taking an unfair advantage of a mere child, and not allowing her to be a free agent. . . . I have been <u>wrong</u> very <u>wrong</u> to let your mind dwell so much upon the whole scheme." Mary is sure that any indication of marriage at his early stage is damaging to Minnie, who cannot possibly reflect with maturity on such a prospect; that such a prospect is unlikely to be fulfilled because of the changeability of a man's youthful passion; and that thus the situation is doubly damaging to her daughter, who will be disappointed and potentially the subject of scandalous loss of reputation.

This all might seem like a mother's sensible response, coupled as it is with a straightforward refusal to let Edward approach Minnie with any proposal. But things are quickly far more complicated—and Mary's complicity far less comfortable for any modern reader. For Mary also encourages Edward to write to her daughter and praises the effect of their correspondence: "I think, my dear Edward, that you may fairly lay claim to the incipient (at any rate) development of Minnie's epistolary powers, for I do not think she ever wrote so good and so neat a letter without the least assistance." Praising the "neatness" of her girl's letter-writing brings her childishness awkwardly to the fore in what is for Edward at least potentially an exchange of intimate letters. Although she has put a bar on his expression of feeling, she also imagines for him the relationship continuing: "Of this I feel <u>quite sure</u>, that after 14 or 15, this interest must be shown guardedly and carefully, so that shd your feelings or rather your opinion change,—[she] may never suffer from the change." At fourteen or fifteen, Minnie will be becoming more mature, and then—but not now?—there will be a need to be guarded and careful. Then—and only then—will there be recognition in Minnie of the sexuality involved, and the potential for scandal or psychological upset becomes real. "It would seem almost ridiculous," she reflects, "to prescribe the degree of interest which it would be safe to show a child of 11 years old," and she hopes that Edward would "gradually give up such childish fondlings as were only suited to a childish age," at least "<u>for a time</u>." Mary raises the possibility of regulating his fondling of her eleven-year-old daughter, only to reject such an idea as ridiculous. It would bring what in a pre-Freudian world is seen as an impossible or impossibly explicit sexuality into the relationship.

Mary writes—repeatedly—that their correspondence has become too focused on what she calls "The Subject," yet also constantly teases and prompts more response from Edward: "If I am wrong in my surmisings, dear Edward, tell me so—but somehow or other I have a sort of feeling that you have some misgivings in your own mind concerning the subject of our many letters." Or: "I am aware that I do not reply so methodically to your letter as you do to mine. This is perhaps but a woman's way. It's a very good one. If I leave any point untouched upon, mention it to me again"—this after suggesting that so much discussion of "The Subject" is unhealthy. The more she talks about how his feelings will change, the more she bolsters him in them. When he appears to make a joke about something Minnie wrote in a letter, she writes immediately to tick him off. There should be no jokes about marriage: "she made the remark . . . in absolute simplicity." The two older figures are linked knowingly above the girl's innocence. And then, an hour later, Mary writes a second letter to make sure there has been no misunderstanding between them. It is not that she thought Edward read the letter aloud in an inappropriate way but that any suggestion of a premature eroticization of discourse is to be regulated: "I do believe in the power of rightly directed education to keep every feeling in its proper place and not to suffer any to be prematurely developed. I should wish Minnie to feel for you as for a very kind cousin, taking much interest in her improvement and thus most justly entitled to her love." Mary both bars Edward and encourages him; pushes him away and praises his involvement; writes repeatedly about how there is too much writing between them on "The Subject" and goes back over their exchanges obsessively. The private language of "The Subject" forms an intimate bond of complicity between them.

Above all, she writes to Edward about how she, as a mother, has been testing and scrutinizing Minnie's feelings: "I have often observed in Minnie that she has much difficulty in the expression of her deepest feelings—remarkably so for a child of her light-heartedness—and yet she does feel strongly and warmly, I am sure." She brings up the subject of Edward getting married to someone— and writes the story cutely to Edward: "She said 'I cannot fancy Edward married at all,' and when I asked if you would like it she said "<u>Perhaps</u> if the lady was very nice and I liked her,' and then after a pause she added "no, I <u>don't</u> think I <u>should</u> like it at all—but I know I am selfish to say so. It is all selfishness I know it is for me <u>not</u> to like it." She even tells Edward how Minnie responds to the idea of being engaged: "Mama, it would be curious for me to be engaged now, I shd not like it, because I wd not be able to think <u>properly</u> about it." She writes also to tell him that her sister Henrietta quizzed her about Edward and Minnie's relationship, informs him that she gave her approval for a future marriage, and then adds: "I think it better to say nothing on the subject to anyone at present." It is almost as if Mary is titillating Edward's feelings, as she demands that he restrain them: let me tell you more exciting details of how we talk about the forbidden topic . . .

This reaches a head in October, after Mary has reported that other people have begun to notice and even comment that "if Minnie had been a <u>little</u> older, I should have been disposed to form quite a <u>romantic idea about her and Mr Benson</u>." We must, she writes in the language of a secret and illicit affair, "be careful." On October 9, Mary dismisses any idea that when she has any "mercenary thoughts" when she talks of the need to wait until Edward is more settled. It is a question, for her, of simple principle: "My simple object in dear M's education is to bring her up—that she may be good, happy and useful in whatever state or station of life may be her appointed lot. And should she marry I have always hoped that her husband might be a good and superior man in such a station as her own." This cliché of parental propriety seems surprisingly to have produced something of a crisis in Edward. He writes about his intense grief about not being able to speak to Minnie. He is in discussion with Mr. Martin about what he should do. Mr. Martin thinks he should marry before he is thirty. The combination of his intensity of feelings—grief, anger, passion—has become, it seems, by now too much for Mary, and the threat he makes of breaking off all contact is for her the breaking point. With characteristic ambivalence, she confesses that she did not mean Edward to give up on his plans altogether, and that he should do what he thinks right, only not till they have talked face-to-face: "It will be a pain to me to <u>give up all idea</u> of it. This I never intended: still if it will be more for your happiness and peace of mind to be decided one way or the other— pray do what you think wisest and best: only promise me this one thing that you will take no strong resolve until I have seen you." It is this, finally, that gives Edward permission to sit Minnie on his knee again, start to talk and take her hand, and get "quietly to the thing."

Over these eight months, Mary is not merely bullied, cajoled, and persuaded; she conspires, encourages, and toys with the idea she calls "<u>wrong</u> very <u>wrong</u>." It seems that eventually that she cannot bear the idea of a complete break with the emotional entanglement—to "<u>give up all idea</u> of it." She allows the proposal to go ahead for *his* peace of mind, she writes, to avoid *her* pain: Minnie has slipped from sight. As his children knew all too well, Edward could be scathing, angry, imperious, and he withdrew his affection and approval in a way that made them feel wrong, inadequate, and miserable. Mary writes how she feels terrified and miserable that Edward is "grieved beyond satisfaction." The dynamic between them is emotionally manipulative, divisive, knowing, and pained. And leads to Edward's proposal and kiss.

Minnie's age in this discussion is not a simple question of evident cultural acceptability. Mary is clear from the start that a proposal at this age would be an assault on the girl's agency; she thinks that an engagement of seven years, these seven years of psychological and physical development, is at best a precarious, at worst a gravely dangerous, enterprise. Yet it goes ahead. Mary struggles to find a framework for Edward's feelings, a process complicated by her already complex intimacy with him. She cannot allow that the eleven-year-old Minnie is sexualized or should or could be treated simply as a sexual object. As her sister Henrietta sees it, Edward's desire is simply not like that; it is "pure and unworldly." So Mary imagines that Edward's fondlings would become in need of prescription only when the girl reaches fourteen or fifteen, although the qualification "*almost* ridiculous" shows that her concern still has a place, and that the case for her is not as easy to categorize as it might seem.

The friends of the family comment on how this *would* look like an affair of the heart, a romance, if only Minnie were older—which reflects a certain unwillingness to see this all as simply normal. Mary tests the ground with Henrietta: what would she think if it were a romantic attachment? She gives her approval, as does Mr. Martin. It would seem that the combination of Edward's paraded propriety and the bizarre nature of his affection produces a confused and confusing uncertainty, which creates the arena for the intense exchange between mother and wooer, with Mr. Martin and Aunt Henrietta commenting from the side. Edward, as he does so often in later life, constructs the boundaries of normality with extreme conviction, holds to them, and forces all in his circle to observe these boundaries on pain of exclusion, disapproval, and anger. In a slippery and confusing moral world, he brings them all into the sway of his certainty.

Bland acquiescence in the normality of this proposal, then—this delightful little Victorian love story—is possible only by repressing the evident anxiety, emotional strain, and troublesome moral feelings of the participants—their *need* to talk about it at length, to worry over its import. Ruskin, for his part, as another man who loved an eleven-year-old, barely brings Rose La Touche into his wonderful autobiographical work *Praeterita* (which we will come back to), and then introduces her cautiously: "Some wise, and prettily mannered, people have told me I shouldn't say anything about Rosie at all. But I am too old now to take advice. . . ." To talk of such things is to go—to express the need to go—against the advice of one's friends. So, Edward's displayed feelings were—socially, emotionally, normatively—discomforting. Minnie's mother's letters show just how difficult it was to share Edward's certainty of the rightness of what he was doing, and just how difficult it became to resist the force of his certainty.

SO WHERE WAS MINNIE'S MOTHER IN THIS STORY? SHE WAS in her room alone at night writing to Edward intimate, emotional, angry, and submissive letters about whether he could speak to her daughter about love. She was talking to her daughter about the possibilities of love and conveying her responses to her undeclared lover, in the name of regulation, but performing with whatever self-consciousness a more intricate complicity. Both during the initial courtship and during the engagement, writing letters was integral, not just to the mother and the wooer, not just to the lover and the girl, but in creating their particular triangulated dynamic. Here is Mary writing to Edward in August 1852, at the fervid heart of the conflict over whether Edward can tell Minnie of his love:

> M. let <u>me</u> read your letter, and said she wished me to do so, and when I askd why she said nothing in reply to the latter part of it she told me she did not like to <u>think about that</u> at all, because she was afraid that you had <u>really</u> thought that she did not behave well. This was said with <u>most</u> tearful eyes—tho' she now believes you have forgiven her and that you will think no more about it.

Mary is vetting Minnie's letters to Edward, although Minnie does not know that her mother is doing this because Edward is a potential lover. Mary is telling Edward how this process works—in a way that seems designed to excite Edward's feelings about the girl's cute moral attractiveness and emotional engagement with his letter, lingering on her *most* tearful eyes, and what she thought he had *really* thought. Mary reads Edward's letter to Minnie, Minnie's letter to Edward, comments to the girl on what she is writing, and offers a different, adult, knowing, manipulative commentary to Edward. The mother as go-between stage-manages the epistolary affair.

Minnie, much later, remembered both her mother's control and Edward's expectations with distress. "Mama wanted me to tell her all that he said, without his knowledge of my promise.—I made a stand, and, I think, rightly." Fascinatingly, Mary wants her daughter both to promise to tell her every detail of the conversation with her fiancé but also not to tell Edward of her promise (what sort of power play is this?); at the same time, Edward wants her to be more expressive of her love—which she then has to lie to her mother about: "I had to strain the truth in order to satisfy Ed. by expressions of love and after was not true to Mama. I was influenced too strongly by him without really loving." The *strain* again, this time of the truth as well as the self. Caught between the authority of her mother and the authority of Edward, both demanding love, truth, and revelation, Minnie in retrospect sees nothing but her multiple misrepresentations of her self: "I wasn't true."

Mary also regulated the frequency of letters between Minnie and Edward after the engagement:

> Dear Minnie, I can see, would write to you very often but really her lessons occupy so much more time. . . . I had begun to fear that the subject was occupying her mind too much. I therefore alluded to it and she said "Mama, I do think of it many times a day, but never at lessons, if I can help it. He said I must not think of it then." . . . Her eyes filled with tears and she said, "O mama, if he wishes it, and really would like me to write oftener, I will do it."

Mary again mediates—stages—her daughter's feelings for Edward. The context is schooling, and Mary is keen to let Edward know that Minnie is trying emphatically to follow his injunctions not to think about marriage during schoolroom lessons ("if I can help it"—the injunction not to think about something is always likely to fail hopelessly, which may be the point here anyway). Her tearful promise to write more often if Edward "really would like" it is a carefully drawn portrait of the pining and obedient lover.

Five years later, however, Edward is less than satisfied with Minnie's still very youthful letters (the girl is by now sixteen). He now writes to Mary with the complaint that Minnie's own letters lack the emotional punch he is looking for:

> Minnie is a most affectionate creature but from her letters one could scarcely think so. Her last letter to me, though otherwise very good and very nice, might have been written to the most casual acquaintance, with the exception of the address and signature. But perhaps this is owing to her letters being still under supervision

and to prudent precaution. . . . I don't mean for a minute that I wish her to write love letters. . . . But I don't write this to hurt your feelings, but only to ask you if you notice it—and above all pray don't hurt <u>her</u> feelings by saying that I was surprised at it.

Again the dynamics are extraordinary. Edward writes to his fiancée's mother, complaining about the lack of affection in her daughter's writing. He wonders if it is because her letters are still under the oversight of her mother (Mary describes sitting and watching Minnie write out a long letter, before reading it: the act of writing— her body language of feeling—as well as the content, was under surveillance). He is quick to deny any wish for any eroticized or embarrassingly excessive emotion—no love letters—and equally quick to avoid any hurt to Mary's feelings. This is a private conversation between him and her about Minnie, which Minnie is certainly not to know about. The mother and wooer together are grooming the girl into the emotional expressivity suitable for marriage.

Clearly Mary did not quite read this letter as Edward hoped, and he writes again to assure Mary that it was not her actual emotions but her writing of them that he is criticizing:

You don't think my letters to her improperly affectionate, and yet I am sure they would not appear so wholly uncoloured with any tincture of regard for my correspondent.

Don't mistake me. I only speak of her <u>style</u>. That she <u>is</u> most affectionate I know. . . . But I think it is a sad pity that she should not, as I said in my last letter, "write herself down better."

Edward rather pompously describes the affection, with which he very properly colors his prose, as "the tincture of regard." But what is at stake here is something more than just style. She is not succeeding in "*writing herself down.*" It is the gap between her style and her true character that makes her prose a misrepresentation. He does not feel the truth of her emotion (which retrospectively makes him an extraordinarily perceptive reader). A letter is to be a window on to the soul—a colored, carefully designed window, but one where the truth of the lines matters.

So he writes fervidly on a scrappy piece of paper to Minnie after some crisis between them to offer his forgiveness. "Believe me though, you will not be <u>really</u> nor <u>permanently</u> comfortable and happy till you know that you <u>deserve</u> your own respect, and mine, and that of others, by a regular unsparing Crusade against the faults you speak of till indulgence is conquered and unselfishness is a clear ruling principle—till you begin <u>self-formation</u> in earnest." "Writing oneself down better" is part of the self-representation that is also the crusade of self-analysis that is essential to "self-formation." The meditation she undertook after her husband's death, "Good Lord, give me a personality," is a process of writing the self that began in "writing herself down" for her husband, under the watchful eyes of her mother.

Edward's evangelical Protestant background echoes through his prose here. The faults of self—summed up as "selfishness"—are to be conquered by a moral crusade, "unsparing" in its rigor. Only then will she have "self-respect" and the regard of others. That is how the self is to be formed, molded, shaped: inward self-analysis and correction. For the young Minnie, this work on the self is matched by the education of the classroom, her hated lessons in architecture and physical geography—the styles and meanings of church buildings and the map of the Holy Land, no doubt, an education into a physical world in which to live a Christian life of unselfishness. This training is also an education into her place within the family, her role as daughter and future bride, directed by her mother. For her wedding day, Minnie received from her mother a long letter of moral precepts about how to be a wife, the culminating letter of moral instruction. The Victorian genre of *"Life and Letters"* has such a pull on the nineteenth-century imagination because of this religious, educational, and social commitment to "writing oneself down," to express and explore the self in letters.

The significance of the moment when Edward at last expressed his love formally to Minnie had been prepared for, then, and resisted, tested, argued over between her mother and him over several months of intense letter-writing, "writing the self down," establishing the narrative in which this discomforting act would make sense, or could make sense within the family, as a social and emotional story. When Fred Benson comes to write his versions of the romance of his parents, or Arthur Benson offers his grimmer reticences, or Minnie her pained recollections, or Edward himself puts down his triumphant account in his diary, these are all continuing written attempts to get the story right, or at least told acceptably, with their own partialities, concealments, and misunderstandings. Fred and Arthur are sons trying to understand their parents as young people, and, in particular, their mother as she has revealed her retrospective understanding of herself as a child—which has quite changed their own reminiscences of their earlier life with her: their own childhood and youth, retold. Family history, of course, always takes shape within such storytelling, its narrative and meaning constructed and fought over. But with this family, the material technologies of writing—letters, diaries, biographies, meditations, letters about biographies and diaries, letters about letter-writing—create a factory of competing and supplementary public and private narrative forms; and, what's more, the process of intergenerational misunderstanding and recalibration is vividly and self-consciously on display. When a son writes of how he has misunderstood his mother's feelings over the death of his father, or a woman in later life recalls bitterly how she was brought up and molded by her mother, the problem is not merely that any proclaimed objectivity of biography must be filtered through strategies of self-deception and self-representation. Rather, the issue is, more precisely, how reticence is formulated within a self-conscious, familial, intergenerational story of changing comprehension. What is at stake here is an ongoing education into social and emotional articulacy. Or, if you like, between growing up and speaking up, the question is how to bring up the subject.

4

Fifty Ways to Say I Hate My Father

SO WHY DID FRED BENSON WANT TO WRITE A BIOGRAPHY of his mother, to rewrite the romance of her childhood, and to write it all in the celebratory style he adopted? One simple answer—and no doubt an oversimplified one—is that he hated his father.

Now, if it was ever a simple or easy matter to publish the sentence "I hate my father," it was certainly not the sort of sentence that was going to come in any direct form from the pen of any of the children of the honored and respected and admired Archbishop of Canterbury. Nor would such an aggressive directness make sense of the complexity and powerfully conflicting feelings that characterized all the Benson children's interactions with their parents. A highly articulate indirectness, however, runs as a parallel narrative necessity to the reticence and joyful hagiography of public biography. *Of course* the Benson boys don't hate their father.

How to be a father was the topic of much Victorian writing—novels as much as advice literature, up-to-date articles about modern parenting as much as plays, which loved to stage clashes between the generations. The Oedipal crisis may be the master plot of literature, but because Victorian culture was so self-conscious of a *generational* sense of "the New," when parents and children clashed about religion, morals, styles of writing, dress, it provided not just an interfamilial tension but an argument about the values of modernity itself. The grim image of the whiskered Victorian patriarch—a familiar stereotype from genres of melodrama as well as from later and more self-serving reconstructions of Victorian grimness—is a stereotype that modern histories of the family, differently self-interested no doubt, have greatly softened. Yet the normative expectations of fatherhood throughout the century certainly included a profoundly felt sense of paternal authority, often expressed as a precarious but enforced need for obedience, which was buttressed by physical punishment as well as an economic and social control. Fathers did express their expectations of authority, vehemently. Within such a range of expectation, Edward White Benson stands out—in his children's eyes—for his fierce moral disapproval of any flippancy or waste of time, the severity of the expression of such disapproval, and the sheer fearsomeness of his personality. He was, it seems, terrifying to them all.

Yet what language was available to express their feelings, what form of expressivity? Two remarkable books from the turn of Victorian into Edwardian society offered contrasting and paradigmatic models. Both were written by men who came from evangelical religious and educational backgrounds similar to the Bensons' upbringing, in terms of spiritual fervor, highly regulated familial life, and literary hopes, nourished by school, university, and social milieu. Both were men who struggled privately with their erotic desire for men. Both had parental relationships that they felt defined their lives, and that they struggled to explore through writing.

Edmund Gosse's father was Philip Gosse, a naturalist and an expert on marine biology, who was elected a Fellow of the Royal Society for his research papers and was a leading member of the Plymouth Brethren (a Low Church, evangelical, Protestant sect of fundamentalist belief, committed to *sola scriptura*, the absolute authority of biblical writings, and to a pure fellowship of believers, subject to grace). According to Edmund Gosse, his upbringing was relentlessly strict, with a ban on all novels and fiction, a constant scrutiny of morals and behavior, and compulsory regular participation in Brethren meetings as well as visits to the poor and sick. In 1857 Philip Gosse published *Omphalos: An Attempt to Untie the Geological Knot*. This was an attempt to reconcile the deep-time chronology of the new geology, led by Charles Lyell, with a literal reading of the biblical account of creation. He argued that as Adam had been created with a navel, although he had no need of one, in order to be the perfect man in image of God, so, too, the fossils could have been created as fossils at the moment of creation, signs of life that had never existed. The book was treated with scorn, not just by scientists, but also, for example, by Charles Kingsley, a committed Christian and marine biologist (and friend and walking partner of Darwin), who could not contemplate that God would thus write in nature a "lie for all mankind." The book became an object of ridicule. The same year, Philip Gosse's wife died painfully and slowly from breast cancer. These two blows, her death and his intellectual humiliation, dominate the narrative of Edmund's understanding of his father's increasingly extreme piety and increasingly extreme demands on his son—although Philip Gosse also continued to publish in learned journals articles on technical marine biology.

In 1890, after his father's death, Edmund published a standard and rather dull biography, with all the piety of a good son. But in 1907, with an act of rewriting and reevaluation that finds so many echoes with the Bensons, Gosse published *Father and Son*, in which he now depicted his father as a God-haunted neurotic, who could despise the Christmas pudding his servants wanted to give his son as "flesh offered to idols." It is a searing narrative, an uncompromising picture of a sensitive boy escaping the control of a domineering and intensely religious father into a world of literature, society, and a silenced rhetoric of hell and duty. It was published anonymously till its success allowed Gosse to take credit—and it has remained undoubtedly Gosse's most read and most influential book. Edmund Gosse was in the process of becoming a historian and writer of distinction, who introduced Ibsen to England and became an arbiter of taste for literary London—librarian of the House of Lords, a cushy sinecure, and knighted for his services to literature in 1925, a grandee of London's cultural life. Henry James, a close friend, captured his intellectual style nicely when he declared Gosse's "genius for inaccuracy," and Virginia Woolf, no friend and keen to dethrone the gatekeeper of literary value, sniffed that he was "as touchy as a housemaid and as suspicious as a governess."

In *Father and Son*, Edmund Gosse immediately announces the truth of his new portrait of his father: "At the present hour, when fiction takes forms so ingenious and so specious, it is perhaps necessary to say that the following narrative, in all its parts, and so far as the punctilious attention of the writer has been able to keep it so, is scrupulously true." (That modern scholarship has found out his genius of inaccuracy here, too, should have been no surprise. . . .) He offers this biographical story as the "diagnosis of a dying Puritanism," a "record of educational and religious conditions, which, having passed away, will never return." As with Fred Benson's *Peep Show*, this view of his own family's past crosses a chasm toward a now-lost religious as well as personal world. Like so much of the Benson writing, it is also an attempt to understand a child's view of a father from the perspective of a sophisticated adult. "It seems to me now profoundly strange," Gosse writes paradigmatically in the epilogue, "although I knew too little of the world to remark it at the time, that these incessant exhortations dealt, not with conduct, but with faith." He can now think of his father as out of tune with the times even then, "like an old divine." Arthur Benson, always sensitive to such dynamics of untimeliness, recognized in his diary that *Father and Son* is "beautiful . . . Really perfect art"; "a book I should really like to have written."

The portrait is strikingly damning of the effect of his father's religious fervor on the child's education, emotional, intellectual, and spiritual, as viewed from the perspective of later escape. Gosse speaks out clearly against his father's way of having him grow up. The effect is made all the more moving and persuasive by the care with which he evaluates his father's emotional and religious convictions and motivations, and the generosity of feeling he parades in the epilogue for the "unique and noble figure of the father." The exchange of letters here plays a key role, as the son struggles to find himself in London, away from the immediate control of his father, who nonetheless "kept the spiritual cord drawn tight . . . jerking into position the head of the dejected neophyte." Almost every day the father sent him a letter—a "torment of postal inquisition." "The letter, the only too-confidently expected letter, would lie on the table as I descended to breakfast . . . in its threatening whiteness, with its exquisitely penned address." It destroyed his taste for food. "I might fatuously dally with it, I might pretend not to observe it, but there it lay. . . . I knew it had to be read, and what was worse it had to be answered." Gosse describes how he would write in reply what was wanted, or he would evade answering, or demand to be left alone— but how the exchange never let up. When his father confessed that it was only his anxious paternal love that made him write, Gosse confesses that he is "not ashamed to say that I sometimes wept . . . tears commingled of despair at my own feebleness, distraction at my want of will, pity for my father's manifest and pathetic distress." The material business of engaging in a written correspondence—its very physicality as much as its emotional content—the tear stains on the page that he still holds in his hands after all these years—forms the story of their distanced interconnection.

Edmund Gosse was one of Arthur Benson's closest friends, and Arthur's diary heaves with meetings with Gosse in town, at the club, and shared trips to stay with his mother and Lucy Tait at their house at Tremans. It is an intimate, gossipy, often feverishly disagreeable relationship. (Portraits show them both in tweeds with large mustaches, staring seriously out with furrowed brows.) Virginia Woolf, with the condescension typical of Bloomsbury's attitude toward the previous generation, especially where biographical reticence is concerned, mocked Gosse, in terms that could be applied easily to Arthur Benson: Gosse, she wrote, "hints, he qualifies, he insinuates, but he never speaks out. . . . [He] is kept by his respect for decorum, by his decency and timidity, dipping and ducking, fingering and faltering on the surface . . . always a little afraid of being found out." Yet *Father and Son* did speak out, and the paradigm of resistance to an evangelical parent through biographical narrative was available to Fred and Arthur and Hugh. Gosse ends *Father and Son* with a truly remarkable claim, that he had taken "a human being's privilege to fashion his inner life for himself." The act of self-fashioning requires a narrative of the rejection of the father. Gosse's book posed a challenging, empowering, worrying question to the children of Edward White Benson. For Arthur—who dreamt about his father, who wrote about his father, who reflected at such length in his diary on his father's influence on him—to be able to assert the "privilege to fashion his inner life for himself" was indeed something he "should really like to have written."

In 1903 Samuel Butler's remarkable *The Way of All Flesh* was published. It begins, "When I was a small boy at the beginning of the century . . . ," as if it were another autobiographical narrative of a lost religious and cultural era (this will also be the story of a century . . .). The narrator, however, is only the godfather of the book's very conflicted hero, Ernest Pontifex, though he worries that he may have been too much like a father to him. The name Ernest Pontifex makes its point—"Serious Priest"—and the novel traces Ernest's collapse into a loss of faith, unwilled bigamy and a mistaken sexual assault, and recovery from imprisonment into the writing of polemical literature, all in the context of the bitter hypocrisy of Ernest's pious and horribly respectable father, Theobald, and his family. Their separation is described as a "bitter pill to Theobald to lose his power of plaguing his first born." At his father's death, Ernest in his turn feels bitter not because of the old grievances, but "because he [Theobald] would never allow him to feel towards him as he was always trying to feel": his father's meanness prevents filial decency. In any situation, he feels, "his father's instincts showed themselves in immediate opposition to his own. . . . If he met with any check his father was clearly pleased." Theobald and his family stand in explicitly for the Anglican Church, which is lambasted for its "absurdities and unrealities." Butler, unlike Gosse, angry still, aims his bitterness at the present as much as at the past.

Ernest's loss of faith, however, does not lead to his destruction, as so many novels had enacted, nor to the life of literary success that Gosse reports, but leaves him as a lonely voice of decency and commitment in a sordid community. Butler's novel fictionalizes the horrors of a corrupt religious family's effect on the earnest young man, and his refusal to have *The Way of All Flesh* published during his own lifetime only emphasized the evident desire to have it read as a novel not just of the sign of the times but of his own familial experience. Much as Gosse sought to fashion his inner life for himself, Butler's hero is beset by demands to give over his inner life in grim confession and submission to his mother: "Of your inner life, my dear, we know nothing beyond such scraps as we can glean in spite of you, from little things that escape you almost before you know you have said them." This invasive desire to know the inner life, coupled with a fear of giving oneself away, goes deep into the heart of the paradoxical (auto)biographical logic of the book. With characteristic self-consciousness about the revelation and concealments of biographical writing, the narrator, Edward Overton, worries, "Every man's work . . . is always a portrait of himself, and the more he tries to conceal himself the more clearly will his character appear in spite of him. I may very likely be condemning myself, all the time that I am writing this book, for I know that whether I like it or no I am portraying myself more surely than any of the characters whom I set before the reader." The figure of the writer in the novel not only encourages the (self-)recognition that writing always reveals the self of the writer—all writing in this sense is autobiographical—but also, paradoxically, may act as a type of fictionalizing protection for Butler himself: as with Pontifex's mother's gleaning of scraps, his image of the hated father emerges "in spite of him," and not just as spite. "In spite"—with the inevitable double hearing of "unwilling" and "with malice"—is the anxious watchword of talking about the (hated) father.

THE TRANSITION FROM THE VICTORIAN TO THE EDWARD-ian era could be shaped as a violent severance between the religious fervor of an older generation and the need to escape such oppression or hypocrisy by a younger. At a crossroads, Oedipus needs to murder his father. Arthur Benson's biography of his father, however, is calm: "I do not think," he writes, "that my father was conscious of the terror he could inspire." He suffered, he explains, "from a great deal of acute mental depression, which in early days had a blackness and fierceness of misery that must have been very trying to those most nearly connected with him . . . in these moods his rebukes were terrible." But he quickly adds: "And when my father was gracious, who was ever so gracious? His eager deference, his anxiety to take up any subject that seemed likely to interest his companion, made him the most charming of entertainers. And these qualities grew every year." Even such passages of carefully balanced psychological narrative, where every negative description is quickly followed by a forgiving, positive image, are few and far between in the more than a thousand pages of biography. The chapters on daily life, for example, have little on the daily interaction of the archbishop with his children, and nothing on the consequences of his depressions. In his second, long account of his father in his much later autobiography, *The Trefoil* (which ends with his father's death), Arthur balances his father's fearsomeness for him as a child with a growing sense of his father's greatness and concludes, "In spite of the fact that for the next twenty years my father talked very freely and openly to me, yet his heart and mind remained, and still remain, a good deal of mystery to me." It is this that makes a passage in Arthur's first novel, *Memoirs of Arthur Hamilton, B.A. of Trinity College, Cambridge,* so riveting.

The book was published anonymously in 1886 when the author was only twenty-four years old. It is structured as a memoir, "extracted from his letters and diaries, with reminiscences of his conversation by his friend Christopher Carr of the same college"—that is, a fictional version of a common nineteenth-century format of memorial. The hero, like the author, is called Arthur. Like the author, "Arthur" has a terrible encounter in a college room, which he will not fully explain, but which he refers to repeatedly over the coming years in his diary as a seminal moral crisis. Like the author, "Arthur" becomes a dissatisfied teacher and wonders about what the right system for training a boy into manhood might be. Like the author, one of "Arthur's" siblings dies when he is at school, and his parents are "overwhelmed with anguish." And "Arthur" loves music. Like many a first novel, it is all too easy to see this as a thinly described autobiographical fiction (and no critic has resisted the temptation so to do). It is this that makes the descriptions of "Arthur's" father telling. He "was a very religious man, of the self-sufficient, puritanical, and evangelical type that issues from discipline; a martinet in his regiment, a domestic tyrant, without intending to be." When the child "Arthur" is found by his father practicing the piano early in the morning, he "asked him rather sharply why he couldn't do something useful"—a story that appears in exactly the same form in the autobiographical *The Trefoil*, now with Arthur himself as the child. When "Arthur" does not do well enough at Cambridge to pursue an academic career, his father writes to inform him that "he had suspected all along that he was misusing his time and wasting his opportunities." These briefest snippets seem all too applicable to the author's own father and his celebrated distaste for "wasting time." What, then, of this poignant anecdote?

> He disliked his father, and feared him. The tall, handsome gentleman, accustomed to be obeyed, in reality passionately fond of his children, dismayed him. He once wrote on a piece of paper the words, "I hate papa," and buried it in the garden.

One way to say "I hate my father" is to write a fictional memoir in which a character with your own name writes as a child "I hate papa" on a scrap of paper and buries it so that nobody can see it. "In reality passionately fond of his children" is a hopeful plea for forgiveness. Having the child write and bury the hatred, which the author then publishes, could scarcely better capture the author's ambivalence, the thrill and difficulty of writing out the words "I hate papa."

When Fred Benson published *The Challoners* in 1904, Arthur, like all the children, quick to enter into a competitive possessiveness over their parents' stories, commented in his diary, "Mr Challoner—though drawn too superficially from Papa—is an interesting character. But Fred fails purely from lack of sympathy with and knowledge

FIGURE 2: Edward White Benson in his pomp.

of what really could be inside a man like that." (Fred, himself, many years later, wrote of his father, "I never got a true perspective of him.") *The Challoners* has a simple plot. Mr. Challoner is an intense, evangelical Christian. He has twins, both beautiful, charming, and talented. The boy is called Martin, and he is passionate about music and beauty. He deserts the possibility of doing well in his exams in Cambridge; his love of beauty leads him to convert to Roman Catholicism in rebellion at the aesthetic ugliness of his low Protestant upbringing; he performs in one brilliant solo concert that takes London by storm and becomes engaged to a nice and sensitive girl. But—perhaps, *of course*—he dies young on the book's final page, as his sister tries to make his father, still resistant to the idea of a Catholic priest visiting the house for the final rites, attempt a reconciliation. (Hugh, Fred's brother, had converted to Catholicism; Martin, Fred's brother, had died young: what does it take to write a book in which the talented young hero called Martin dies young, when your talented young brother called Martin died young? A cue or clue to what is being *brought up* here?) The daughter, Helen, falls in love with—and the name again could scarcely be more obviously significant—Frank Yorkshire, who is a reasoned atheist. Her father demands that she choose between himself and her fiancé, and it is only a period of intense suffering and sacrifice that leads the father to accept Yorkshire as a good man for his daughter—though they are far from married when the book ends. In a short story published the same year, called, tellingly, "Two Generations," the same plot device with another "stern, vigorous and masterful" father who "secretly longed for love" results in the girl choosing her lover and just walking out, leaving the father alone in his misery.

The Challoners is not a great book, but its engagement with its author's own life is fascinating, as was immediately apparent to his brother. As with Arthur's *Memoirs of Arthur*, music and the waste of time is the immediate cause of tension between father and son: "I deplore . . . his general slackness." The representation of Mr. Challoner does indeed have many superficial similarities to Edward White Benson. He is horrified at a female member of his family smoking. He upbraids his son for drinking (as Edward did to Fred, repeatedly). He is passionate about duty. The portrait echoes not only Arthur's "Arthur's" descriptions of his father, but also Arthur's official biography's descriptions: "He was so intensely serious that at any given moment it appeared to him that there was probably something better to do than to laugh, and a moment's thought easily discovered what it was. Of work he was insatiable. . . . All pleasure, except that which was to him the greatest pleasure in life, active religious work and religious exercises, was put away." As with all of these paternal portraits, the true misery of the father is his impossibility of winning the affection he desires: "Herein lay the secret tragedy of his life; he longed with the same intensity with which he served God for the ordinary human affections and relationships, but through the armour-crust of his nature, an armour, be it noted, of welded work and duty, his human hand could not break its way to clasp the hand of others." For Arthur, the book fails because Fred cannot really get inside the character, the "mystery" he felt he himself could not penetrate of his father's "heart and mind." The motivation of Mr. Challoner indeed appears as little more than a total religious commitment: "His passion springing though it did entire from his own intense and fervent Christianity, had suddenly shot into a bitter and poisonous blossom . . . ," which is relentlessly low Anglican (he regards joining the Catholic Church "as wanton and wicked as a violent crime"). Nonetheless, the conflict between Martin and Mr. Challoner early in the book is memorable.

Mr. Challoner is outraged that *The Mill on the Floss* is being read in his house and that Martin has muffed his exams. (*The Mill on the Floss*, as one of the seminal books about how to bring up a son and a daughter, is, of course, another rather clunky symbol of what is at stake in this story—a sufficiently modern book that Minnie was thought rather daring at Lincoln for reading it aloud to her children.) The interview he demands—the demand for an interview is one of the moments of fear that all the Benson children recalled with horror throughout their lives—is the moment at which Martin is finally goaded into speaking out: "You get angry with me and you frighten me; I think you do it on purpose. You have frightened me into silence all my life, now you have frightened me into answering you." The conversation stages the first and, it turns out, irremediable breakdown between father and son. It is, strikingly, focalized through the father's eyes, with the author's imprimatur: "He felt and felt truly, that just now Martin almost hated him." So another way to write "I hate my father" is to publish a novel in which an evangelical father recognizes, and recognizes *truly*, that his son—named for the author's father's idolized perfect and dead child—"almost hated him."

In 1925, the same year that Fred Benson published *Mother* with his account of his father's wooing of his mother, he also published a novel, *Rex*. The plot has some familiar elements. A fervent evangelical father who "married a girl half his age"; a son who wants a literary career as a dramatist, a choice regarded by his father as a shameful dereliction of social and religious duty, and a waste of time; a terrible breakdown between son and father; a father who dies before his time of a heart attack; a mother who is generous and loving and religious, not like her husband's beliefs, but with an inner intensity and surety. The book that precipitates the first row in the novel—the father rips his son's copy in disgust—is Ibsen, as clunky a symbol as *Mill on the Floss*, as the novel spirals into familial psychological violence. The would-be dramatist son reads aloud his whole script to his mother, who criticizes it (somewhat to his dismay). The son finds success not as the serious dramatist he wishes to be, but through a brilliant, frivolous comedy. And in case all this is not clear enough, when the hero's best friend reads Rex's first play, he comments, "There was Rex's mother among them [the characters], disguised it is true, but unmistakable," and laughs. "Why, he's got your father's name, by the way. It certainly is you, but it isn't like you." Reading an author's family in his work is what the characters of the novel do. Indeed, Fred Benson's novels were well-known for including thinly disguised friends in them. *Dodo*, his first novel, starred Margot Tennant as Dodo: though Fred disingenuously denied the identification, her future husband, Prime Minister Asquith, thought he deserved a good kicking, not least when the Prince of Wales referred to Margot as Dodo in public. "Edith Staines" in *Dodo* was delightfully accepted as a portrait of the composer Ethel Smyth, who was a friend of the family. The Cambridge novels are full of recognizable Cambridge characters and events. Fred's fictions revel in their reality effects.

The book opens with Rex's distaste for his father. "He was aware that between him and his father was some deep-rooted animosity." Although Rex is still a young man, he is disdainfully conscious of how his feelings are changing: "Never from his earliest days onwards had he felt any sense of comradeship with him; once he had been appalling and omnipotent, now he was merely disagreeable." When Rex and his best friend aim to spend the day swimming and relaxing, his feelings and the author's voice are silently overlapped in a sardonic rejection of the father's religiosity: "If only Sinai and its thunder-clouds were not there to menace them and keep them careful." At the moment of culminating conflict, the conversation is so bitter that the author has to distance himself from his hero:

> "You're no son of mine." "That's a relief to us both." There was never a more evil word spoken, nor one so little regretted.

Even when his father has died and Rex goes to see the body, he merely worries "would the mouth open, and frame such syllables as 'I thought, Rex, that I had told you not to do that.'" One way to say "I hate my father" is to write a novel where the son and father disown each other, where the father's rage precipitates his death, and where the son's cynicism and selfishness offer a threadbare cloak of self-loathing.

But in 1925 Fred Benson had also read his mother's diaries. In *Rex*, Mrs. Goodwin, we are told, "had not, it would seem, been in love with him [the father], and she had yielded, rather than known the imperious need of the one man: his tumultuous desire for her had swept her off her feet, even as it had swept him. Anything so strong and so menacingly sure of itself had something of the force of destiny about it." The menacing certainty of a father's desire for a much younger girl, a force hard to resist, leads to a wary marriage where "all that concerned her husband was a matter of her watchful and eager duty," but "she had never come to him with the white-hot fire, but what was in her power she gave him, warmth and tenderness, and as the years went by the pity that is akin to love." In the same year that Fred Benson was writing of his parents' delightful Victorian romance, where Edward White Benson appears as "masterful, convincing and convinced," "sure in his own soul," he was also writing of a hated father, whose sense of sureness is menacing, and a mother who did not love her husband, but came round, thanks to her warmth and tenderness, to a sort of pity. Is this a way of saying "I hate my father"?

I suppose one could say that when Fred Benson wrote in *Mother* about his parents' first kiss, it was not all he was writing and thinking about such things. The past is not written once. In different narrative forms, different modes of indirection, the mother's wooing is written out in fragments: a romance in the truth of biography, a yielding to menace in the fiction of the novel. To say "I hate my father" produces what Freud would call *Spaltung*, a splitting, a fission, a division—a splitting of representation, a divisiveness and division within narrative, a fissure in emotional self-positioning. There are only multiple and indirect ways to write "I hate my father."

5

Tell the Truth, My Boy

EDWARD WHITE BENSON HAD AN OVERWHELMING DISLIKE
of lying. He saw it as a fundamental moral failure, and he made
truth-telling a principle of the fiercest observance, especially amongst
his charges. One pupil at Wellington remembered with lasting terror "the awful sight" of the headmaster preparing to cane a boy in
front of the gathered school for being a liar. His son Arthur believed
it was because lying had been his "own boyish temptation" that he
so relentlessly combated the sin in others, especially with humiliating public corporal punishment. (His father's first autobiographical
memories, written in Cambridge in 1849, dwell on him being "sadly
addicted to lying" and how he was whipped for lying when he told
his mother the sort of imaginative nonsense that children often tell.)
As headmaster of Wellington, he wrote to his wife in Germany that
he had "returned to find hideously bad lying on the part of three
boys who had misbehaved." He expelled two of them and stopped
a half-day holiday for the whole school as a collective punishment
for the persistence of untruth—a collective punishment he also
defended as exactly the right course of action: "If society punished
itself instead of 'making examples' there would soon be no examples
to make." His fervent Protestant Christianity privileged truth as a
religious and spiritual necessity, and the pursuit of truth through
self-scrutiny and rigorous introspection undergirded his practices of
self-formation and social regulation. Hence, one of the really telling sentences in the biography of the archbishop—a sentence that

finds echoes in all of the scenes of demanded interviews in Fred's novels—is Arthur's observation of his father that "real candour, which he made very difficult, entirely disarmed him." The spectacular observance of truth-telling, in the quietly sardonic insight of Arthur, was not always compatible with personal or emotional honesty, which fear and anger barred—and such candor threw his father off course.

In his father's eyes, Martin, his eldest son, was a paragon, not least because "I never, his mother never, no master ever found any falsehood in his life." Fred—who named the hero he killed off in *The Challoners* Martin—was a different sort of talker. "I can never be sure whether credence is to be attached to anything he says," confesses Arthur to his diary, and he complains repeatedly that Fred's rattling talk flits from subject to subject, brittle, and often self-evidently full of fibs and exaggerations. This is not just that the society novelist was delighted by gossip, always happy for a witticism or smart observation to overtake the serious business of understanding the world (as Arthur would have it in his graver moments). Rather, Fred's face to the outside world was the most inscrutable:

> I know less of what Fred <u>really</u> thinks than of almost anyone whom I see much. I expect he is rather a pagan, but a most zealous conformist. He is a very highly-strung superstitious person, and has a great terror of speaking at all frankly or giving himself away. Indeed, he seems to me <u>never</u> to speak frankly.

For Arthur—who was also envious of Fred's bronzed, whistling healthiness and, above all, his success as a popular writer—Fred's reticence is a sign of superstition, a constant awareness of the danger of "giving oneself away" that frankness brings—as if to reveal the self is bound to be an act of shameful exposure. Not that Arthur thought that Fred would find a sophisticated or profound language of revelation: "Fred is a <u>simple</u> man, not having gone far into the labyrinths of the mind."

Minnie too, as his mother, worried that Fred was never willing to reveal to her whom he was seeing or what he was doing. She laughed off his reticence—in a term that has now a retrospective brilliance—as "Freddian." So perhaps his delighted romantic description of the first kiss is what we should expect from Fred, giving nothing away, another sign of a life of a "little writing and much irresponsible amusement," a fearful resistance to frankness. When E. F. Benson writes about his family's founding romance, is he just being Freddian?

Arthur saw in all the Benson children "a touch of something morbid," which he defined as a "diseased self-consciousness." Across the 179 surviving volumes of his diary (one has been lost), he provides a remarkably complex language of reticence and confession, frankness and tact—an intricate framework of "diseased self-consciousness," as it traces, also, his collapse into mental disease and hospitalization. He prides himself on his un-Freddian frankness: "I write to my friends, men and women alike, with brutal frankness." He notes with satisfaction that Miss Cholmondeley, the author, writes that "she didn't credit me with the grim self-knowledge my letter displays." "Serious," "interesting," "candid" conversations are recorded as high points of any day. He is proud of his family's self-scrutinizing talk: "I don't think that many families w^d have discussed an absent brother with so much genuine admiration, and so much candid justice." He reflects on the diary itself: "One thing I claim. It has made my own weaknesses more and more clear to me. . . . Well, I know pretty well what my faults are: I am pretentious, sensitive, unsympathetic, indolent, self-indulgent, weak-minded, liking rewards better than deserving, self-absorbed, ambitious, sceptical. I have on the other hand humour, intellectual dexterity, interest in character, a strong sense of beauty, tolerance, kindliness. But my virtues won't wash. I write this with my eyes open." Just as he analyzes himself with announced frankness, so, he writes, "I like to know people's interiors." Emotional candor between friends is a paraded ideal of the diary.

Yet the slippage is inevitable—and fundamental. In *Memories and Friends*, another book of (auto)biographical reminiscences, Arthur admits that his writing "makes no claim to be complete or even *true* impressions, but they are *my* impressions, faithfully recorded." In the diary he wonders, "if I am posing all the time," and, even when he praises his own frankness, he has to withdraw a little in the name of honesty: "What an odd book this diary is! So full now—and so very <u>nearly</u> the whole truth. Just not, of course." He refers to two crucial and fundamental aspects of his life that he definitely will not discuss, even and especially in the exposure of a diary: "I can't speak or write of two thoughts that dwell within me mainly, and to any-one who like myself talks easily of all that is in the mind, this is in itself a discipline." His discipline, explicitly foregrounded, inevitably prompts our voyeuristic guesswork (as he must have known). Four years later, he repeats the comment in a more theoretical manner:

> I reflect that, intimate in some ways as this, there are at least <u>two</u> thoughts, often with me, that greatly affect my life, to which I never allude here. I suppose people's ideas of privacy differ very much. Some people's minds are like a wide park, with a high wall and lodges—no-one but callers admitted—the house in the woods. Some are like suburban villas on the street. I don't think my sense of privacy is very general—but it is very strong about one or two things—and I have a carefully locked and guarded strong room. Anyone might think they could get a good picture of my life from these pages, but it is not so.

The descriptions of houses and landscapes run throughout the diary, and Arthur's love of domestic spaces, his romantic longing for secluded pastoral nooks, his visits to churches—are central to his narratives of self-formation. His autobiographical book, *The Tre-foil*, is structured around three houses—Wellington, Lincoln, and Truro—each lavishly described. The house at Tremans features as the very structure—emotional, social, as well as physical—of their later family life in his imagination. In *The Thread of Gold*, he writes movingly of a house, "So near to my heart came the spirit of the house, that, as I mused, I felt as though even I myself had made a part of its past, and as though I were returning from battling with the far-off world to the home of childhood": the fictionalized house takes the musing author back into an as-if of childhood, a fantasized return via the spirit of the house into his own inner life. So the extended analogy of minds and houses is a deeply charged expression for the threats and privileges of privacy: it goes to the heart of the socially embedded, embodied person. Neither the grand park nor the suburban villa will capture Arthur's internal life. He has a "carefully locked and guarded strong room," an inner sanctum that goes beyond even his representation of the secluded don or recluse, as his persona in so many essays and fictions has it, the view from a college window. This "strong room" means he is—if not proudly at least with a flourish of self-pronouncement—unknowable. When you have read the four million words of intimate diary, intimate "in some ways," actually you will not get a "good picture" of his life. His secrets are such that without knowing them—and nobody may— there is no chance of producing a biography, an image that matches the truth. His diary, he confesses—frankly?—is at a fundamental level "not a good picture."

Percy Lubbock took another view on the inaccuracy of the self-representation. He was the first person to read all the volumes of diary (there have only been three others, including me, as the librarian told me: Lubbock; David Newsome, Arthur Benson's biographer; and the master of Magdalene, to check that the diaries could be made public). Percy Lubbock was Arthur Benson's most regular companion, a younger, well-connected man who made his way in the world of literature as a reviewer in the *TLS* and as a biographer, ending up with a CBE for his services to letters. The diary itself records that "Percy says I make phrases so easily, I forget how pungent they are. 'It's different in talk—there's something anti-septic in talk! You wouldn't say these things, just think them.'" Lubbock expresses to Arthur the view that conversation, face-to-face, has its own protocols, for all the prided frankness of exchange, and the written diary is false because it reveals the rather too sharp hidden and unexpressed thoughts, which should have remained in the recesses of the mind, in the strong room. As a demonstration of this dynamic, elsewhere Lubbock himself writes down a different thought: "In fact, he never knew himself well enough to record himself aright." This is not so much a slur on Arthur's self-conscious scrutiny, as a recognition that nobody sees themselves being seen by others as in fact they are: "He failed to see [his own geniality] as others always saw it." Nonetheless, Arthur is characteristically tetchy when his flaws are teased by someone else. Fred sent him a parody of his "intime style in which I appear as a pompous, selfish, hypocritical, elaborate poseur." No doubt the parody upset him because these terms were all ways he chose to criticize himself.

The materiality of the diary reveals Arthur's growing into a pattern of disciplined reticence as the boundary to frankness. An entry in volume II is scribbled out with the note, "A sordid entry. I therefore erased." His handwriting becomes neater and smaller when he meets royalty and needs—wants—to behave with exquisite manners; the writing becomes florid and uncontrolled as he rants about a dinner party insult; the approach of mental illness cramps the pages with claustrophobically small writing for the descriptions of minute changes of black moods. Longhand writing embodies mood, and when Arthur indulges in his rare crossings-out and corrections, the work of careful self-presentation, recalibrating appearances, is physically evident.

Throughout, indeed, he remains deeply suspicious of improper self-presentation as a sort of showing off. He snorts about Gosse's writing: "But the sticking of the autobiographical element in, in patches, is not nice: it gives an evil aroma. It is the need of skipping and posturing before the people; of bowing them into the show; of wanting to get a recognition of your own cleverness, and this is distressing." He recommends to a budding poet that he should not in his verses give himself away. He is very sniffy about his chum, the bibliophile, Cambridge don, and dodgy poet, Charles Sayle, for his self-revelations: "Sayle dined and gave himself away as usual." "Sayle rather horrified me. . . . I hated to see a man so give himself away." To admit directly or in an uncontrolled fashion to a passion, to display one's desire out loud, to squeeze up against the fences of convention worried Arthur Benson. The self is not to be given away.

Tact, discretion, decency must police the display of frankness. Arthur was delighted, therefore, when he took on the difficult subject of writing about Walter Pater, to hear secondhand a reader's remark that "he committed no indiscretions, and yet one who knows the whole story can tell that B knows it too." To those who know, he talks with knowingness, and knowingness shared is precisely discretion in action. "This was high praise and pleased me very much," smiles Arthur. So in personal exchange when Howard Sturgis confesses to him that "the most terrible thing that has ever happened to him in his life has happened . . . the nature of the event he cannot hint at," Arthur responds with a gesture of comfortable sympathetic tact, "I do not want to know, poor soul." It is important to know when not to want to know, when not to allow voyeuristic curiosity free rein. A. C. Benson was chosen to edit Queen Victoria's letters because he could be relied on to know what could be put into the public eye.

His immense diary is thus both a performance and a discussion of the awkward and constantly shifting boundary between frankness and giving oneself away.

In 1916 Fred Benson published one of his most successful novels, *David Blaize*. It is a schoolboy story, set in a great British public school, and is focused on the intense and eroticized relationship between David and his friend Maddox. They read Greek together, swim naked, and promise to go to Greece when they are a little older. But it is their innocent intimacy itself that the book holds up as an icon of a lost glorious world of Edwardian summer, looking back from the grimmer perspective of the First World War. Much later, the book's popularity, especially for soldiers in the war, prompted speculation about the author's investment in the fiction, not least for its homoeroticism. In 1935 Fred gave an interview to a journalist, who, like so many tidy-minded or prurient readers, wanted to disentangle the interplay of fiction and the autobiographical and read through the one to the certain purity of the other. Pressed on the scenes between the two boys, Fred explained their force simply enough: the book was, he said, "a genuine piece of self-expression." Especially when a creative writer fictionalizes boys daydreaming about Greece, the obliqueness of fiction, as Freud knew, allows the censor to be bypassed. For Fred, it would seem, the self was most genuinely expressed in the concealments of fiction.

IT IS HARD TO IMAGINE A FAMILY MORE MUTUALLY ENGAGED in the process of writing the self as a family history than the Bensons. The family, many years after the archbishop's death, even started a joint diary, for which each person wrote their own entry and circulated it to the others. "The three ladies most perceptive," commented Arthur in his parallel diary, "the only thing they must learn to do is not to be afraid of speaking of each other." When many years later he read his mother's personal diary for the time of Maggie's breakdown, he was shocked not just by how censorious and exacting Maggie became; rather, "it distresses me," he adds tellingly, "that my name is only once mentioned." Not being a named figure in the story takes Arthur outside the family trauma; not into the tactful silence of not needing to know, nor under the aegis of the discreet knowingness of withholding vulgar revelation; but in the emotional hinterland of wondering whether and how he mattered to the story. In a family, as in the games of celebrity, there is, as Oscar Wilde knew, only one thing worse than being talked about.

Telling the truth is too simple an expression for how the Benson family was obsessed with writing the self—descriptions, debates, criticisms of their own and others' internal lives—and how they discussed equally obsessively the dictates of politeness, rigor, tact, and insight that controlled or should control such explorations of the privacy and exposure of family dynamics. So when Fred Benson decided to write the story of how his parents became engaged, his position in these family dynamics inevitably frames his writing. He writes as the family member he is. The amused and superficial anecdote of a distanced world, highly conscious of how "genuine self expression" passes through fiction, and what the costs of candor can be, means that his tale of a father loving a mother can only turn out to be deeply Freddian.

All self-presentations are organized around concealing something from the world, and Fred Benson's romantic image of his parents' first kiss has its all too obvious repressions—of what he had read about his parents, and what he felt about them, and his own feelings about himself, then and now. But writing this primal scene as a delightful anecdote is also a gesture of appropriation. Henry James, the friend of Fred and Arthur Benson, when he was accosted for changing the words of his brother's personal letters in a memoir to make the prose better, commented, "I did intuitively regard it at last as all my truth." Fred Benson has made the story of the kiss his own, a Freddian moment, where the world is made in his image, his own truth, all his, at last, against the family.

6

A Map of Biographical Urges

IT IS A STRANGE DISTORTION, FOSTERED BY THE BIASES OF
modern literary genealogy, that the novel is so often seen these days
as the dominant and privileged genre of the nineteenth century.
The Victorian novel, as a new and, of course, modern exploration of
the self through narrative, has become an integral part of our story
of modernity's culture. This story certainly has some solid foundations. There can be no doubt that Walter Scott's historical fiction
formed the cultural imagination of a generation, not just in Britain but across Europe and America. Novelists were indeed lions of
literary society and creators of narratives by which the world was
understood and lived: it is not without his usual and precise self-
consciousness that Oscar Wilde in *The Importance of Being Earnest*
mocks the literary ambition of Miss Prism as a "three-volume novel
of more than usually revolting sentimentality."

Yet such a literary history distorts and diminishes the cultural
significance of at least two other forms or genres, which in the nineteenth century were no less fundamental as narratives of the self,
and which the novel is in constant dialogue with. The first, simply
enough, is poetry. One of the best-selling and most loved books from
the end of the first quarter of the nineteenth century is *The Christian Year* by John Keble, whose famous Assize Sermon on "National
Apostasy" was often taken as the beginning of the Oxford Movement. Despite the controversy of his Tractarian theological leanings,
this book of poems, one for each day of the calendar, was read and

learned off by heart by an extraordinary number of people. By the 1870s, it had gone through more than a 150 editions and sold more than 375,000 copies. It is barely read today even by scholars of the nineteenth century. Yet its spiritual framework informed and nourished the internal lives of an extraordinarily diverse and extended public. Keble described poetry as a sort of God-given balm, "medicine divinely bestowed upon man," which brought "healing relief to secret mental emotion." John Henry Newman, his Tractarian colleague, wrote that "the taste for poetry of a religious kind has in modern times in a certain sense taken the place of the deep contemplative spirit of the early Church." Poetry, for Newman, "is our mysticism." *The Christian Year* was the iconic example of this idea.

Similarly, Wordsworth's epic and lyric poetry—*The Prelude* and *The Excursion*, that is, as much as the lyrical ballads—was taken to provide an especially inspirational, transformative journey of self-discovery for his Victorian readers. Writing in the 1880s, William Hale White, whose pseudo-autobiographical fictions we will come back to, captured the religiosity of the experience of reading Wordsworth: "Wordsworth unconsciously did for me what every religious reformer had done,—he created my Supreme Divinity, substituting a new and living spirit for the old deity, once alive but gradually hardened into an idol." So earlier in 1841, Sir John Simon—surgeon, medical professor, and the first Chief Medical Officer of England—wrote a fan letter to the seventy-one-year-old Wordsworth: "Instruction in all, which it chiefly behoves to know— humbler reliance in the Divine rule—fuller love of Man—deeper & holier sympathies with Nature—in success, self-diffidence—in trial & suffering the stay and comfort of religious wisdom—are lessons which I, in common with thousands—owe to those works [of yours]." Like the chief medical officer, the philosopher John Stuart Mill found in Wordsworth, rather than in philosophy, "a medicine for my state of mind." Charles Darwin read *The Excursion* repeatedly, and Charles Kingsley, who walked on excursions with both Darwin and Edward White Benson, celebrated Wordsworth as "preacher and prophet of God's new and divine philosophy—a man raised up as a light in a dark time." The Bensons went on holiday often in the Alps and, as Wordsworth taught, roamed through memories and desires as they walked, tracing the anatomy of their inner beings—what Freud would have wanted to call the walking cure. And all the Bensons wove poetry into their diaries, expressions of the most intense moments of reflection and memory. Arthur's first four published books were all volumes of his poetry, and the only part of Minnie Benson's papers that she herself marked "private" or "intensely private" are not her diaries or meditations, but her poems. Poetry as a narrative of self-formation—reading it, writing it, learning it so that it is inside you—is fundamental to nineteenth-century *Bildung*, an education into a cultured life. Edward White Benson and Minnie Sidgwick were reading Tennyson's *The Princess* together as a dawning of love. Like so many of their friends and social acquaintances, each of the Bensons read, reread, and absorbed—as a soundtrack to their emotional self-expression—Tennyson's *In Memoriam*, which for a generation and more provided the privileged exploration of memory and the articulate memorialization of grief, of an (inner) life of desire buried in loss, and a striving need to make sense of it all.

But Victorian writers and readers also declared that theirs was a new age of progress in biography as in all else—the second flourishing genre that constantly informs the novel—and, as with poetry, biography is a fundamental way in which the process of "writing down the self" was expressed. So the thoroughly undistinguished journalist Robert Goodbrand wrote in 1870, with clarity if not truth, that until recently "there has been no biography at all. It is a modern attainment, and Goethe and Rousseau have opened the double valves through which the world has arrived at it." Goodbrand's drastic shortcut in the history of life-writing is justified by Rousseau himself, who begins his *Confessions* with the startling announcement, "I have conceived an enterprise that has no model at all." So much for St. Augustine. What is important here is not to correct such self-serving and misleading claims, but to try to understand how they could possibly have come to be made in the first place. The high priest of classical scholarship, Ulrich von Möllendorf-Wilamowitz, who certainly knew the ancient biographical tradition of Plutarch and Suetonius and Libanius, offers a telling clue as to what is at stake here, when he declares that ancient biographies offered *no representation of the self.* The modern self needs its own story.

In the eyes of Victorian writers, especially toward the end of the nineteenth century, there is a new sense of self-consciousness at work in British culture, for which a new form of life-writing plays a fundamental role. We will need a basic map of how biography develops over the century in order to find the proper place for the Bensons' prolific contributions to this genre, but first even the barest outline of how this new sense of self-consciousness took shape will provide a necessary if preliminary framework.

At one level, made familiar now by a host of recent cultural studies of the nineteenth century, we can see in Victorian writing a new awareness of living in a particular historical moment, a sense, that is, fostered especially after the French Revolution, that contemporary society—and each person's place in it, therefore—is different from the past *as an era.* The most obvious and repeated sign of this awareness is articulated in the myriad proclamations that a special modernity has arrived—"the girl of the period," "the spirit of the age," "the era of progress," "the foundations of the century," "the behaviour of today." This rhetoric of modernity, however, is formulated against a background of large-scale theoretical models of political, historical, and imperial development, which are typical of a Victorian intellectual agenda—from Maine's or Marx's social theory to Darwin's biology to Marshall's economics. This sense of history on the move—and its effects on a person's experience of time, social placement, and the significance of action—grounds the huge series of biographical volumes that memorialized the heroes of empire, the political leaders of the age, the artists of the era, of which Thomas Carlyle's *Heroes and Hero Worship* is the most sophisticated, the most theoretically rich, and, more surprisingly, the most influential example. It is in part because of the dominance of Carlyle's paradigmatic understanding of a life's exemplary value that the ancient authors such as Plutarch seemed so easily dismissible to late Victorian thinking about how to write the story of the self.

New theoretical models of psychological development, however, are equally influential in this changing sense of self-construction. Scientists and theoreticians of the mind—of which Freud is only the most starry example—were producing instrumental and wide-ranging paradigms of psychological development as models of individual growth or as models of social transformation. How the child would or should become an adult—sexually, morally, socially—was becoming a question argued through at a particularly heated juncture between social science, educational theory, and medicine. Life-writing became the test cases of such intellectually explosive theorizing. Theories of psychology duly became systems of upbringing, which stimulated in turn a literature of resistance and questioning. For the Bensons in particular, as teachers, writers, and children locked in an obsessive response to their own father and mother—not to mention their deep involvement with a giant of moral science such as Henry Sidgwick, or of the literary portrayal of the psychology of a child approaching adulthood such as Henry James—the desire to anatomize, repeatedly, their own childhood was a pressing and overdetermined injunction.

Yet this new understanding of psychological development was intercalated with an old tradition of religious writing—and a contemporary sense of religious self-expression. Long-standing models of Protestant conversion narratives or Catholic hagiographic saints' lives were attacked—and imitated—at two levels. From one perspective, critical history's assault on the authority of the Bible was precisely an attack on the reliability of a biographical tradition—epitomized in David Strauss's *Das Leben Jesu* or Ernest Renan's *Vie de Jesu*. As a novel such as Mrs. Humphry Ward's *Robert Elsmere* vividly depicted—to the scandal and fascination of the British reading public—critical reading about ancient life-writing could undermine the story of one's own religious life—one's religious self. From another perspective, a burgeoning and seductive line of loss-of-faith stories offered a counter-history of the self—to be relived and retold. In such an environment, one of the most worrying publications was the book *Ecce Homo*, originally published anonymously but eventually revealed to be the work of the (future) great historian John Robert Seeley. *Ecce Homo* purported to be an autobiographical account of religious reflection that was so poised that it proved hard to tell if it was a book of a Christian losing his faith or of an agnostic growing toward God. Doubt about the trajectory of religious doubt was the most upsetting uncertainty of all; but one that Arthur Benson in particular could appreciate all too personally and painfully.

What's more, the educational models inherited from a reading of classical literature as well as from within the institutional structures of schooling demanded that the exempla of great men and women should form the basis of social formation. "Diet yourself on biography, the biography of good and great men," wrote Edward Bulwer Lytton in *The Caxtons*—with his finger as ever right on the pulse of the just trendy. The narratives of the self were to be read as part of the diet of self-formation, to provide the models by which a life could be lived and narrated. Because it is a diet, (auto)biography, as Arthur Benson knew, needed discipline. In short, "pressures of secularization and psychological theory unsettled the categories of biography and autobiography." The new sense of self needed new forms of storytelling. How lives can be told or written will always be of cultural significance, and life-writing needs its deep contextualization within social, intellectual, and political frames to take on its shape of significance. So how did biography find a form within this shifting development of a new sense of self-consciousness?

BIOGRAPHY WAS A BEST-SELLING GENRE OF PUBLICATION in the nineteenth century. It is good to remember that in the 1850s when *David Copperfield*—a fictional autobiography—sold 25,000 copies to critical and popular acclaim, the Reverend William Brock's *A Biographical Sketch of Sir Henry Havelock, K.C.B.* sold 46,000 copies. *David Copperfield* begins with an amusingly knowing nod to (auto)biographical form: "Whether I shall turn out to be the hero of my own life, or whether that station will be held by anybody else, these pages must show." Brock acknowledges his public in quite a different style: "In deference to a very generally expressed desire for some authentic information about Sir Henry Havelock, the following biographical sketch, having special reference to his religious character, has been prepared." General Henry Havelock, a career soldier, was best known for his recapture of Cawnpore during the Indian Mutiny and the relief of the siege of Lucknow. He also introduced cross-rank Bible classes into the army and distributed Bibles to the soldiers. He was a national hero for whom Tennyson wrote after his death: "every man in Britain / Says 'I am of Havelock's blood!'" As a paradigm of the overlap of evangelical zeal and imperial militarism, it is expected that the public might want some "special reference to his religious character" to ground his heroic deeds. What sort of a man—and thus what sort of a religious man—was he? How is he is to be understood—narrated? What sort of an exemplary figure?

Life-writing—and life-reading—was a nineteenth-century obsession. A beginning and prime example can be found in Thomas Babington Macaulay, whose celebrated history of England gave the English a sense of their own place in history and a new Whig version of progress toward the triumph of England as a dominant power in the world, as a sign of the triumph of civilization. It is a brilliantly stylish piece of writing, which owes a great deal to Walter Scott's historical fiction as well as to the classical historians Macaulay read and reread and loved (biography, the novel, and history writing are in constant generic interaction through the nineteenth century). His biographical essays, which seem like polemical outtakes or preparatory studies for the history, often focus on a single figure—Hastings, say—just as in the history itself there are some remarkable portraits of villains, such as Jeffrey, the hanging judge, a picture that reads like a character sketch out of Tacitus, melodramatically evil and locked into a narrative of rise through corruption and fall into humiliation, like so many of the powerful freedmen in Roman history. Biography here consists in an account of a public life, explored as a testimony of the paradoxes of motivation. *Ethos* is revealed by public activity and by contribution to a national narrative. Macaulay, writing in the middle of the nineteenth century, gives a perfect example of the reception of classical models of ancient historiography, elegantly informed by an English nationalism, a paradigmatic Victorian self-consciousness about historical time in an age of progress, and a sense of the excitement now needed in historical narrative after the huge success of Scott's historical fiction.

But Arthur Benson's biography of his father fits into a quite different model of life-writing that crams the shelves of the last years of the century, the two-volume "Life and Letters." Almost every major public figure, and quite a lot of frankly minor public figures, had biographies of this type. They are usually edited or written by a wife (since most public figures are male) or by a son; they tell the facts of the public life, rarely with anything like the racy prose of Macaulay, and weave their narrative in and out of the collection of letters that every Victorian worth his salt wrote every day to friends, colleagues, and family. This form of biography has no intention of producing the sort of paradoxical character insight of a Macaulay. Rather it offers an archive, a memorial, and record of a life, lived out in public, and in the semi-public, semi-private world of published letters. A training in how to write letters—as Edward demanded of Minnie—is always with an eye on the act of self-presentation for an outside world and, for public figures, with an eye on their future publication. Preserving letters is the expected ongoing archive and memorial of a relationship; returning letters the *damnatio memoriae* of an exchange and the physical, violent denial of a history: the return of letters materially embodies disjunction, just as the continuing holding and reading of the tear-stained page materially embodies a present interaction.

The narrative of such a "Life and Letters" is always linear, always chronological, and aims to provide a coherent, multifaceted jewel: my husband's glorious career. The biography is written by someone intimately connected to the subject, but intimacy is not what is on display. Rather the genre is committed to complicity, control, and the production of public image. One adjective embodies this strategic reticence: "sacred." As soon as anything intimate is approached—letters to a lover, say—the author/editor will say: "This is too sacred for revelation here." Sometimes, even for the most austere and public-minded figures, this veiling seemed excessive in its hesitancy. As Prime Minister Gladstone sniffed about George Eliot's biography, written by her husband, John Cross: "It is not a Life at all. It is a reticence in three volumes"—a line delivered at dinner to Minnie Benson and quoted by Fred in his own biographical reminiscences (where reticence plays its thematized role). Such a biography sets out to say something quite different from Macaulay about what a life should be, how the story of a life can be told.

In the last fifteen years of the century, one of the great imperial projects, *The Dictionary of National Biography*, also gets under way, under the leadership first of Sir Leslie Stephen, father of Virginia Woolf. The early editions of this masterpiece of encyclopedic thinking—and encyclopedias are always linked to conceptual if not political imperialism—are a real joy to read. They offer usually quite brief accounts of a life, often no more than a paragraph or two. But what makes them so much fun is the combination of the bare outlines of a career with a couple of telling anecdotes or scurrilous details. This is biography as dinner party conversation. That is, if someone mentions Hastings, it is not necessary to know any deep paradoxical understanding about his character and the relationship between his motivations and the political narrative of the English: what is needed is the barest facts, to know who he is, why he matters, and a couple of racy anecdotes to drop into the conversation. *The Dictionary of National Biography* is a sort of handbook for passing muster in polite society, a collection of anecdotal snapshots to get you through as a cultural insider. Extraordinary stories circulated to promote and project a shared sense of the normal. This is typical of university biographies, as evidenced by the obituary columns, which also flourish in this period: a life reduced to academic successes, future career, and two stories by which we remember our former students or colleagues—a witticism offered, a quirk recalled, an amusing accident. . . . In contrast to the archive of the two-volume "Life and Letters," here we have biography as anecdote and thus a quite different sense of what memorializing and remembering might look like. Such snappy biographies offer a very particular charm but, more importantly, an insight into how a life should be conceptualized, what counts in making up a biography. Arthur read the *DNB* in bed to send him to sleep. He dreamt most often of his famous father.

For Edmund Gosse, "The true conception of biography" is "the faithful portrait of a soul in its adventures through life," a form that he terms, typically for the period, "very modern." (He also, slightly more wickedly, aimed to be "as indiscreet as possible within the bounds of good taste and kind feeling.") The "portrait" becomes a key term of biographical writing in the late nineteenth century, of which the *DNB* entry is a miniature of calculated, elegant oversimplification. Portraiture was changing materially through the lifetime of the Bensons, with the formal portraits of high Victorian art giving way to the blurry inwardness of Impressionism, the realism of photography and the jagged lines and abstractions of Post-Impressionism. A. C. Benson was drawn by "Spy," the famous cartoonist, and found the process of being stared at and reduced to the simplest lines a very uncomfortable experience. The Bensons' friend Henry James wrote *The Portrait of a Lady*, and Walter Pater, whose biography Arthur Benson produced, had composed *Imaginary Portraits*, a set of autobiographical short stories, the influence of which stretches beyond the nineteenth century and into the impressionism of a writer such as Virginia Woolf, who found an intellectual father figure in Pater—and in her *Orlando*, a biographical narrative as far as possible from her father's baby, the *DNB*. Oscar Wilde's *The Picture of Dorian Gray*, with its central trope of the concealed portrait, could not have been conceived outside this nexus of tensions between art and literature, between an inner life and an outer image to the world, between different models of transition into maturity, between new psychologies, new sexualities, and old moral certainties. Arthur Benson also wrote volumes of portraits—shortish biographical accounts of people he had met and known, his impressions, as he called them, of the figures in his life. The question of the portrait—its aim, success, and failure—was never merely its lifelikeness but always also its ability to reveal a concealed inwardness, to fashion the inner life for oneself.

Pater's displacement of autobiography into the imaginary portrait was only one of many nineteenth-century strategies of (auto) biographical writing, a compositional richness that makes Paul De Man's celebrated statement that "autobiography and fiction is not an either/or polarity" seem a very late theoretical observation of what had been thoroughly well-known and explored in practice by many great writers. Thomas Carlyle, who made history "the essence of innumerable biographies" and who wanted biography to be thus the great didactic genre of the age, also called fictional (auto)biography "the lowest of froth Prose in the fashionable novel"; but his own *Sartor Resartus* is perhaps the wildest biographical fiction of the era, based as it is on a crazy German philosopher's treatise on clothes: its success as a story of self-formation is surely one of the most bizarre turns of Victorian literary culture. William Hale White wrote *The Autobiography of Mark Rutherford, Dissenting Minister* in 1881. Like Arthur Benson's *Memoirs of William Hamilton* (and *Sartor Resartus*), the text comes to us via a fictional editor, Reuben Shapcott, who claims not only to have found the manuscript but to have added some parts from diaries and other papers left after his friend Rutherford's death (a ruse that allowed for a sequel or two after the discovery of more papers). Rutherford tells us that his education, no doubt in the Edward White Benson mold, had given him "a rigid regard for truthfulness," yet it is precisely with the dubious referential boundaries of truthfulness that the book plays: is it a novel of loss of faith like *Robert Elsmere*, or is it a pseudonymous autobiography of its author, pseudonymous to protect its author from giving himself away? As one contemporary reviewer wrote, "We hardly know whether to call them fiction, they carry so deep a sense of truthfulness." Hale White was explicit, however, that he did not care to reveal his inner life: "It would be too dangerous," he wrote. Leslie Stephen, yet another well-connected member of the British intellectual elite who theorized about biography as well as founding the *DNB*, reflected how "the story of my own life is somehow altogether wrong." When he goes back and rereads old letters—as the Benson brothers did, with a similar sense of self-redefinition—the fading pages revealed how his memory was "ever since letting facts drop, and remoulding others, and colouring the whole with a strangely delusive mist." Between the fantastical self of Thomas Carlyle's *Sartor Resartus*, the fictionalized self of William Hale White, and the mistaken, misremembering self of Leslie Stephen—not to mention the 54-book series of the publisher Fisher Unwin called the Pseudonym Library or George and Weedon Grossmith's smartly parodic *The Diary of a Nobody*—it is easy to see why a critic can write that through the last decades of the nineteenth century and the beginning of the twentieth, both "reference and resemblance" seem under increasing attack as the self-evident mainstays of the autobiographical mode.

Despite such self-aware experimentation with the narrative gaps, self-deceptions, and rhetorical self-positioning in (auto)biography as a form, then, when it came to it, *reticence* constantly structures the frankness praised by Arthur Benson, even when the piety of reticence is derided by Gladstone, always well aware of the social protocols—which allow a mocking of tact at the same time as displaying a horror of any actual transgression of it.

As ever, the tacit regulation of social normativity is most obvious at the site of transgression. James Anthony Froude, whose *The Nemesis of Faith* was such a scandal when he was a young man, had become a respected historian and man of letters. He was Carlyle's literary executor and commissioned to write his biography, with unique access to his personal papers as well as long personal contact, especially with Mrs. Carlyle after her husband's death. Like so many fictitious biographers, he found in Carlyle's papers a self-penned memoir of his marriage, which Froude duly included in the biography. Froude's biography, however, with Carlylean bluntness, crossed a boundary and revealed the bitterness and sexual unhappiness in the Carlyles' marriage. Reviewers were horrified: it was, as Mrs. Oliphant paradigmatically declared, "a betrayal and an exposure of a woman's weakness." The fuss that followed—a family brouhaha, public outrage, and even a law case—led Froude to write a pamphlet that was published by his children ten years after his own death, in which he stated in an even more outright fashion that Carlyle was impotent. To give away the sacred inner truth of a marriage undermined the social decency of the biographer.

Morley Roberts found that fiction was no defense, either. In 1912 he published *The Private Life of Henry Maitland: A Record Dictated to J.H.: Revised and Edited by Morley Roberts*. It is typical of the instability of reference and resemblance in life-writing of this era that Roberts offers a text that he claims to have edited, from a text dictated by one J.H. to him, about a fictional character, called Henry Maitland—but all contemporary readers seem to have been quite assured that the book was about the recently dead George Gissing, a friend of Roberts. The title's promise of a private life is undoubtedly a come-on, and the preface anticipates a portrait without hagiographic reticence: "This is not a British statue done in the best mortuary manner. There is far too little sincere biography in English. We are a mealy-mouthed race, hypocrites by the grave and monument." Like Gladstone, Roberts pokes fun at the British, who offer nothing but mealy-mouthed reticence about the dead. Unlike Gladstone, Roberts went on to write a "sincere" biography (if sincerity can be applied to a fictional, dictated memory of a fictional figure), a biography that enjoyed revealing the subject's flaws and transgressions. The allure of the "sincere," "private life" depends precisely on the prurience and reticence it claims to refuse. Ford Madox Ford called it a "bitter bad book" but quickly added— with equal bad faith, one might fear—not because it "gave away a number of confidences of the poor dead Gissing," but because it lacked "invention." Its resemblance was too close, its reference too dishonestly—or transparently—concealed. Morley Roberts, too, had crossed a line: he gave away his fictional masks and Gissing's confidences, without the necessary reticence. He couldn't dissemble or disavow successfully enough.

So looking back in anger at the Victorians, constructing the "real gulf, vastly sundering" between the two eras, also meant redrawing the boundaries of the privileged genre of biography. Lytton Strachey's *Eminent Victorians* constructed and reveled in that gulf of separation. His book consists of five essay-length biographies of Victorian grandees, but now the project of life-writing is undertaken by an outsider, an outsider who revels not in his complicity with the subjects of biography, but in his distance—an ironic, revelatory, and critical distance. He opened the sacred to the snide. Biography becomes a means of criticism of a generation, an uncovering not just of foible or sin, but of self-deception, political bad faith, and unpleasant intimacies. Lytton Strachey, from the highly charged, highly sexual heart of Bloomsbury, within the extended family of Sir Leslie Stephen, reconstructed biography in his own image: bitchy, clever, dismissive—demanding a quite different complicity or knowingness with his readers. Telling a life now means revealing what the subject did not know about herself, what she could not see by virtue of her historical position, her psychological blindnesses or political misprisions. Rip off the public self-presentation and look beneath, to show the unpleasantness beneath the skin. This is knowingly another, quite different sense of what telling the story of a life can mean or stand for. Strachey's book made a biography like Arthur Benson's memorial of his father, the archbishop, look desperately out-of-date.

THIS MAP OF (AUTO)BIOGRAPHICAL LIFE-WRITING ACROSS the nineteenth and into the twentieth century has been no more than a map. As with a map, the terrain is more complex and varied than its representation, and, as we will see, with Arthur Benson in particular what it means to write a life is especially intricate and multilayered. But enough has been said even in outline to indicate that when Fred Benson comes to write biography and autobiography, the choice of form comes loaded with an internal history of a genre and with an integral commitment to an understanding of how public and private, revelation and concealment, familial piety and intergenerational anxiety are to be managed.

Fred Benson had written a biography of Sir Francis Drake—a character far from his usual range of interests, except perhaps as a hero of English history—which begins with a nod to the genre as genre, in characteristic lighthearted manner. It is something of a melancholy embarrassment for a biographer, he confesses with mock horror, that he cannot say where his subject was born. He is fully aware of the easy cliché of the *genius loci*, which opens so many Victorian biographies: he was born in Kent and that gentle county which he loved formed his character. . . . He also wrote a biography of Edward VII and of Queen Victoria, following in his brother's footsteps, carefully constructing a public image of royalty for a kingdom of subjects. In all three volumes, none read today except for professional reasons, I suspect, the air of conventional restraint is marked. Especially for Edward VII, whose gambling played a role in Arthur's biography of the archbishop and whose other gestures of disdain for standard Victorian proprieties were ripe for the analysis of a Lytton Strachey, Fred Benson proved a safe pair of hands. In *Final Edition* (1940), his final book, subtitled *An Informal Autobiography*, looking back he gives perhaps his most telling and even most theoretical statement on life-writing. Of an autobiographer's fictions, he writes with charming insouciance, "It was not his memory that had failed but his imagination that had flowered. I think it would be pedantic to call such a result a falsification of fact: it was rather an enhancement of fact." As his family always knew, Fred was an expert in the imaginative enhancement of the facts.

So when Fred Benson comes to write his own life story and the story of his parents' first kiss, the form he chose should seem overdetermined. The narrative of elegant anecdotes, amused distance from himself and from others, his wry awareness of the foibles—rather than the sins—of the world take shape against a Victorian tradition of biographical decorum, and a modern tearing down of such veils; against a Victorian fascination with inner life as a dangerous area of religious and moral revelation, and a modern psychological uncovering of psychosexual urges; against his brother's life-writing and the genre's awareness of self-fictionalization. It is unlikely to be by chance that this autobiography is called *As We Were*, but his book *As We Are* is a novel with no immediate connection to any aspect of his family's life: another form of distance from the immediate revelation. The anecdote of the delightful romance of his eleven-year-old mother, as a form, reveals Fred Benson's insistent desire to see life one way and to write it so. It is an act of resistance.

7

To Write a Life

IF WE WERE TO DRAW UP A MAP OF BIOGRAPHICAL URGES, Arthur Benson would inhabit a particular place on it. He was an intimate friend of Edmund Gosse and Henry James, who from their different angles drew the boundaries of the late Victorian portrait. He wrote a biography of Pater, master of the aesthetic imaginary portrait; he wrote a biography of Ruskin, whose autobiography *Praeterita* provided the paradigm of the paradox of both recalling what is past (*praeterita:* "what has passed") and confessing to an autobiography's deliberate omissions (*praeterita:* "passed over," "omitted"). He wrote short literary portraits of many of his Cambridge acquaintances. He loved reading biographies and diaries, and did so with a sharply critical eye: "read Haydon's Diary, a bitty, unbalanced, sordid book, which made my heart ache," he notes in his diary; or, with his teacher's commitment to the fore, "Herbert Spencer's Autobiography is the strongest argument I have yet seen against irrational education"; or, for the genial and donnish Dean Farrar's biography, written by his untalented son, he snidely practices his phrases, "I have been reading the <u>Life of Farrar</u> with the sort of joy that Mr Bennett got out of Mr Collins, when he said he was as fully absurd as he had hoped. The book has every disadvantage—it is full of misprints and errors; it is compiled by a man (F's son) who has neither taste, judgment, [n]or literary skill. It is full of ridiculous letters which F received. . . . [H]is son does not see his faults and the result is grotesque." This high dudgeon, a Victorian reviewer's panache, leads into his own character sketch of Dean Farrar, to show how it should be done. By contrast, Scott's diary reveals: "Such a sweet, simple, tender-hearted, faithful man," though he can't resist adding, "but not an <u>artist</u>." These four diary entries are taken from just a couple of months in 1904. He also read (auto)biographies of Carlyle, Kingsley, Morris, Newman, Burton, Jowett. . . . In the back of Minnie's copy of Mrs. Oliphant's *Autobiography*, which I found in a secondhand bookshop, he wrote out in fair copy the paragraphs he would publish in his own published portrait of her, his biographical commentary on her autobiography. Arthur lived in the midst of life-writing.

Reading diaries, as he wrote his own, was a self-conscious act of self-exploration, and one journal in particular mattered to him. *Extracts from the Letters and Journals of William Cory* was published in 1897, the year that Arthur Benson started his diary in earnest, and he claimed it was his inspiration: "It is the answer to all people like myself who want to write and cannot." This was also the first year after his father's death, which is one of the reasons why we will have to come back to the lament that he cannot write but will be able to start now. Cory's memoir was printed by subscription, and the twenty-three subscribers include not only A. C. Benson, but many of his closest friends from the Eton circle. This is very much an insiders' book. Inevitably, Benson added a biographical introduction to the reprint of this volume, though, tellingly, Herbert Paul, himself the biographer of Matthew Arnold and James Anthony Froude, and someone who know Cory well, thought it "an interesting ingenious little essay, on a character evolved from Benson's own mind"—an imaginary portrait. Cory, who had changed his name from William Johnson according to the terms of a legacy, had been a teacher at Eton and a poet, whose book *Ionica* achieved a mild celebrity not least for its beautiful and haunting translation of Callimachus, "They told me, Heraclitus, they told me you were dead." Cory had been forced to leave Eton because of his too evident affection for beautiful boys (the very title *Ionica*, to the cognoscenti, screams its lyric roots in Greek desire). Nobody doubted he was a great teacher—a self-serving commonplace in such stories, even when true—but his charisma and charm meant that he left behind him something of a cult of romantic friendship among the boys, which both engaged and exercised the masters. Arthur writes of Cory with more direct passion than he finds for most living people, "I really love W.J. and I cannot help feeling that my love helps him somewhere. . . . This is very transcendental; and yet it is very real."

This very real thing of love for a man through his prose, a man never met, is nourished by Benson's repeated reading of Cory's journal—and by writing down his own feelings. In 1899, struggling to capture his sense of sublime emotion, he writes, "I read a few pages of Cory, which always brings up by cords of pathos and delight the deep well-water of the poetry of this life. I can't express what that book does for me." Three years later he is still wondering about this feeling: "I wonder why the thought of Wm Johnson is so often with me and stirs the deepest founts within me"—and offers an answer, "It is, I think, that with a perfectly furnished mind, strong, virile, self-possessed and liberal, he yet deliberately put the intellect far behind the affections. Hence comes the coolness and depth of his poetry—the romance, the heart-hunger, the eye for beauty . . . the tenderness." Arthur Benson, who always worried that his over-intellectual persona might be no mask, knows the virtues he would like to find in himself, and finds them winningly in Cory: "He hated all that was cold, or low, or mean, or petty, or ungenerous, or hard. I think it was a very beautiful soul." Yet this beauty and attractiveness are tainted, and for once—feeding idealism and suspicion alike—he could not find out all the details he wanted to know from the still-reticent staff who had known Cory. But he knew enough to see that this idealized figure had been "pulled off its pedestal by the foul cur he could not control"—both his desire and the response around him to it. When the very real hits the very idealized, the tension must be painful, the repressions hard work. He recognized that Cory "was bursting with suppressed sentiment—how hopelessly he spoilt his favourites, who took <u>any</u> liberties with him." He felt painfully that "the letters about his boy friendships are very touching," but "those lost and haunting presences of whom he writes—those boys with serene eyes and wind-stirred hair . . . stand in these pages in a magic light which no mortal could ever have for me." Benson simply cannot feel like Cory, cannot reach out to such happiness and such pain—or cannot let himself feel like Cory. Not least because "no one sees the dangers more clearly than I do." And with his characteristic gesture of disavowed longing, he concludes, "I almost wish it were not so."

It is in the "almost" of that expressed and suppressed wish that the work of Arthur Benson's exploration is being enacted—recognizing and denying what he wants but feels he cannot have. It is also in the thousands of pages in his diary of detailed anxieties about his own and others' romantic attachments to pupils at the school where he teaches, as he articulates his own life against the template of Cory. "W. Johnson says that the passions, the imprudences, are the things that one is glad and proud of afterwards. I wonder if this is true? I have no means of knowing"—a characteristic mixture of wonder and self-pity in the face of another's expression of desire. While he was trying to imagine being proud of imprudence, he was told by an older colleague that Cory "had his favourites and associates. . . . while he was in the school, yet he was at least prudent and self-controlled, but that his helpless adoration of certain boys afterwards became too absurdly patent." To be "too absurdly patent" catches neatly the constant fear that limited Arthur's pursuit of frankness, not least because "adoration" is a word he uses of his own feelings for particular boys. Yet he can also hanker for the clarity of Cory's emotion: "I wish I could feel the sort of ordered tenderness that W.J. felt and wrote of. But I am up and down; sometimes very wretched; sometimes dry as dust." The choice he grants himself for his emotional life, between wretchedness and unfeelingness, leaves him longing for a sentiment he fears. Two years later, though, he is reading Cory again in bed and "felt truly ashamed of my paltry, weak, trivial, sentimental, ignorant mind." Yet when he talks to Mrs. Coleridge about Cory, "I could not tell her of the shadow, and how dark it was." It is through Cory, it seems, that Arthur Benson reads and rereads the magic light and dark shadow of his own emotional experiences.

Gwendolen in the *Importance of Being Earnest* announces, "I never travel without my diary. One should always have something sensational to read on the train." Arthur Benson never travels without Cory and his own diary in dialogue with one another as a textual mirroring against which to calibrate his own turbulent feelings, his own recognition and concealment—from himself and from others—of his desires and passions, his own business as a teacher of boys, a teacher who repeatedly reflects, as the teacher in his book *The Upton Letters* depressively puts it, "I am here, a lonely man, wondering and doubting and desiring I hardly know what. Some nearness of life. . . ." Cory's letters and journal, as an account of the precarious boundary between his inner life and his public imprudence, is used by Benson as an emotional *vademecum*, a testing ground for a self-history in the making. This, rather than merely the revelation of a life lived, is what such life-writing is for, what it means for a written life to be exemplary.

This intricate and continuing use of Cory's life-writing as an exploratory model of self-understanding can be tellingly set against another fascinating text. John Addington Symonds has become something of a hero in modern histories of sexuality, to a good degree thanks to his frank and anguished memoirs, which were published, after his literary executor's embargo, only in 1984, when their time had indeed come. Symonds has much in common with Cory, at least at a superficial level. Symonds wrote *Studies of the Greek Poets*, volumes of literary essays that deeply influenced Oscar Wilde and his generation at Oxford because of their treatment of so-called Uranian love—the desire of men for male youths. He also privately published and very selectively circulated *A Problem in Greek Ethics*, a serious attempt to describe and comprehend ancient Athenian male sexual practice. As a young man, he published lyric poetry and other literary essays, and he was instrumental in making the epigrams of *The Greek Anthology*, and their translation into English, into a minor genre of Uranian artistic endeavor (to which Arthur Benson's *The Reed of Pan* makes a contribution). Like Cory—and many of the late Victorian period—Greek philosophy, Greek poetry, and Greek art were ways of talking about their own transgressive desires that they could not speak of otherwise, publicly. But unlike Cory, Symonds was also deeply connected not so much with the world of the public school's elite education, but with the growing science of sexology. He was a close friend and collaborator with Havelock Ellis, especially on the subject of what in these decades came to be called homosexuality. In his *Memoirs*, along with tales of how, after much painful self-struggle, he finally discovered physical pleasures with guardsmen in London, Symonds strives to theorize his masculinity and his desires: which is why his time had come in 1984, as Foucault's *History of Sexuality* was emerging, a hundred years after the invention of homosexuality.

His literary executor, Horatio Brown, did publish a version of Symonds's biography in 1895, which carefully hedged around the question of his sexuality. Symonds had married, retired to Davos in Switzerland, and had four daughters, which made the task easier. Edmund Gosse further expurgated the volume and, after Brown's death, burnt all of Symonds's papers, except the autobiography, according to Brown's wishes. Symonds was also well-known to Arthur Benson because of the Vaughan affair at Harrow, which he wrote about at length in his diary. Back in 1858, Symonds was sent a letter by a young friend, who told him how the headmaster of Harrow, Vaughan, had made sexual overtures toward him. Symonds, deeply disturbed, in turn told his tutor at Oxford, the classicist John Conington (who had given Symonds a copy of Cory's *Ionica*). Despite his own feelings on such matters, Conington advised Symonds to tell his father. His father confronted Vaughan, required him to resign, with the threat that if he ever tried to take a job of responsibility again, he would reveal the truth. The threat was enacted later when Vaughan was offered a bishopric, which he rapidly—and to outsiders, bafflingly—declined shortly after accepting it. For Benson, at Eton, worrying about romantic attachments, the Vaughan scandal was the paradigm of the terrifying humiliation that could be the result of being "too absurdly patent."

Symonds was especially close, what's more, with Henry Sidgwick, Minnie Benson's brother and Arthur's uncle. Henry Sidgwick read what Symonds wrote, including the life, and was a constant friendly adviser and confidant, from his own odd marriage. Symonds, that is, was a figure in Arthur Benson's network of imaginative associations. Perhaps predictable, then, that he would write it up: in 1912 Benson gave a paper on Symonds to a small group in Trinity College. Bertrand Russell and Lytton Strachey, "a strange man," were there. "It was rather a fiasco; I was tired and stupid. There was no discussion." Symonds, like Cory, was good for Arthur Benson to think his life with.

But his *Memoirs*—and I assume it was Brown's version that Benson was reading—certainly did not lead to any feelings of sublimity or love. He read and reread them, it seems, but with disturbance of a quite different sort: "To bed, but could not sleep; read most of J.A. Symond[s]'s life—a horrible, tortured affair, which <u>vexes</u> me more the oftener I read it." Symonds—who theorized his desire, allowed himself eventually physical expression of it, who married and had children—is indeed an emphatically vexing example for Benson, who never married, found sexual physicality a shuddering fear, and who hesitates even when hospitalized to reflect on desire as a causal element in his mental collapse. Reading between the lines of Symonds's biography, chatting with Edmund Gosse and with Henry Sidgwick, recalling Symonds's role in the humiliation of the headmaster of a great school, giving ill-received papers on Symonds—Arthur had much to vex him with Symonds. But he seems to have kept going back to the horrible, tortured affair of his life. He kept going back to the mirror of Symonds's life, but unlike the narrative of Cory, he could not process it inspirationally into a calibration of idealization and danger. In some mirrors, one can only look uncomfortably askance.

"If I were a great writer," reflected Arthur Benson, "I would try to overthrow this tyranny of form, for a tyranny it is." "Form" obsessed late Victorian and Edwardian writing about writing, not just as an aesthetic issue for the long history of modernist experiments with prose form, but also as a key expression that links such aesthetic developments with social morality ("good form"), with ideas of cultural order and regularity ("social forms"), church liturgy ("forms of service"), and even education ("sixth form"): the space that overlaps literary form and the formalities of social life. For one contemporary critic at least, A. C. Benson made a significant contribution to a formal innovation in life-writing. Stephen Reynolds is best known today for his account of his life with poor fishermen, called *A Poor Man's House*. In 1906 he wrote an article with the extraordinary title "Autobiografiction"—a term since reinvented more than once as a term of art for postmodern arguments about the necessary intertwining of fictional form and self-representation. In this piece he took three main examples, *The Autobiography of Mark Rutherford* by William Hale White, *The Private Papers of Henry Ryecroft* by George Gissing, and—above all—*The House of Quiet* and *The Thread of Gold* by A. C. Benson. As forms of life-writing, *The House of Quiet* (1904), along with *The Thread of Gold* (1905) and *The Upton Letters* (1905), changed A. C. Benson's life, because they were each volumes that sold over 100,000 copies, that brought him to a vast new readership, and that created a new public persona for him. He became something of a celebrity, and the gap between his hopeful, reflective public persona and private waspishness caused his family and friends some amusement and some thought—and caused Arthur himself a good deal of self-reflection. Life-writing did not merely express the self but became a way of creating a persona that informed the life of the self. Writing a life changes a life.

Stephen Reynolds gave a long and eloquent explanation of what he meant by autobiografiction. "A man, usually of an introspective nature, has accumulated a large body of spiritual experiences. He feels he must out with it." But he cannot write fiction, pure and simple, because the story would swamp the spiritual experience and the complexity of self-expression would be too daunting. But he cannot write autobiography, either, because there is too much extraneous material in a man's life. Essays are too discontinuous; and going on too much about spiritual experiences is bound to be tedious. So the solution is to mix some autobiographical material with some fiction, and "on that he builds the spiritual experience," diluted, made coherent and readable. "The result is autobiografiction, a literary form more direct and more intimate probably than any to be found outside poetry."

It is much easier to see the "intimacy effect" than the directness. Although even at the time and even for the author himself, let alone his wry and competitive brother, it was easy to dismiss A. C. Benson's style of writing as bourgeois and indulgent self-reflection for a middle-class and largely female audience (an empirical as well as stereotyped sneer), nonetheless the books did deeply affect their readers precisely because they created a sense of intimate, introspective, and consoling self-expression; and, as we will see, A. C. Benson had to field many letters from women who felt passionately about him through this beguilingly intimate prose. An undergraduate asked Benson simply about *The Upton Letters*: "But isn't it almost indecent to be so intimate?" As Arthur Benson fell in love with Cory, so, to his surprise and discomfort, he became the object of fantasy and desire for his unknown audience.

Direct is a less self-evident term. *The House of Quiet* is subtitled *An Autobiography* and first appeared anonymously. Its conceit was that it was found in the papers of a dead cousin by one J.T. The cousin is identified only as Henry, and then only toward the end of the book. The first preface in 1904 ventures "to express a hope that identification will not be attempted, because the book is one which depends for its value, not on the material circumstances of the author, but upon the view of life which he formed." This view of life is framed by a religious despair at Cambridge, followed by depression and introspection in a life of quiet retreat demanded by doctors. He gradually acclimatizes himself to this life of "mandarin gentility" and allows himself to fall in love with a woman. On his way to propose to her, however, he is struck by the fatal illness that ends his life and the book—a story that is rather too absurdly patent for Benson's own feelings about marriage, to which we will have cause to return. In 1906 the second edition (and seventh printing) included a second preface signed now by "A.C.B." He explains that he is now prepared to own up to his authorship, since it has become an open secret. But this leads to an extraordinarily guarded version of the writer's contract. "There may be some people," he writes, "who will think it disingenuous to give what is in a sense a fiction an air of veracity." The book is "*in a sense* a fiction," which opens the door to the idea that the "air of veracity" may be more than mere air (in a sense) which might be thought disingenuous. . . . Indeed, he explains that it is his lack of experience that turns him toward such a personal subject, and "the intimate nature of it gives every excuse for my attempting to take refuge in anonymity." In what sense, precisely, is it, then, a fiction? And he continues for three pages to deny the seriousness, solemnity, or sacredness of his project; it is no more than the sort of story one might tell a friend by a warm fire. Not only does this demurral sound much like the voice of the narrator of the book itself, but now the frontispiece reads, *The House of Quiet: An Autobiography by A. C. Benson.* The preface seems designed to hold up the precarious veil of fiction to the light and to disavow it in the same breath.

In 1907 a third preface was added. It begins with the author reading "a paper that has lurked for years in an old collection of archives, a preface. . . ." *The House of Quiet* itself begins with a diary entry that reads: "I have been amusing myself by looking through some old papers and diaries of my own. . . .": a preface about reading old prefaces, for a book that opens with a diary entry about reading old diaries. Now, however, he goes on to explain that he wanted to create a character as an example for "all those whose life, by some stroke of God, seemed dashed into fragments, and who might feel so listless, so dismayed, that they could not summon up courage even to try and save something from the desolate wreck." As A.C.B. puts some distance between himself as author and the character he has depicted, he once again finds himself describing what sounds a lot like his own depression. It is perhaps unsurprising that readers read this book as intimate, autobiographical if not an autobiography, and consoling. It is hard to see its strategies in any straightforward sense as "direct."

Such formal games with authorial identity continue through-out these three books. In *The House of Quiet*, J.T. adds an editorial note halfway through explaining that the following passages were "either extracted by the author himself from his own diaries" or are taken "from a notebook containing fragments of an autobiograph-ical character"—selected and arranged, that is, either by Henry or by J.T.—an instability of agency that allows the book to shift between biography and autobiography. *The Thread of Gold* is even more episodic—extracts of a journal of reflections, each prompted by some event of the day or something read. The thread, the thread of gold, that links them is a consolatory hopefulness that comes close to a religious optimism, which is awkwardly combined with an aesthetic love of beauty. The book's title page announces it to be by the author of *The House of Quiet*, which allows the fiction to come home as a spiritual portrait of the author's perspective on the world.

The highly successful volume *The Upton Letters*, a series of let-ters to one now dead Herbert, published by their author T.B., is a more literary and socially engaged exchange—though the conceit of anonymity was swiftly pierced and led to another apologetic preface, again to the second edition and seventh reprinting. The picture of Eton in this book caused specific upset, though Benson denied any applicability of his descriptions to reality. Yet in the *Upton Letters*, T.B. writes to his friend, "I do not know if you have come across a book—I must send it to you if you have not seen it—which moves me and feeds my spirit more than almost any book I know—the *Letters and Journal of William Cory*," and he goes on to praise its "hard intellectual force and passionate tenderness," though he val-ued "these gifts" of intellect "very little in comparison with feeling." He also comments on the lives of Farrar and Spencer in the same words he used in his own diaries. When T.B. echoes *Arthur Benson's* diary so closely, it is easy to see why Stephen Reynolds wanted to coin the ugly portmanteau term "autobiografiction" to indicate this fictionalized, aestheticized version of self-expression.

A. C. Benson continued with this winning formula for his read-ership. *From a College Window* (1906), *The Altar Fire* (1907), *The*

Silent Isle (1910), and *Along the Road* (1912) followed. He wrote and rewrote this fictionalized persona of a depressive, reclusive, sensitive, introspective man, offering hopeful consolation in beauty, inward struggle, and a gleam of religious feeling. Their formal games with authorial identification and veiled intimacies may seem to antici-pate a postmodern fictionality, but their perspective of infirm gentil-ity and lofty judgmentalism makes them mawkish, unpleasant, and repetitive to most modern readers. But the very act of rewriting a life story—along with its rereading—is integral to Arthur Benson's obsessional practice.

His own diary repeats stories of him rereading old letters and the diary itself, usually with a (mis-)recognition of a no longer recog-nizable self. "Read old letters of my own (very priggish) from Eton and King's." Someone shows him "a bound vol of my old letters . . . such old ghosts . . . speaking with an alien voice. . . . [W]as I like that?" He reads old letters by M. R. James: "I was horrified at them so solemn, so awfully priggish," and then, in a way that anticipates his published books, "I found a bundle of old papers—beginnings of stories and a longish autobiographical kind of romance, about a man who joins a brotherhood. I could not remember having written one single word of it." His own life and self appear through his dis-covered ignorance in a fresh light: "I read Maggie's Letters. What I did not know was what a big, fresh, uncommon sort of life we were living at Truro. . . . I see myself in a detestable light, selfish, pre-occupied, unkind"—this more than thirty years later. The memo-rial of a diary also becomes the performance of a constantly failing memory of self, a surprised recognition of a lost and changed self. The development and inconstancy of the self was a major theoret-ical concern of contemporary psychologists; the diarist, especially the diarist who lapsed into the fragmentation of mental disease and repeatedly looked back in wonder across the abyss of major changes in his life to an unremembered but self-recorded past, acted out this concern to the full.

When Arthur comes to read his mother's papers after her death, then, rewriting the life story is an inevitable part of his obsessional and familiar response—as is the recognition that he no longer recognized the past of his memory. *The Trefoil* (1923) is an account of Edward White Benson's life in three houses: Wellington, Lincoln, and Truro. The explicit rationale for another volume after the 1,000-page biography that he has already produced, is that the *Life* of the archbishop allowed less space than necessary for the life of a father before his great duties took over. But rewriting is the compulsion. I have already quoted Arthur's new sense of bafflement before his father: "In spite of the fact that for the next twenty years my father talked very freely and openly to me, yet his heart and mind remained, and still remain, a good deal of mystery to me." He also movingly recalls his father's despair at Martin's death. In the piety of the biography, he had described his father's grief with awful, clichéd insufficiency as "perfectly tragic." Now he writes, "What awful depths of darkness and bewilderment his spirit had descended," and remembers "my father struggling with moods of blackness and tortured irritability. The calamity was so overwhelming to him and so unintelligible—I think to the end of his life Martin was never out of his mind." Of Lincoln, in the biography he had written, "My mother was ill at the time we moved, and was much away." Now he redrafts, "I learned long afterwards she was herself much unsettled at this time in mind and thought," and goes on to explore her transformative religious feelings at the time (though not her passion for Miss Hall, of course). Arthur is finding his way toward a more painful, intimate, and un-reticent account of his family history. The unpublished 200-page manuscript of biography of his mother is another step in the ongoing process of rewriting the lives that make sense, intimately and (in)directly, of his own.

Between reading his own diary as fragmented shards of a lost self; and reading and rereading (auto)biographies to orientate his own self-narrative; and constantly rewriting the life histories of his family and friends to make his own place within the networked dynamics of a social life, Arthur Benson's life-writing is very much a work in progress—a process of rewriting.

The brothers Fred and Arthur had different responses to the

experience of discovering their mother's papers. They agreed, it seems, when talking it through, that there had been a real darkness, a failure of love between their parents, at the start of a turbulent marriage. Both recognized, too, and struggled with the fact that they had not understood the torment she had experienced after their father's death, and the depth of her religious response. They both wrote and had to rewrite the story—both in the sense of giving more than one version and in the sense of scripting it according to their own agenda. For Fred, in *Mother* (1925), he begins his portrait of his mother with and from his father's death, and although he recognizes his mother's later comprehension of the difference between her and his father, he determinedly sees it as the beginning of a growth toward an accommodated love and duty. There was no "mistake"— "for if her marriage was a mistake, what marriage since the world began was a success?" (asks the unmarried son). In *As We Were* (1930), the "mistake" has become differently idealized as a "little authentic Victorian love story," perhaps "remote enough from modern ideas of mating," but "tenderly and exquisitely" conducted. "Modern ideas of mating" may ironically echo trendy eugenic discourse, which tried to keep love out of the equations of pair-bonding, just as the "mistake" of marriage may recall the celebrated newspaper controversy whether "marriage is a failure," as the *Daily Telegraph* asked of the institution. Trendy touches, then, but definitely a soft focus backward look. That is one way to write a life.

For Arthur, who dreamt so much of his father, it is the father's story that baffles and is first rewritten, from the grim official biography (1899) through to *The Trefoil* (1923). His father becomes a darker, more oppressed, more psychologically tormented figure. Writing even the first biography, Arthur now confesses, produced "considerable tension." He had also in between read Hugh's religious autobiography, *Confessions of a Convert* (1917), where the father is once again portrayed as a "personality . . . so dominant and insistent that the lack of this understanding [of his children] made very little difference." Hugh talked with precision of the "kind of despairing impatience" with which they were treated, the "rather oppressive disappointment when we were listless or stupid," the paralysis he felt from "the appalling atmosphere of my father's indignation." When he died, wrote Hugh—and the relief of confession is palpable—"I felt . . . as if the roof were lifted off the world." What could be said within the family and said publicly was shifting. The patterns of reticence with which the story of the marriage is told also begin to slip, as Arthur allows a very small inkling of his mother's religious transformation to emerge. In the unpublished version of his mother's life, left unfinished at his death in 1925, she is beginning to have, as he puts it, "a life of her own." "They were not wholly happy years for my mother." "She formed a very close friendship with a Miss Hall, so close indeed that she seems to have had scruples about the degree to which it absorbed her." And—with knowledge from experience—"she was in the frame of mind when any emotion whether pleasurable or sorrowful jangles the fine chords of the brain and leaves sickening melancholy behind it." It is a real struggle for a son, even as an adult, or conscious of the transformations of adulthood, to imagine his mother's inwardness. This is another way to write a life.

Neither Arthur nor Fred could be Martin, the adored and paradigmatically good son, and both were made acutely aware of this. Neither could win enough of their father's approval or their mother's love; both expressed to each other their ambivalence and even hatred of large parts of their earlier lives at home. Both brothers understood the codes of reticence, and manipulated and explored them, from Fred's first literary foray with *Dodo* or Arthur's *Memoirs of Arthur Hamilton* through to Fred's novels of oppressive fathers and musical children and Arthur's autobiografictions. Both found fiction crucial to self-expression. They also both wrote with an eye on each other, and their own family dynamics, their own competitiveness. Within these intricate webs of reticence and fictionalization, writing a life is also making a family history in which to have a place. Biographers love to say that writing a life takes over your life: you are living with the subject. But for brothers to write and rewrite their own parents' lives is rather writing *from within a*

FIGURE 3: Arthur, Hugh, and Fred in their uniforms, at Tremans, ready to write.

life, a complex act of self-fashioning through life-writing, within a family's interrelationships.

Fred vividly captures this hothouse in one of the most remarkable and funny scenes in *Final Edition*, the last autobiography of the family. The three brothers were all at Tremans, each writing a thoroughly typical book. It was suggested that for a day they would each suspend their labors to write a parody of one of the other brothers. The competition in the game is clear enough: "Though they all took their own work very seriously, there was not a vestige of mutual admiration between them, and they thought it would be very pleasant to give frank expression to the lack of it." The Oedipal scene, with its Bensonian frankness, gets a biblical dressing: "Like three Cains each preparing to murder an Abel . . . they sharpened their dagger-pens." In the evening, Arthur reads out his parody of Hugh, Fred of Arthur, and Hugh of Fred. Each is hilarious to everyone except the victim—and Mother, the judge, "was laughing helplessly and hopelessly, with her face all screwed up." When Fred reads, "I became aware of a draught or a frost or something inclement in the room, and looking up, I saw a pained expression on Arthur's face. . . . ." When Hugh reads, "Really the composition made no impression on me: I could not see the point of it . . . ," as the rest of the family weeps with laughter. But Minnie, the center, gets the last word: "'Oh you clever people,' said my mother, 'Why don't you all for the future write each other's books instead of your own?'"

In comedy, truth. The three brothers, each writing distorted, appropriative versions of each other's individual traits, to make their mother laugh, in a triangulation of competition, sharp humor, and failure of self-recognition . . . recalled now, at the end, ironically by Fred. Perhaps this is the perfect image for this family of what it means to write a life.

8

Women in Love

IN JANUARY 1907, AFTER THE SUCCESS OF *THE HOUSE OF Quiet*, *The Upton Letters*, and *The Thread of Gold*, Arthur Benson notes laconically in his diary: "I dictated about twenty letters, mostly to female admirers." He had become a figure of the imagination for a host of female readers, who wrote to him, and to whom he replied, without the distaste he expressed in private for the business. "My actual reputation as a writer is far more humiliating than gratifying," he sighed, and lamented the "dreadful mass of confidences from morbid spinsters" that he received, or even what seemed like declarations of passion: "The <u>most</u> curious letter from a virgin of 30 . . . seemed to me as if it might have expanded at any minute into an offer of marriage." One of his female friends, however, brought home to him painfully what might be at stake in his disingenuous fictions with an air of veracity.

Mary Cholmondeley was a well-connected writer. Her book *Red Pottage*, a satire on religious hypocrisy—which also reflected provocatively on the idea of the "new woman" and her sexuality—was a notable success for a short while in England and America, although it faded into obscurity swiftly. She was an unmarried woman who lived with her two sisters and elderly clergyman father in Knightsbridge, where she held dinner parties for literary types. Percy Lubbock, Arthur Benson's close friend who edited the first published extracts from his diary, also wrote a memorial of Mary Cholmondeley, and Fred Benson portrays her affectionately as a very funny and smart correspondent and friend. She stayed at Tremans and was fully part of the Benson circle.

Arthur Benson and Mary Cholmondeley had a particularly intimate and intense relationship. As it developed through long and personal conversations, Mary Cholmondeley wrote to Arthur about their relationship. "Now this is a very difficult letter to answer," he wrote in his diary. "I am entirely a person of <u>male</u> friendship. Don't like exultations, agonies. . . . I like a friendship where I can say exactly what I like, as much and as little; speak angrily or affectionately— and never be misunderstood—<u>the bond must be unconscious</u>. I could not bear conscious bonds." These clichés of misogynistic male bonding lead to a rather desperate and odd ending: "If the worst comes to the worst, I must get MB to help me out of this. She is star and sun to Miss C." He seems to think that his friendship is being taken at a mistaken level of seriousness and worries he may need to get his mother to put things straight (this is a man in his forties). The correspondence continues, and Arthur comments, "I am uneasy in these relations, afraid of sentiment, afraid of making professions which I can't carry out, and letting people establish claims. <u>Liberty</u>, again." Arthur had the rare privilege of being allowed to visit Mary without an invitation. The intimacy he had invited he found he had to repel. At the end of their relationship, he wrote into the back cover of one volume of his diary, "Marriage would solve it, but the adventure with Miss C makes me feel more than ever how little I understand women, and how alien, even disagreeable, the female temperament per se is. I suppose this is because I haven't really got the masculine temper!" Marriage would be a solution for the problems of his life, he fantasizes, but his experience with Miss Cholmondeley has confirmed for him that, unlike John Addington Symonds, he was not the marrying type.

But the true break in their relationship was not just because of his compulsive push-pull need for psychological intimacy and withdrawal. In 1906 Mary Cholmondeley published her next novel, *The Prisoners*. The chief character of the book is what Fred delightedly called "an exquisitely selfish and complacent prig" called Wentworth. This odious character finds that his passive self-satisfaction and indulgent judgmentalism prevent him from forming a decent relationship with a woman—and in the course of things, he happens to quote many sentences that Arthur Benson had said to Mary Cholmondeley in private, and many others that were recognizable versions of what had become trademark observations of the author A. C. Benson. Mary Cholmondeley, like so many male autobiografiction writers, defended herself by saying that she was drawing a type, not an individual, and a fiction not a biography. As Fred noted, "Quite a high percentage of middle-class bachelor friends . . . claimed or complained that they were her models for one of these respectable gentry, whom with manifest glee she exhibited in this very popular book." Fred's evident pleasure in the story (and the popularity of the book) is because he knows that this defense of hers cut no ice, and he rather enjoys his brother's discomfort, along with the irony of the autobiografiction expert caught in another's autobiografiction. Minnie Benson, whom Mary Cholmondeley revered, thought—according to Fred—with the greater insight of her closeness to Mary Cholmondeley, that Arthur had been "grossly and intentionally caricatured" out of a vengeful malice. It was "a piece of savagery on Mary's part: she wanted to scratch." Arthur, once again performing his reticence, noted, "MB in private propounded a theory of her [Cholomondeley's] behavior to me which I had better not put down." The two women remained friends, mind.

The savaging certainly worked. Arthur was dismayed by the portrait. "What sent me into a gloom," he wrote in the diary, "was the indescribable and irresistible conviction that she had me in mind for Wentworth, the dilettante egotist. . . . [He] says, in a hateful manner, so many of the things I say in my little books." He winged off letters of complaint to anyone who would listen—"a vicious, harsh, indelicate thing, and one is asked to believe it is not inconsistent with being high-minded and benevolent!"—and nastily upbraided Miss Cholmondeley. He was declared no longer welcome to visit. As Fred concluded, "The whole thing was a storm in a tea-cup, but the gale was violent and a great deal of hot tea was spilt." Ten years later, Arthur confided to his diary that he thought Percy Lubbock was at last disillusioned with Miss C. Lubbock added a firm note when he read the diary: "not at all." Arthur was still hankering to have the story read his way.

To be represented—in a cartoon, in a parody, in a nasty portrait—made the autobiografictioner glum, self-aware, intensely miserable. Writing a life is also a question—as Humpty Dumpty put it to Alice—of which is to be master. How one appears in print—in a life story—is not something over which one can have total control. Arthur fails to recognize Hugh from his own letters to converts, or Maggie in her father's biographical portrait, or his own self in the past. He knows that his image as a writer is a public and distorted—even humiliating—thing; but that his private diary, for all its frankness, conceals the essence of his inner life. To be written about is another dangerous strand of the misrepresentations that make up the portrait of a person. For Arthur, the trouble with Mary Cholmondeley's novel was not that he was made unrecognizable, however, but that he was recognizable.

For some years after his first severe mental breakdown during 1907–9, he had been corresponding with a Madame de Nottbeck. She was wealthy in her own right as a scion of the Astor family and had married a rich husband. Unlike many other of his female correspondents, she seems to have been able to write in an engaged and engaging way that showed an understanding not just of A. C. Benson, the author whose books she had read, but also of Arthur Benson, the Magdalene man, or so he felt. Out of the blue, she wrote to offer him $200,000 as a gift without any strings. "I don't think any writer ever had a more extraordinary offer," he mused (though I know many who think they would like their writing to prompt such a response). He refused the offer, of course, but she persisted. Eventually, as Percy Lubbock recorded, "the gift passed from the one to the other as simply as a birthday present between friends." The letter Arthur Benson wrote indicates that it remained more complicated emotionally than Lubbock could realize. It was, recognized Benson, "unearned"; by most lights, unneeded; but it would be, he felt, "churlish to go on putting an unreasonable unwillingness of my own in the way of your kindness." They continued to write to each other, and she made many other smaller gifts, both to him and to Magdalene College. In particular, when Arthur died, Fred arranged for her to endow the so-called Benson window in Arthur's memory at Rye Church. And she herself organized for William Nicholson, not yet perhaps quite the celebrated artist he was to become, to paint a portrait of Arthur—a really striking piece now in the Fitzwilliam Museum in Cambridge, with Benson in his black gown sitting back on a scarlet chair against a scarlet and gray screen and a scarlet carpet, perhaps a delicate echo of Matisse's red rooms.

Yet Madame de Nottbeck and Arthur Benson never met. She was married, and although they both traveled, she never came to Cambridge and they never arranged to meet even in London. Their relationship was conducted entirely through letters: a written life. "I do feel a brotherly regard for one who has trusted me with so many of her secrets, consulted me so much, depended on my words": words, precisely. The money she gave for the college or for Arthur's holidays or for his portrait was in exchange for more words. "I shall desire to remain in communication with you, if you will allow it, to tell you what I am doing and how I have used the power you entrust me with." Perhaps for the compulsive diarist, this was the perfect relationship. With Mary Cholmondeley, the collapse of their intimacy was precipitated by her writing a portrait of him, denied, veiled, but all too recognizable; with Madame de Nottbeck, his self-portrait in his books (denied, veiled) led to an exchange in which they both wrote themselves into each other's life as portraits in words, an exchange of intertwined narratives (and finally a painting on the wall, Arthur, alone staring out at the viewer, askance). Life-writing becomes a life of writing.

9

Graphomania

EDWARD WHITE BENSON PUBLISHED MAINLY SERMONS, A
genre that can be heard dimly throughout Arthur Benson's "through
a college window" style of reflective essays with their complacent
moralism. He also wrote hundreds of minutes and letters and decisions as Archbishop of Canterbury, a full archive of an official life.
Minnie Benson wrote sporadically, in crisis—though she also produced and read to her children a humorous autobiography and many
letters, mainly now lost. Maggie Benson left her technical work on
Egyptology and some strange stories; Nellie Benson, a couple of
volumes of observed life. The three brothers became celebrated and
prolific writers, individually and as a trio of brothers—hundreds of
books, as well as all the other published and unpublished material.
But it is not simply this staggering output that prompts a diagnosis of graphomania. Many other Victorian intellectuals left huge
archives of letters and published volumes, though perhaps few families have quite this profile. Victorian society was the first in Britain
to be structured around the circulation of the printed and written word: letters, articles, newspapers, books, reviews, diaries took
up a newly insistent proportion of middle- and upper-class life—
writing, reading, reviewing, discussing. The diary of Arthur Benson
reveals only a very extreme example of what made up for many a
daily life: receiving and reading letters in the morning; writing letters in response; the hours of reading, writing, and discussing during
the day, at home, in the club with Edmund Gosse and Henry James,

walking with colleagues and friends in the Cambridgeshire lanes; the early or late evening diary; reading aloud to young friends; reading alone late at night in bed: familiar scenes of the literate world of nineteenth-century culture.

Rather, I take my cue from Fred Benson's description of the three brothers at Tremans—"all madly writing." There is a self-consciousness in the family that knows that even within the bounds of Victorian expectation, their relation to the written word was queer. It is fascinating that Arthur Benson described himself in 1897 as one of those "who want to write and cannot." He had already published four books of poetry and a novel. At one level, he is referring explicitly to the business of self-representation through a diary and his model of William Cory. It is also, that is, about finding a place between articulation and reticence, imprudence and frankness, for someone who is especially aware of the dangers of self-expression, its sentiment. Writing is not merely a mechanical or even an intellectual task. "Writing" also means, however, writing something of substance: he claimed that he only learned how to write well after he had written the biography of his dead father. But it cannot be by chance that it is in the year his father dies that he begins his vast diary with this plea now to write. Writing is also a pathological response to being in a family, but one, it seems, that can only start properly with the death of the father. *Mother* begins with the death of the father; and all of Fred's (other) autobiographies revolve around it. For Hugh Benson, it was as if the roof of the world was lifted: he, too, wrote a string of successful, long novels before he was forty. This family's intense and prolific writing seems to have been released in a particular way by removal of the oppressive presence of Edward White Benson. There was no longer a need to write notes about feelings and bury them under a tree. A different psychic economy of revelation and repression took shape.

For Arthur Benson in particular, this pattern of revelation and repression goes beyond a quirk of literary style or social convention, and toward what could be properly called an *aesthetic of reticence*. This is not so much a question of not expressing things, as of obsessively writing about how hard it is to turn the ineffability of emotional feelings into self-expression, and how worryingly important concealment and revelation are when self-formation must not involve giving yourself away. This aesthetic of reticence links Arthur's literary persona and his games of autobiografiction with his pride in veiling gossipy truth only for those who know, and his constant care about not becoming "too absurdly patent" while privileging the frankness of conversation. Social exchanges and the desires within them have many drives that dare not speak their name, not merely one particular vice. At one level, this aesthetic of reticence is a very secular and social restructuring of the inexpressible that haunts the Romantic sublime. But it is perhaps better to see it as a response to the mid-nineteenth century's commitment to earnestness. Where Edward White Benson from the start boldly spoke out against a racist insult and found in the sermon an inevitable form of self-expression—where he could moralize directly to his captive congregation, especially of schoolboys, in the manner of his educational heroes—and saw in the strict letter of personal ethical and religious instruction a natural form of address to his children, Arthur and Fred found indirection, self-consciousness, and the masks of social form an integral mode of emotional (in)articulacy. It is this aesthetic of reticence that connects the Bensons with an iconic writer of modernism like their friend Henry James, great master of the filaments of nuanced, introverted, and anxious expressivity, and, more surprisingly, with the younger and trendier generation of a Virginia Woolf. Arthur Benson's veiled memoirs of reflective self-absorption are paradigmatic—and popular because they captured the moment so paradigmatically—of a shift from the high Victorian moral revolution to an Edwardian epigonal doubting. This is not merely a literary gesture of withdrawal, but—style is the man—a structuring of self-formation.

Even when hospitalized the first time, Arthur wrote long, harrowing, repetitive accounts of his desperate depression and his painful attempts to recover—as part of the condition and its cure. It was only with the second crippling hospitalization that the diary is silenced. The awfulness of the loss of self in complete mental breakdown is enacted in the loss of writing. Otherwise, the diary entries stretch up to eighty pages to record a single day. Arthur Benson even wrote his own death, as close as he could come. The final volume notes, "I have just woken up with a terrible pain in my left arm. I hope I die with dignity like Dr Arnold." Rather than calling for help, he is duly writing down the heart attack that killed him and once again comparing his image with someone else. *Final Edition*, Fred's last book, was completed, desperately, from the hospital bed where he was dying. Just as Arthur's last words are written, as he dies, in the diary in and through which he fashioned his self, Fred's last act is another, final correction to his life story. This is their graphomania. The compulsion to write to the end. Right to the end.

This is a family that compulsively wrote and rewrote itself.

PART
II

BEING
QUEER

10

What's in a Name?

USING A PARTICULAR NAME NOT ONLY IDENTIFIES A THING or a person, but classifies them too. There was for me—though I suspect this experience is not unusual—a sense of mild dislocation when, for the first time in an academic context, I read about myself in print referred to only by my last name, in a review of my first book: "Goldhill argues . . ." In the past, only my friends or teachers at school—as was normal in those days at that sort of boys' school—called me by my last name, a habit that sporadically continued in a slightly mannered fashion in college. By the time I had published my first book, in social exchanges almost everyone called me by my first name, Simon, or, in more formal and public occasions, by a title and name, Dr. Goldhill (except, perhaps, when being summoned by an official voice for an appointment or something similar). I suppose I might be "Goldhill" in a newspaper report or the like, as I had been when I played football well enough to be reported. But being called simply "Goldhill" in print in an academic context positioned me at last as an author: in Althusser's productive vocabulary, it interpellated or hailed me as an author, for the first time in this public medium. This sense of dislocation has never quite passed, even though it is pretty well only in the formalities of academic discourse, now all too repeated, where I am called, starkly, "Goldhill."

Minnie Benson was christened "Mary," like her mother, Mary Sidgwick (and like her daughter Mary Eleanor, always known as "Nellie"), and although her mother and future husband called her "Minnie" when she was being courted, after her marriage she reverted to "Mary" as a public persona, although Edward continued to write "Minnie" occasionally, when "my wife" or "my dear wife" did not seem to do. For a woman in the traditional patriarchal systems of the West, changing names is a charged and particular part of social integration, always inflected by the system of marriage and kinship, the naming system *par excellence*. Women, unlike men, are still socially expected to change their name with their marital status. In his diaries, Arthur often uses initials for his parents, EWB and MB, as he does for many characters, but the children usually called MB "Little Mother": that's how the volume of Margaret Oliphant's autobiography is inscribed, "To Little Mother, from her daughter." With her most intimate female friends, Minnie was nicknamed "Ben" and signed herself as "Ben" in letters to them: a masculinized tag, an abbreviated and ironized version of her married name, a special name for a special relationship. In return, she called Mrs. Mylne, one of her most significant loves, "Tan." Each name, each act of naming, performs a relationship, classifies the named, and puts the namer in a reciprocal position. Conventions of naming change over time too, of course. It would be thought thoroughly perverse today for a husband to sign a letter to his wife as "Your Loving Husband, E.W. Benson," especially when she called him Edward in day-to-day life—but that formality is pervasive in Victorian familial letter-writing. After decades of friendship, Edmund Gosse was always "Gosse" to Arthur Benson. Although I have used "A. C. Benson" as a way of distinguishing Arthur's persona as a public figure from Arthur in his less public guises, there is no straightforward solution of how to name the figures in a book like this—and even more so in a biography. Neither the proper formality of "A. C. Benson" nor, certainly, the intimate forwardness of "Ben" for the archbishop's wife seem adequate or suitable, consistently, across the range of arguments and narratives. It matters what names are used and how conventions regulate social exchange.

All the more so in the language of friendship and sexuality. There is no unmediated, degree-zero language of sexuality, no proper names: medical, legal, religious, playground, familial, marital, barroom, comic discourses (and so on) jostle and compete with and echo each other within any modern community (sexual intercourse, make love, make out, have, fuck, screw, take, copulate, marital relations, bonk, and so forth . . .). And shift across time, in raw referential meaning as much as in social register or moral import. Words such as "comrade," "make love," "beastly," "gay" need dating before reading. And there is perhaps no other region of human social interaction where the assumption of "nature" and "naturalness"—the cross-cultural, transhistorical truth of human beings—is so pervasive and yet so markedly at odds with the conventionality and localness of language's usage and the evident social variety of practice and belief. It's a very old joke indeed: already in the most lascivious and knowing of the ancient Greek novels from the second century CE, *Daphnis and Chloe*, the two young lovers who are so innocent that they do not know even the word "love," and certainly do not know what to do to satisfy their physical longings, do, however, naturally know to throw apples at each other as a sign of love—a sign as natural, it seems, as giving a single red rose on Valentine's Day. Longus, the author, loves to play games with our perceptions and silliness about what is natural and what is as conventional as can be, when it comes to our own sense of how to be in love—what we do. Caught between what is determinedly most private and most open to social regulation, between what is most determinedly a function of all humanity, and most imbued with particular religious, spiritual, social significances, between rule-making and playfulness, sexuality always provokes linguistic stress and narrative complicity.

It is, then, no straightforward matter to name the queerness of this family.

Of course, writing—our sources for the family—always swathes in veils the expression not just of desire but also of physical experience. When it comes to sexuality, writing what we want and writing what has happened to us or what we have done are tasks disingenuous, self-deceptive, and dissatisfying enough; but when the writing comes from other people, and other people of a past generation, the problems of knowing what we want to know multiply vertiginously. As the rabbinical sources declare, the Talmudic student in his search for knowledge can go so far as to sleep under the rabbi's bed, but can never sleep in it. For the Benson family, what is more, there is a local reticence that exaggerates even the norms of Victorian propriety. The story of the Bensons excites a certain voyeuristic prurience, I fear, but it had better be clear from the start that there won't be much sex in what follows.

Now there were options in Victorian and Edwardian genres for more explicit writing on sexuality, though this explicitness is often surprisingly different in its economies of reticence from modern equivalents. At one extreme of the scale—and a production highly unlikely to have been encountered by any of the Bensons—a book such as *My Secret Life*, signed *by Walter*, perhaps written by Henry Spencer Ashbee, has become among historians of sexuality the best-known example of written pornography that circulated among an elite audience in the market for erotica. Massively long (eleven volumes), poorly written, resolutely episodic, and repeatedly unpleasant, it traces the multiform sexual experiences of Walter. Following the biographical model dominant in the era, it starts from his earliest memories—his childhood discovery of a problem with his foreskin as he begins to explore male and female sexuality—and moves through his sexual abuse of a maidservant in the family into an increasingly fantasized pornographic world where every woman he meets is easily drawn into his leering pornographic gaze. His description of his brief time at public school is far removed from William Cory or Arthur Benson, and fulfills the worst fears of headmaster Edward White Benson, with descriptions of boys indulging openly and aggressively in masturbatory sessions. Less pornographic in generic aim and in their anxious struggle about desire, the memoirs of John Addington Symonds or of Goldsworthy Lowes Dickinson, say, which mention physical sexual experiences as significant transitional moments in their lives, were not intended for publication during their own lifetime, any more than were the letters of men who met with Walt Whitman or Edward Carpenter, which describe sexual encounters more freely, sometimes with an explicitly libertarian stance.

Medical texts were more likely to have entered the life of the Bensons, especially those treatises with a sociological bent. William Acton, for example, was more widely read on prostitution than on his technical investigations into genito-urinary diseases, and although his treatise was sometimes thought to be too morally generous toward prostitutes, it was also one of the volumes—its subtitle specifically included garrison towns—that led discussion about the notorious Contagious Diseases Acts. These acts attempted to prevent the spread of venereal disease by allowing the police to stop and give a medical examination to any woman they deemed suspicious. The sexism of making women rather than men the spreaders of disease was secondary in the public debate to the horror of a respectable woman being humiliated by a policeman. The bitter arguments over these acts from the 1860s through to their repeal in 1886 brought sexual morality, prostitution, and disease to the forefront of public attention. This debate was brought home for the Sidgwicks and Bensons in the intimate world of Cambridge by a figure such as Millicent Fawcett, who campaigned vociferously against the Contagious Diseases Act and rose to become not only a famous suffragette but also a cofounder of the all-female Newnham College with Henry Sidgwick, Minnie's brother and favorite uncle of the children. Public scandals such as the arrest of Boulton and Park, two young men whose shocking habit of dressing as women opened a vista in court of a confusing circle of countercultural sexuality; or the male brothel at Cleveland Street with its apparently aristocratic clientele; or, of course, Oscar Wilde, most scandalous in part because it physicalized and made real the long taunted sneers about aesthetic effeminacy; all brought male desire for males into a lurid spotlight of publicity—exacerbated by campaigns for sexual and social purity, fostered by W. T. Stead's outraged articles entitled "The Maiden Tribute of Modern Babylon," which revealed the buying and selling of children into prostitution into London, and which were instrumental in raising the age of consent from thirteen to sixteen. The emphasis on particularly strident forms of masculinity in the same decades—muscular Christianity and the like, to which we will return—also functioned as a stark contrast to the scandalous visions of sophisticated city miscreants. Of all these scandals, only Wilde features with any intensity or concentration in any of the Bensons' memoirs or diaries. Fred Benson copied out by hand the whole of Wilde's *The Ballad of Reading Gaol*, including passages excluded from the printed version, into a notebook that he kept in his private papers. Arthur expressed undisguised if dismayed disgust at Wilde's behavior, not least at its being so absurdly patent. And in terms that would have hurt Wilde, theorist of the beautiful, he adds: "He does not feel the ugliness of his vice."

Novels, too, in the final decades of the century in particular, were pushing against the perceived restraints of an earlier generation. Arthur Benson was well acquainted with Thomas Hardy, his older friend and colleague, whose *Tess of the D'Urbervilles* with its challenging subtitle, *A Pure Woman Faithfully Presented*, offered a heady image of corruptly motivated sexual pursuits, failed idealism, and tragic destruction arising from an emotional commitment to notions of purity. It disgusted and fascinated many of its earliest readers. Mrs. Craigie is less well-known today, although in her day she wrote plays that starred Ellen Terry and novels that sold 80,000 copies in the first few weeks of publication, under the name, to begin with, of John Oliver Hobbes. In 1904 she sent a copy of her new novel, *The Vineyard*, to Arthur Benson. He set down his response in his diary: "Mrs Craigie has sent me *The Vineyard*, and I don't know what to say. It is a sexual book, like Hardy's. . . . I am not at home in this region at all. Do all properly constituted men feel like that? A wild and rather brutish pursuit of a mate? And are women so morbidly passionate too? I have never felt this, never come across it." Clearly he wrote his impressions to Mrs. Craigie, who replied, "saying that her view of the 'sexuality' of life is not exaggerated, a provincial life at all events."

It is worth lingering a moment on this exchange because it captures so well a founding problem with the Bensons and the language of sexuality. Arthur is sent and reads a book by a fashionable and successful female writer, and is at a loss for a response. He recognizes the problem immediately, that the book is "sexual." "Sexual" and "sexuality" are terms he never uses of himself. The word is still sufficiently novel and touched with its scientific roots in the nineteenth century to sound trendy or at least alienating. Hence his use of scare quotes in his second comment: sexuality needs careful framing as an idea, careful distancing as a notion by punctuation. It marks a new way of thinking, something "of the era." But Arthur is "not at home in this region at all." There is no place, no sense of fitting in when it comes to sexuality, not just as a subject for literature but also as a way of writing a life. It is not where he is at home. This is because he cannot empathize with the erotic feelings that Mrs. Craigie represented. Is desire something for "properly constituted men"? His language is inherently if fuzzily medicalized and moralized. Perhaps, he suggests to himself, it is only men who are sick or improper who have such feelings. This sort of feeling seems to reduce humans to animals, "wild and rather brutish," when desire is comprehended as no more than the "pursuit of a mate." The eugenics movement would want to reclaim the word "mate" for a new understanding of the need for selective breeding, but for Benson here it is what human animals do when not elevated to the ideals of religious marriage and purity. This is heightened—of course—for women. They seem to be, he reflects, "morbidly passionate": that is, necessarily transgressive by virtue of their passion, an idea familiar enough from the medical writings of Acton, say, who famously declared proper women to be "not very much troubled with sexual feeling of any kind." Benson has some normative authority from the earlier years of the century to ground his anxiety. He concludes, however, that he has neither himself felt nor recognized such emotions in others: it is all beyond his ken. Mrs. Craigie, however, continues to disagree, and it is perhaps with a certain comfort that the whole problem is all placed finally for him in the snobbishly dismissed retreat of the provinces.

Arthur Benson is struggling for comprehension at two levels here. He is first of all trying to recognize in himself or even in others signs of the disruptive passions of sexuality and can only mark his intellectual and emotional distance from and incomprehension of such feelings. Is he, or the person whom Mrs. Craigie depicts, to be counted as a "properly constituted man"? He seems to be aware that his distance from the ordinary marks him out as different, though he cannot give up the idea, which everyone holds on to rather desperately, of his own normality. But, at a further level, he is also struggling for the language to express this struggle. He is uncomfortable with the words as much as the emotions of sexuality, but cannot simply revert to an earlier framing of "love" and "sentiment." The pathologizing of sexuality is a process under way in the years in which Benson is writing, thanks to sexology, psychology, the law, and medicine, and we can see the drive toward such generalizing in his worry that "women" might be "morbidly passionate"—"morbid" is another nineteenth-century, scientifically tinged term that Arthur Benson in particular is partial to; but his uncertainty about such generalizations and the time-honored concern that sexual feelings, especially those of women, should be locked away show up very old patterns of thinking. Arthur feels that what Mrs. Craigie depicts in her novel is different from what he regards as his sense of an internal life but cannot quite find the words for it. What are the proper names for a properly constituted man? The right words, now?

Arthur Benson's aesthetic of reticence exacerbates both such anxieties about what is proper, and the complicity that structures erotic narrative—as this sort of sexual narrative always relies on the reader's imagination for its seductiveness to work. So he describes a beautiful evening walk at Eton, "There was a window lighted up, full of flowers: the room inside still: but just as I came past there came a boy in a nightgown to the window with a candle, put it down, and began to move the flowers, smiling." He is enchanted by the picture, and by the fact that the boy was "so unconscious that anyone saw him." But he concludes: "And then came a further surprise, of which I will not speak, but which I shall not easily forget—*inter lilia.*"

Arthur takes us with him to the window as voyeurs, and then cuts us off from the story, teasingly. He refuses to say what he saw or felt or did—but insists it is unforgettable. We are left to ponder even whether he is withholding a sexual or some other sort of secret. The final words, *inter lilia*, "among the lilies," is a clue, though: the phrase refers at one level to the boy—the surprise—among the flowers, but it is a quotation from the *Song of Songs*, "Your two breasts are like two fawns, twins of a gazelle, that feed among the lilies." The boy among his flowers, with a sly wordplay, reminds him of the great erotic, longing poem of the Bible.

In 1882, his second year at Cambridge, some traumatic event happened to Benson in his rooms, H1, King's College. In his diary he regularly records "the anniversary of my great misfortune" on November 9. He never reveals exactly what happened or even what the bare bones of the trauma were. Twenty-one years later, he is still affected: "my darkest hours—it hardly does to think of, even now—and yet it was all so fantastic and unreal." In the *Memoirs of Arthur Hamilton*, however, the narrator tells the story of a trauma that happens to the hero on November 8, 1852, which he first commemorates in his diary with a prayer for salvation on November 9. The narrator explains that he has read some intimate letters written by Arthur, since destroyed, from which he has tried to reconstruct the story. These letters were "so passionate in expression, that for fear of even causing uneasiness, not to speak of suspicion," he will not quote them directly. But the story is simple enough. Arthur has at school formed a relationship with a "weak, but singularly attractive boy." This relationship is quickly glossed as "truly chivalrous and absolutely pure"—although expressed as being like an ancient Greek friendship—an intimacy of "a kind as cannot even exist between husband and wife"; and the narrator speaks "from my own experience . . . when I say that these things are infinitely rewarding, unutterably dear." But this boy had fallen into a bad set and come to grief. When he visited Arthur in Cambridge, the narrator declares, "what passed I cannot say"—but goes on: "I can hardly picture to myself the agony, disgust, and rage (his words and feelings about sensuality of any kind were strangely keen and bitter), loyalty fighting with the sense of repulsion, pity struggling with honour, which must have convulsed him when he discovered that his friend was not only yielding, but deliberately impure." It is quite unclear whether anything physical took place in this discovery, but Arthur is singled out as being peculiarly keen and bitter in his "words and feelings" when it comes to sensuality, and this helps explain his violent repulsion from a confession of the willing physical expression of male sexuality with other males, the deepest impurity because deliberately undertaken. This impure desire for males must be utterly elsewhere and declared to be not Arthur's, however suspicious his now destroyed letters might make a reader feel: "The other's was an unworthy and brutal nature, utterly corrupted at bottom." Utter corruption is "the other's," *de l'autre*, of and for the other—and it is a corruption "at bottom," a phrase hard not to over-read knowingly as a disgusted fear of "the beast below the waist." But this simple tale, concludes the narrator, is all inference: "I do not wholly know the facts and never shall." It remains something that is not to speak its name.

So in his novel about another Arthur, an Arthur who has a different relation to sensuality from others, the narrator tells us repeatedly that the complete facts of this trauma are not available—but it was certainly devastating to the young man. Between what is "unutterably dear" and what is "utterly corrupted," there lurks something not to be uttered, not utterly at least. This careful fencing—a novel with a narrator, who cites indirectly letters, from which he inferred a story that he knows he cannot fully know—again leads the reader to the window of revelation and closes the curtain at the last moment. A scene of confession is the setting of the trauma but does not lead to a full and frank confession by the writer. The struggle about speaking out is all too vivid.

So there are at least four silencing forces here that muzzle Arthur Benson's speaking out. First, we are dealing with the vice that dares not speak its name. Legal restraints, which shifted and intensified, were designed to produce fear; and, combined with the real threat of

career-ending scandal for a schoolmaster, and of disastrous destruction of reputation for a writer and public figure, such implicit and
institutional regulation worked to make physical or verbal expression of male desire for males, whether younger or older, a genuine danger, which well-publicized scandals and emphatic models of
normative masculinity highlighted. In the decades around 1900, it
did take daring to risk prosecution and humiliation to name such
desires, let alone to claim them actively for oneself. Well into the
1920s and beyond, novelists were prosecuted for writing books with
plots that included same-sex desire.

Yet, secondly, "the vice" went under various names and descriptions, and not merely because of the periphrases of propriety. The
decades from the 1880s through the 1920s are the period in which
sexology, psychology, medicine, and the law were initiating a developed idea of sexuality as a pathology where one could be a homosexual in oneself, rather than be prosecuted for sodomy as an illegal
and immoral act. But the language of homosexuality itself took a
long time to become the dominant frame of reference that it has
now become. Inversion, perversion, Uranian desire, sodomite, the
intermediate sex—and so forth, including terms for women and
a different range of expressions in other European languages—
attempted to proscribe what a properly constituted man was, and
constructed a sexual constitution, as it were, by which a man could
be defined and scrutinized. For Arthur Benson, it is not clear what
name would or could have been used even if one dared to speak it.
The map of sexual naming is shifting and recognized to be shifting
across this era.

But—and this is the third force—at any particular moment
within a period of rapidly changing cultural value, there will be people who are behind the times, just as there are people retrospectively
viewed to be ahead of their times. A sense of untimeliness, of not
fitting in, of being singular is often expressed by Arthur Benson, for
all that his very career as a student at Eton and Cambridge, teacher
at Eton, working for the palace at Windsor Castle, returning to
Cambridge as a don and eventually master of a college might seem

to proclaim a comfortably secure position in the establishment; and his books seem to place him by the number of their sales and the attraction of his self-portrayal as a paradigm of Edwardian cultural imagination. What is normal and proper for men was a central and contested question in this era, driven not merely by sexual issues but also by imperial, religious, civic demands. Arthur Benson and his pals were repeatedly vexed and vexing on what a real man and his vices were taken to be. Both the shifting landscape of sexual behavior and sexual language and the personal sense of not finding one's own place on this moving map produce an unstable place from which to speak out. There were people at the forefront of psychology or sexology, even in Cambridge at the time, who were developing the language that would become dominant for the comprehension of male desire in the twentieth century and beyond—but, although by the 1940s Fred Benson could mention Freud, there are precious few signs that this language was ever an absorbed part of the Benson family conversation.

Finally, Arthur Benson himself has his own personal reticence, which he thinks singles him out as especially unwilling to experience sexual feelings, psychologically or physically, despite the long history of young men he says he loves, and friends who shared some of his predilections. He worries how he is not at home in this region at all, not like other men, not one of the boys. In *Arthur Hamilton*, the opposition between the pure, chivalric, unutterably dear relationship of boys at school and the utterly corrupt recognition of sexual desire, willingly and willfully indulged, constructs a polarized architecture, which hundreds of pages of reflection in his diary testify to be hopelessly naïve. *How* Arthur Benson thinks he is queer is the question: how normal, how sexual, how ugly, how corrupt, how odd, how typical?

This what I mean when I say it is far from straightforward to name this family's queerness.

11

Though Wholly Pure and Good

TRUE TO FOUCAULT'S OBSERVATION THAT THE VICTORIANS talked nonstop about (not) talking about sexuality, it may be hard to name this family's queerness, but in Arthur Benson's diaries there is an extraordinary gallery of figures—characters and forms of speech—that calibrate very fine distinctions between types of male desire.

Despite the fantasy of purity and chivalry in *Arthur Hamilton*, the teachers at Eton in Benson's circle talked—and talked and talked—in far more nuanced, less idealistic and more self-implicating ways about boys. Benson refers to his own special friends, but with an ever-present need for propriety: "Talk of a Rabelaisian kind does not necessarily imply any moral depravity. It is the perennial anxiety, and it makes me shudder." Like Arthur in *Arthur Hamilton*, his shuddering is a sign of his "strangely keen and bitter" response to sensuality and its potential embodiment in words. He certainly had his crushes, which he reflected on afterward with melancholic pleasure: "I can never think of Mason without a glow of the heart—and also, alas, without some tears of the mind. There was something so beautiful and intense about his growth. I can never be thankful enough for his kindness to me." The boy's accession to adulthood also prompted an almost despairing recognition of the passing of time as a coarsening of the beauties of youth—which is a familiar theme of the epigrams of *The Greek Anthology*, examples of which Arthur Benson translated and published. Fred Benson had other translations in his library; and translating the *Anthology* linked many Uranian writers in a shared hankering for another, Greek-tinged world. (It was John Addington Symonds who was instrumental in making these poems fashionable for more than one generation.) So Arthur Benson meets Harry Cust many years after he had taught him: "But, oh dear me, my heart beat no longer at the sight of him, as it would have long ago. He is nothing, he is a corrupted roseleaf, a singed gnat." "The corrupted roseleaf" is an image redolent of Greek erotica's obsession with the fading of youth. These passions had little physical expression, it seems—he looks longingly at the sight of boys walking arm in arm as an impossibly casual physical intimacy for him. From the perspective of his later life in Cambridge, these fixations, which took up so much imaginative energy at the time, seemed unformed and undirected: "Then there was the Arthur Mason adoration . . . and Reeve . . . and Martin . . . and the opening up of Eton life. How utterly purposeless one was then. I know what I want now, though I can't get it." Desire, it seems, however understood, is barred.

This pervasive and snippy frustration takes shape with a good measure of self-disgust. As he himself grew older, he worries that he is fat and slow and lumbering—a "Walrus"—but his distaste goes deeper. He writes occasionally devastating single lines in the diary, that open a vista of misery, particularly as he moves toward one of his breakdowns: "I woke early with much repugnance of the flesh" (a thought his father, laboring at his studies of Cyprian and of the other Church Fathers, might well have approved). This self-disgust is matched by an intense distaste for the actual physicality of boys at school, whenever it seems sexualized—or rather, to keep within his vocabulary, when it stopped being romantic, edged toward the dangerously sentimental, and finally slipped from vice into the shamelessness of vice: willed impurity. So while he admires the casualness of boys at school walking arm in arm, there is an immediate danger of degeneration into something else, where casualness becomes lack of awareness: "Boys do not know the ugliness of what they do, or how it taints their lives, and their reputations too." The link between beastliness, Baden-Powell's favorite term of sexual horror in *Scouting for Boys*, and the bestial is always lurking, and such potential bestial feelings are integral to male behavior, or so it seems to Benson in his more desperate moments: "Can one trust any boy not to lapse into animalism? No, one can't: and I can forgive a sudden fall, a distortion of passion, even a habit of evil; but when this is added to a foul and ugly shamelessness of vice, the most corrupting of things, it makes one wonder that the brimstone does not rain down." The religious language resounds with his childhood education—"lapse," "fall," "evil," and, of course, the brimstone that destroyed Sodom and Gomorrah—but the emphatic emotion of his words also reveals how deeply this fear and disgust has been integrated into his emotional makeup. You cannot *trust* any boy not to slip into a physicality that is like the animals: there is a betrayal at work in the body. He can imagine and forgive a spontaneous momentary error, though it is still called in a telling phrase a "distortion of passion"—and he can even allow that this moment might be repeated—a "habit of evil." But as in *Arthur Hamilton* or his judgment on Oscar Wilde, what truly sickens him—with a crescendo of charged moralism—is the foulness and ugliness of a vice which does not recognize its own horror, that is, the true corruption of *deliberate* and *willed* sin.

In contrast with such physicality, Arthur Benson also idealizes the relationship between boys at school or university (they are all "boys" to him), and between boys and older men. While at Eton, Percy Lubbock, then captain of Benson's house, became friends with Howard Sturgis, who had already published the mawkish *Tim: A Story of School Life* (1891), which was dedicated to the "love that surpasses the love of women" and depicts the romantic attachment of two boys at boarding school. Sturgis had been at Eton and at King's College, Cambridge, like Benson—and was twenty-four years older than Lubbock. Benson, as Lubbock's housemaster, comments: "P.L. is making a romantic friendship with H.O.S.—I think it will do him good—he wants sympathizing with." There is for him no question, it seems, that it might be inappropriate for a schoolboy (though Lubbock was actually nineteen at this point) to form such an attachment. It is just good for him. And there seems in later years to have been no particular anxiety—at least about this aspect of their relationship—in the long and deeply felt friendship of the three men.

The edginess between romance, sentiment, and something further is, however, a constant threat. The story of O., a boy whom Benson mentored at Cambridge, flirts with crossing the boundary. O. has a "naturally wholesome and good nature" and is "deeply affectionate," but risks getting into more worrying territory: but "he is very little to blame, for he tells a further story to G. of that sentimental donkey N., who was not only sentimental, but now turns out, I fear, to have been worse." The extended, gossipy circle of men (familiar enough to need just discrete initials) is linked by the scrutiny of sentimental attachment and its discontents. O. has told G. of a story that perhaps exonerates himself because N., not an evil man but one on a slippery slope (a "donkey" rather than a degenerate), has allowed his sentiment to become something worse. B., exonerating O., records the pattern of exchange as a participant in a constant relay of anecdote and judgment—the mix of gossip, testing of norms, wondering about feelings that makes up a sexual discourse in action.

The lines of the map of acceptable feelings are constantly being drawn and redrawn in Benson's struggles about his own feelings and those of others. In the single month of October 1909—he is forty-seven years old—he records first, and typically, "I think my selfish nature is really incapable of love! But such as I have, I have given to her." The "her" here is Beth, his nanny. He strikingly excludes both his parents and his pupils—although there are innumerable expressions of love for both in his writings. A couple of days later, he is worrying about "free love" as an idea—it's part of a discussion he had one night with some chums—and although he does not condone promiscuity (as he carefully glosses), he does think that love "justifies carnal passion," and high-mindedly declares of marriage that "intercourse without love seems to me a far viler thing because so much more shameless": the shamelessness of willed carnality is once again the most despised sinfulness for him.

Very soon after, he has news that Henry James has fallen for Hugh Walpole, one of his own dear friends. "But it <u>must</u> be very surprising to have Henry James fall in love with you," he reflects with dry wonder. He then hears of another story that has come out, of a schoolmaster writing to a boy: "These are very odd semisexual affairs, full of the mystery and excitement of sex, yet with a sort of moral aspiration behind them—they are largely physical, I think." The difficulty of delineating feelings that get closer to his own is apparent: "sex," a word, as always, for others, has mystery and excitement, but in this case is only half-sexual because of a moralized tone—but is also "largely physical"—at least so he thinks. His incoherence is the sign and symptom of his struggle to match words and feelings, to get his feelings down. He then goes to a feast at King's and marvels at the undergraduate behavior—all men, of course: "The public fondling and caressing of each other, friends and lovers sitting with arms enlaced, cheeks even touching, struck me as curious, beautiful in a way, but rather dangerous." The move from surprise ("curious") to envious admiration ("beautiful in a way") to concern ("rather dangerous") is an archetypal transition of his emotional longing toward self-policing. In the space of a few days, he records a panoply of contested, judged, and confused emotional responses: in the family, in theorized discussion, in gossip about his friends, in the public eye, in the college life of men together. The diary is not just a record but a performance of the effort to find out *how* he might find his place in a region where he can never quite feel at home.

And with a return to self-disgust, Benson finds himself dismayed—with whatever disingenuousness—both at his own potential feelings in such circumstances and even at his willingness to reflect on them:

> I feel that I c^d <u>almost</u> be sentimental with this boy who would respond to sentiment very swiftly—but just could not. It might amuse me, but it w^d be like an emotional flirtation, or emotional sensualism. I should not want to give anything, only take a little ripple of emotion—how hideous to talk so!

He catches himself flirting with the possibility of flirtation and is horrified by the selfishness—again—that he knows he indulges. Many years before, he had bluntly dismissed the triviality of "pretty, irreproachably dressed young persons, *deliciae*, in no way interesting except as young creatures to be petted and patted"; and now he tries to reject such toying with boys, such pursuit of a "ripple of emotion," and even so wants to bury the anatomy of feelings he traces in himself: "how hideous to talk so!"

Yet he was also capable of listening with care and sympathy to boys who matched his sense of struggle. He describes how one boy came to him to talk and how the conversation moved from earnestness, to frankness, to revelation: "There comes one of the most <u>intime</u> confessions I have ever heard, which I must not speak of here. The boy is in very deep waters. . . . I don't think he is giving in. He said with a shudder, 'I could manage it all, if it weren't for my dreams.'" *Managing* emotions is exactly the aim and the problem: the dreams—longings, fantasies, desires—continue to well up within, and produce the shudder that marks the painful mixture of desire and revulsion: the slippage in the management of feelings.

After a lecture, a "graceful, ardent, impetuous creature" of a boy wrote to him "a letter such as I have never read in my life: if it had been from a woman it w^d have been simply a very ardent love letter." It is fascinating that despite everything, he still seems able to imagine a love letter only from a woman to a man. He admits that "I was not, in the days of my youth, inexperienced in the sensation of being made love to, so to speak, by older people"—that is, he recalls with surprising directness how what he has so often described as the chivalrous, pure romance of his younger days could "so to speak" be called "being made love to"—which implies an emotional, seductive, though still non-physical engagement. Yet this letter feels to him like something else: "But to be made love to in this simple way, with this deep and grateful devotion for nothing in particular except for being what I am, moves and touches me a good deal." There are no more "as ifs" or "so to speaks": he is simply being made love to, simply because of who he is—and he is moved. Moved, but disengaged: "I wrote a simple, elderly letter back to say that these things were better not confessed—partly because they must be transitory, and partly because people were not always to be trusted."This is Arthur Benson through and through. A simple letter of rebuttal, he announces, in return for the simple letter of lovemaking—though the psychological strain, veined with memory and desire, is far from simple. Strong feelings, he tells the boy, are better not to be uttered—reticence, above all—on the one hand, because such passions pass (boys grow up; arguments mar affection) and, on the other, because people cannot be trusted: word gets out, reputations are ruined; sexuality gets in the way; passions distort and disturb— all this, the personal, intimate side of things, produces the anxiety that destabilizes, that prevents trust: betrayal of the self is always looming. This is how emotions are to be managed.

In Arthur Benson's diary, long, twisting, intimate tales of powerfully felt relationships with boys run through certain years and are echoed elsewhere with longing memories, self-criticism, and more bitter turns of loss or disparagement. Benson is tetchy as much as sympathetic, snippily jealous as well as kindly and self-mocking, as rebarbative to intimacy as he is desperate to cherish its delicacy: both revelation and reticence depend on a constant self-anatomizing of emotion, often through a recognition of past self-deception. Much the same could be said for his equally tortuous relationships with Edmund Gosse or with his most lasting and calm friendship with Herbert Tatham, or even with his brothers, Fred and Hugh.

His emotions rarely reach any overt physical sign. His ideal rather was an evening like this with Hugh Walpole: "I was reading some scraps aloud out of Cory's Journals, and he was sitting on the hearthrug. He turned half-round as he sat, and just leant his head on my knee as I read, without either sentiment or embarrassment, as if it were just the most natural thing in the world." Benson sums this up as a picture of how Walpole "has pretty, affectionate tender ways with him." But it is also a telling self-portrait. Arthur sits by the fire reading his favorite Cory—just a few scraps, mind, carefully chosen—to his favorite boy. This, like good conversation or the silence of communing men, is an idealized image of what the proper talk of men is to be. Arthur sees himself as a father, a very different sort of father from Edward White Benson: Walpole "behaves as a son might, without protestations or gush." Because he is like a son to a father, the boy's head in his lap is neither "sentimental"—a sign of expressive or, worse, eroticized emotion—nor "embarrassing"—a sign of being "not at home in this region." The tableau is held. The scene ends, however, with a mix of dismissiveness and anticipation: "Of course I don't suppose this feeling will last. . . . I am a bad hand at keeping up relationships. But it will be a tender sort of memory." The moment is experienced with an immediate awareness that it will pass, and pass into the haze of memory. A moment of pleasure, darkened, as ever, by the melancholy of inevitable loss.

By the same token, when Howard Sturgis gave Percy Lubbock "a long and lover-like kiss" at the end of a weekend of "emotional flirtations," where his friends kept "making little overtures and whinneyings, like dogs and horses" to each other, Benson expresses his deep distaste. "It is only a symbol," he recognizes, "but I don't want that sort of symbol—perhaps I don't really want the thing symbolized." Even among his closest friends, when feelings turned to sentiment and found physical expression, he withdrew in (self-)disgust and relentless analysis.

The contrast of all this with Fred Benson is marked. There is barely a word in any of his surviving papers on any aspect of his internal erotic life. As his mother worried, he tells nothing. He regularly summered in Capri, however, which, since Italy had legalized sexual relations between men in 1891, had become a noted playground for an expatriate community of men who desired other men. He was fully part of that community. Typically, the only description we have is in a novel, *Colin*:

> How attractive was the pagan gaiety of these young islanders! . . .
> Love was a pleasant pastime. . . . They were quite without any
> moral sense, but it was ludicrous to call that wicked. Pleasure sanc-
> tified all they did; they gave it and took it, and slept it off, and

sought it again. How different from the bleak and solemn North-
erners! These fellows had charm and breeding as their birthright,
and, somehow, minds which vice did not sully.

This sexualized idyll of Mediterranean freedom is the precise
inverse of his brother's repression and self-disgust. For Fred, "pagan
gaiety" is simply and directly attractive. "Love," about which Arthur
was so anguished and intent, was no more—or less—than "a pleasant pastime" for Fred's narrative voice. And, in terms to horrify his
brother at Cambridge, there is an easy recognition that not only
were these young Italians quite without morals, but also it would be
ridiculous to worry about any level of sinfulness in such immoral
physicality. So, in *As We Are,* with a self-consciously shocking insouciance, he calls postwar premarital sex "almost innocent shamelessness." Even more horrifying to Arthur would be the blithe assertion
here that pleasure sanctified such behavior—both the claim that
pleasure was the criterion of judgment and that something as upsetting as pleasure could actually "sanctify"—make holy—immorality
is the sort of language that made Arthur despair of Fred's superfi-
ciality and frivolity. On Capri, in a way beyond Arthur's ken, pleasure could be taken and given without cost, guilt, remorse, or consequence. The final insult? Fred happily calls their behavior "vice,"
but equally happily announces that their minds are unsullied by it.
It would hard to invent a more systematic reversal of the deepest-
held categories of anxiety in Arthur Benson's moral, emotional, and
physical world.

Yet for all the talk of feelings in Arthur Benson's diary, there are
very few positive self-definitions in this vast work of self-fashioning
and no language of positive sexual identification. Our contemporary
confessional and assertive language of "coming out," with its commitments to the truth of a sexual identity, its conversion narratives,
is not yet employable by Arthur Benson, nor is it clear that had it
been employable it would have been used. Toward the end of his life,
just as Fred talks of the "real gulf, vastly sundering" him from the
Victorian past, Arthur was certainly aware that things are changing.

In 1924, less than a year before he died, a friend told him how sexual mores were not as they had been: "We spoke of the new ideas of <u>sex</u> that were growing up. He told me a very curious fact, if it is a fact, that 3 freshmen admitted that they had had serious affairs with girlfriends. He said that he looked forward to a far greater laxity under the new scientific methods." The underlining of the word "sex" and his disbelief that three freshmen could have had or could admit to have had serious affairs suggest that he found this information more than merely very curious. "Laxity" and "new scientific methods" are both negative terms in his view of romantic feeling; and his blank reporting of his colleague's hopes drips with a displeased irony.

In the same year, the language of homosexuality finally enters his vocabulary—just. In conversation with Fred, "we discussed the homo sexual question." Spelled as two words, it is marked also as a term of the moment, a Question, like the Woman Question or the Jewish Question—a novel term of definition, which needs new debate. There is, however, no explicit symmetrical recognition of the term "heterosexual," a term that needs homosexuality to become pertinent and marked—an act of self-definition. He goes on: "It does seem to me to be out of joint that marriage should be a sort of virtuous duty, honourable, beautiful and praiseworthy—but that all irregular sexual expression should be bestial and unmentionable. The 'concurrence of the soul' is the test surely." We will see in a while how conflicted a reaction to marriage Arthur Benson maintained throughout his life. But once again here, he marks that he is "out of joint" with the times. He himself had often condemned irregular sexual behavior as bestial and regarded it as profoundly unmentionable—but perhaps the word "all" is what counts. If the relationship is a concurrence of souls, then whether it is a relationship between men or between men and women seems not to matter (a case his father would find hard to countenance). The argument is made, however, in abstract terms—and there seems to be no place within it for himself (who is neither married, nor engaged in irregular activities, nor partner in a concurrence of souls). Indeed, when he uses the vocabulary of homosexuality for the second (and last) time, it is—as usual with his language of sexuality—to find a way to place someone else of whom he disapproves. Charles Sayle died in 1924. Benson reflects that "as long as he had a pretty boy to pet, it mattered little," and recalled a scandal when he had been seen holding hands with a boy at a concert in Oxford and asked to leave. "I expect S. was a homo sexual person, perhaps of perverted fancies, but blameless morals. He went about accosting beautiful girls and boys—fêted them, caressed them, flattered them, but did no one an ounce of harm." The combination of "blameless morals" and "perverted fancies" would baffle the twenty-first century's popular press, especially when embodied in the accosting of beautiful girls and boys (itself an odd phrase after the recognition of his homo sexual tendencies). Yet it is clear enough that Arthur Benson does not wish to see himself as open to description in such terms.

Nearly fifteen years earlier when Sayle was very much part of Benson's circle, he dismisses him in rather different terms. "He goes about *paidoppeuon* and why I dislike his sentiment is because it is all based on looks. . . . It is all very harmless . . . but it is a kind of sensuality." He puts the key term in Greek. *Paidoppeuon* means "looking" or "staring at boys." Hence the remark that he doesn't like "sentiment"—an emotional, expressive, erotic engagement—when it is "all based on looks": a boy's good looks and a man's staring. Benson, as ever, wants more—though, of course, for him the opposite of looking is talking (not touching). Hence, again, he strives to get a precise placement for Sayle: he is, on the one hand, "harmless"; on the other, mere looking is a style of sensuality and thus not wholly without blame. Roland Barthes called the style of rhetoric where two extremes are articulated, leaving an unstated middle ground for the subject's own position, "neither norism." Here the vacillating Benson wants to insist his friend is not dangerous ("just looking"), but also that his behavior is morally questionable ("looking as sensual indulgence"). The struggle to fit the example of Sayle into the Greek talk of male desire ends up only capturing Benson's confused distaste.

Oliffe Richmond, future Professor of Humanity (Latin) at Edinburgh, had been at the weekend party where Howard Sturgis kissed Percy Lubbock with lingering intensity to the disgust of Arthur Benson. Richmond used to hang around the King's College choir-boys because of his sexual tastes. Benson is clear that this is in his eyes not acceptable. "O.R. has a morbid predilection for boys—it is a sort of sexuality, an erotic mania, though wholly pure and good." The negative charge of the words "morbid" and "sexuality" are clarified by the specificity of "erotic mania." Yet Benson can also add "though wholly pure and good." This seems to mean that, because he committed no sexual act, no physical expression of his desires, he has maintained his purity and goodness. Benson is emphatic, repeatedly, that Richmond was in dangerous terrain: "I told O.R. he must drop these boys or that he would for ever be misrepresented"; "I told him today that it was a sexual perversion." It is a vivid indication of the shifting language of erotics that a man's desire for boys can be recognized as a perversion, a mania, a morbid sexuality, and yet be classified as pure and good, because there is no physical behavior, no specific act, that follows from it. It seems a judgment poised precisely and awkwardly between a modern pathology of sexuality and an older definition of sexual transgression based on activity.

A similar tension in his language is evident some nine years earlier in 1915, when he tries to describe one Martindale. He is "naturally pagan, sexual, Epicurean in all ways." "Pagan" is a familiar coded word from Victorian erotic language to indicate a pre-Christian physicality without guilt and, in particular for many, a Greek idealism; "sexual," underlined also, indicates as ever with Benson a pattern of bodily desire that is distasteful in its physicality or expressiveness; "Epicurean" is shorthand for a lover of pleasure, the epitome of a pagan, sexual intellectual. This is a description that could come straight from the coterie of 1890s Uranian poets or neo-pagan circles: an old-fashioned insider's dismissiveness. Yet he goes on: "I suppose this instinct became partially 'sublimated' . . . but I am sure it is all there, horribly suppressed and imprisoned." The scare quotes, as before, mark the self-conscious modernity of a new language, a language from contemporary psychology, which, with the terminology of instinct and suppression, takes us toward a new scientific thinking about the mind and erotic drives. (The English call this punctuation "inverted commas," which adds another grace note to the discussion.) The language, like so many of Benson's feelings about the subject, pulls in different directions; instantiates a moment of historical transition in the normative comprehension of sexuality.

Earlier still, in 1911, Benson can state of Oscar Wilde that he "had a <u>woman's</u> soul inside him—all his characteristics were feminine, his love of <u>men</u>, his dressing up, his pose, his sensuality," which prompts him later to ponder, "I wonder why I have always preferred <u>men</u> to women—some theosophists w^d say it was because I have the soul of a woman in the body of a man." Whatever he suggests of Wilde, as soon as the same thought is applied to himself—his self—it is distanced as the belief of "some theosophists," a marginal and dubious group of modernist theorists. Yet he has also absorbed nineteenth-century psychological theory enough to write at the same time, "The reproductive instinct, and its pleasures, lie a great deal deeper than the superinduced civic virtues." To describe what is inside a man, his deepest sense of self, shifts between different discursive registers, different ways to capture the sense of not fitting into conventional "civic virtues."

Arthur Benson is as often baffled by the sexuality of others as he is by his own. His mother, he writes, "told me several things I didn't know, which rather shocked me—strange sexual delusions": he was fifty at the time, still being told about such things by his mother. When he hears of a man who liked flagellation, he ponders: "I can imagine a man having such a perverted sense—but to confess it and carry it out in public is simply inconceivable." This bafflement is partly because of his deep internal contradictions. He insists—and there are many ways that he says this over the years—"I am pleased to recognize that for me the real sexual problem does not exist. I mean that my relations with women and men alike are of a dispassionate kind, without jealousy or desire. I don't want to claim or be claimed. I want nothing but a cordial camaraderie." Yet he is also less than pleased to recognize that he longs for something more, an imagined world where he was not brought up to believe that there was something sinful, something inherently wrong with sex itself. He is repeatedly distressed by his own failure to discover passion or lasting strength of feeling. He expresses pain that he compulsively withdraws when a relationship approaches intimacy. He knows in this that he is different from others—"I don't think I am an entirely conventional person"—but struggles to define his own oddity except by a constant process of an anxious search for the filigree of differences between himself and others. What's more, his bafflement is compounded by a certain willed silence. He talks with George Mallory, a very special friend, on one of his happiest days, about friendship and declares (in by now very familiar terms), "If one can trust a person absolutely, not to give one away, there is no objection to an easy and natural frankness. I do think we English are absurdly reticent." But within minutes, as the conversation turns to the "darker moral region" of romantic friendship, Benson, even here with Mallory, confesses in his diary, "that is one of the few things about which I do not speak my mind."

But the sense of his baffled struggle to name his desire is also because Arthur Benson cannot rehearse the simple and trivializing modern language of sexual essence and preference, of sexuality as a pathology. He cannot write even the word "homosexual" without a division in it. As it is changing, the language of sexuality is fissured, and Benson's language is pulled in different directions by these conflicting historical—scientific, medical, social, ethical, religious—forces. As we will see, he considers marriage on many occasions; he also expresses unpleasantly misogynistic opinions, while having some close and valued friendships with particular women, as well as profound feelings for his mother and for Beth, his nanny, along with his sisters. He can talk of finding particular women attractive and, usually shortly after, of why this will not lead to further intimacy for him. He can express in multiple ways what he is *not*, and who he is *not* like, but finds it excruciatingly hard to find a positive self-definition. His (ab)normality is always a fleeting object of anxious search. With Arthur Benson, we have an extraordinarily detailed and highly articulate case of how a man who finds males desirable struggles for self-expression in an era before the pathology of (homo)sexuality has become a social or emotional expectation.

It is hard to name Arthur Benson's queerness, then, because, although he cannot stop talking about it, he can never quite find the words for it himself.

12

He Never Married

THE LONDON *TIMES* MADE THE OBITUARY AN ART FORM, with its own brilliances and clichés. One cliché is the final sentence, often in a paragraph of its own, "He never married." It takes the place of the equally conventional "He is survived by his wife, Mary, and four of his six children." "He never married" is both a bare statement of fact and an invitation to read beyond its own reticence.

In 1898, two years after Edward White Benson's death, Minnie was discussing marriage with her son Arthur, already thirty-six years old. "Mama told me today," he recorded, "how constantly papa had wished this—how he mourned the absence of grandchildren. 'Oh, why don't we have grandchildren like other people!'" In his own diaries, Edward White Benson does indeed compare his family with the happiness he sees in the household of his friends the Westcotts and wonders why his own family life, in its religious aspects above all, has so disappointed him, but neither in his diaries nor in the dialogue first of mother and father, and then of mother and son, is there any suggestion that there is a reason easily to be found in the sexual preferences of the children or Arthur in particular. Such pathology is not yet a conceptual option, it seems, culturally or personally. "Well," reflects Arthur on his mother's revelation, "one can't marry to order; and I must trust God in this too. It is not as if I had made light of my chances. But I think He withholds it. It w^d help me in some ways—but it would not in others—so it is well." Arthur havers: of course, a man can't just marry because of parental wishes; perhaps God's will is being done (though it is hard to know how seriously he seeks for a religious lead here); but since the good of marriage is balanced by its demerits—both sides of the equation are scrupulously unspecified—all seems fine to him for the moment. At this point in his life—and on many later occasions too—the question of marriage is raised but not answered with reference to erotic feeling. Like a good Victorian man, he wants to balance the books when it comes to marriage—to draw up the pros and cons and to see if he can afford the expense—but this does not involve "th' expense of spirit in a waste of shame" that "is lust in action." About the same time, he discusses whether it is better to be an old maid or an old bachelor: the old maid is "much happier than the old bachelor, because she presumably had a circle and home ties—no such selfish, ineffective loneliness as the old bachelor. True, I think. I wish I saw my way out." Loneliness, the lack of family, are consequences of not marrying: a social gap, a lack of position, a lack of care, even—but the issue of whether he is a "properly constituted man" does not arise, except, perhaps, deeply buried in his failure "to see [a] way out."

Deciding not to get married was a significant gesture. His great hero, William Cory, some years after he had been asked to leave Eton, found his range of feelings changing. "She is the fifth or sixth that I have fallen in love with since I left London," he wrote jocularly to Reginald Brett, Viscount Esher, whom he had been close to as a boy and young man. Forty-six years old, he begins to reflect that it is "odd that I should begin to like and be liked by mere girls at the end of my life. Too late. But," he adds, with a bathetic nod to the conventions of love, "I can give them lockets and clasps." Ten years later, to his surprise, a young woman, Rosa Guille, a neighbor of his in England, wrote to him in Madeira, where he was living for his health, to confess her love. "I always wanted to marry an old clever man, good, tender and true. You are the man." He reciprocated with a matching declaration of love, "which, as I write it, seems to me incredible." After a suitable delay to test the strength of feeling—he was "subdued by the consciousness of being double-natured"—they married and lived together in Hampstead, London, where they had a child. The marriage seems to have been one of genuine affection and care, although his biographers are very dismissive of her later conversion to Catholicism and taste for frivolous pleasures. "The years roll back," he wrote, "I own my identity." To the surprise of his friends, Cory ended his days teaching Greek to young women, as a happily married man.

John Addington Symonds, by contrast, married Janet North at twenty-four, and they had four daughters. Four years later he met Norman Moor, a young man—in fact, his pupil on his way to Oxford—with whom he fell in love, with whom he had a physical relationship, which did not, however, lead to consummated sex. He had been forced to leave Oxford because of a scandalous accusation of improper feelings for males, before he met his wife; it was some years later that he finally had a fully sexual relationship with a man. His feelings for men and his marriage are painfully intertwined. Henry James wrote that he found the germ of his story "The Author of *Beltraffio*" in Edmund Gosse's description of the relationship of John Addington Symonds and his wife. The story is macabre enough, but it is telling that Mark Ambient, the author of *Beltraffio*, describes his wife's view of their relationship as "the difference between Christian and pagan. . . . She thinks me, at any rate, no better than an ancient Greek . . . she thinks me immoral." Gosse had described how Symonds's wife had no interest in his work, but James expands such distaste further and depicts a woman who has a physical loathing of her husband and all he stands for, and strives to keep their son away from his father to such a degree that she lets the boy die rather than be tainted by him. James enjoys uncovering the violence lurking beneath the veneer of English familial politeness, and it is not by chance that the narrator of the story is a young American writer, a disciple of the aesthetic author of *Beltraffio*. Unlike Cory's happy old age, this portrait of a marriage of difference revels in nasty, self-destructive horror.

Charles Ashbee—to add another contrasting model—was the son of Henry Ashbee, the probable author of the pornographic *My*

Secret Life, and he, too, had been at King's College, Cambridge, in the same year as Arthur Benson. He became a distinguished Arts and Crafts maven and promoter of the Garden City movement, as well as the first Civic Advisor of Jerusalem under the British Mandate. Benson visited Ashbee's Guild, where he produced his work. Ashbee was an intimate friend of Goldsworthy Lowes Dickinson, the Sinologist at King's, and Edward Carpenter; and both led him to recognize his sexual predilections in a way that seems to have been barred to Arthur Benson. In 1897, at age thirty-five, however, Ashbee, too, decided to marry and proposed to the seventeen-year-old Janet Forbes. He wrote to her with a surprising candor, in the local language of male desire before homosexuality. "Comradeship to me so far—an intensely close and all absorbing personal attachment, 'love' if you prefer the word—for my men and boy friends, has been the one guiding principle in life." "There may be many comrade friends but only one comrade wife." "These things," he concluded, "are hard to write about." He hoped that the seventeen-year-old girl would understand. It is not clear she understood at all.

On the wedding night, he kissed her fondly and went off to write a letter to his mother about how he would always love *her* more than any other person alive. (Minnie Benson also confided that Fred had told her he would never marry because he loved her too much.) After three years of unconsummated marriage, Janet fell in love with another man, Gerald Bishop, who was also married and who reciprocated her feelings. But duty and morality prevailed, and this relationship was also unconsummated. After six years Janet, not surprisingly, had a mental breakdown, to which Charles responded with heartening sympathy, and they had four daughters in rapid succession. The letters and diaries of this marriage give a fascinating insight into the daily workings of a relationship caught between the strictures of a public morality and the gradual development of a personal honesty deeply at odds with that public morality. He describes to her picking up a guardsman on the Strand and taking him off on a walking holiday in France; she replies that she cannot deny shedding a tear over his letter, but adds that since he had been so good to her over her difficulties previously, she gave his holiday romance her blessing. The accommodation between two individuals here seems quite different both from Cory and from Symonds.

Marriage was the expectation for a well-connected and wealthy young man, as was a marriage between a much older man and a younger woman. Such expectations were fed by the different models provided by Cory, Symonds, and Ashbee in the extended Benson circle, along with the prevalent cultural recognition that the emotional behavior of boys in the all-male environments of school or university was a deplorable moral danger, but also a recognizable stage of life before the social duties of adulthood. Many a novel—such as Howard Sturgis's *Tim: A Story of School Life* or Horace Vachell's *The Hill: A Romance of Friendship*, both books read by Arthur Benson—feel the narrative and social need to kill off the young man before adulthood, to avoid the consequences of such boyhood relationships continuing. This normative discourse of marital expectation is a constant backdrop to Arthur Benson's havering over the years.

Benson wants companionship but hesitates to seek it in marriage: "I don't like being so much alone as I am; but I do not think I want to be married." He imagines that he might well have married: "Oddly enough if it hadn't been for two chance remarks"— one, of course, from his father—"about the mistake of early marriages, I could have been in love with her [Mrs. Sparrow], if I had stayed a few days longer with them." The "if only" of desire fades into a lost past, just as his relationship with Mary Cholmondeley finally appears not as a humiliation but a lucky escape. He sees in his friends who have married a lack of spontaneity and a crusting of routine, which, like the narrator of Henry James's "The Author of *Beltraffio*," he expresses through the barely repressed erotic language of aestheticism: "He has formed habits, which Pater says is failure in life" (this, from a man addicted to the routine of writing). He wants to break out of his ineffectiveness and emotional passivity— "But I do rather hanker for some <u>nearer</u> tie—someone to whom it would be natural to care and linger about"—but even as he sees the obvious solution, he pulls away from it more firmly: "Of course the obvious thing is to get married . . . but then one can't get married on principle. It's very unlikely that I shall marry." And—this is typical of him—his indecisiveness leads to a remote theorizing about the state of marriage itself. In contrast with the church's rulings on divorce and the significance of virginity, he takes a modern, even a surprisingly liberal view in favor of divorce and remarriage: "The incident of sexual intercourse does not seem to me to render that tie insoluble" (the slightly priggish expression is once again the sign of his awkwardness when the word "sexual" or "sexuality" appears). He gets into a tiff with his mother and Lucy Tait about the issue: "MB and Lucy . . . don't understand an idea of <u>marriage</u>"; "I recognize no moral law except the law of affection. I think that without it, marriage is <u>per se</u> immoral." But this leads to a *froideur* between him and his mother: "MB introduced the personal element and said rather stiflingly that my views on marriage were 'funny.'" Like Telemachus in the *Odyssey*, he is told firmly by a parent that he does not understand the intimacies of marriage.

As late as 1916, when he is well into his fifties, he is still being prompted by the voices of normative expectation and resisting it with a theory that avoids any explicit language of sexuality. The wife of the Master of Sidney Sussex College at Cambridge "said she wondered why so 'dear' a person as myself did not 'bless some person with my sympathetic companionship.' . . . This letter touched me a good deal. But it is a line unintelligible to me—as if one could give oneself away, because one so believed in one's power to help and delight! My idea of marriage is that one calls an angel down!" This idealism, with its echoes of Coventry Patmore's "Angel in the House," is in blunt contrast to his reaction when a woman actually expresses a desire for him: "A very sad letter from Miss A confessing a deep passion; but I feel no answering thrill, merely a sense of discomfort. . . . I don't want to marry—I don't want anyone so near me as that." Sadness, discomfort, distance . . . It is perhaps understandable that as he grows old as a bachelor, he laments, "Why is one brought up in such transcendental ignorance about marriage?"

The Marriage Question became a Question in 1888, when, as I mentioned earlier, Edwin Arnold, the editor of the *Daily Telegraph*, asked his 500,000 readers "Is Marriage a Failure?" He was—in the usual run of journalism—responding to an article in the *Westminster Review* by the novelist and feminist Mona Caird, who had termed marriage a "vexatious failure." Her polemical feminism, even in a middle-class journal like the *Westminster Review*, might well have passed without much ado had it not been for Arnold's publicity, but the response to his question surprised everyone. The *Daily Telegraph* received no fewer than 27,000 letters, which dominated the columns for weeks. Harry Quilter published a selection of them the same year, with a mock-heroic introduction: "England stood aghast at the mass of correspondence which, like a snowball, grew in size as it rolled along." Even Mr. Pooter in *The Diary of a Nobody* records with his endearingly straight-faced simplicity that "we had a most pleasant chat about the letters on 'Is Marriage a Failure?' It has been no failure in our case." The debate—public and widespread—is a sign and symptom of the shifting normative structures toward the end of the century. What prompts so many people to write in to the paper and to discuss the issue at home is not so much the sociological, biological, or political basis of monogamy, which were Mona Caird's intellectual starting points, as the personal involvement of each individual in the implied narratives and lived experience of marriage. For Arthur Benson, as for his mother, father, Lucy Tait, and his brothers and sisters, the comprehension of the institution of marriage was a profound question of personal identity. His repeated anxiety about his decision to marry is not just a question of social form or fitting in, nor an issue of whether he can conceal his true nature from himself or others by a type of *marriage blanc*, but a pained reflection about who he is and wants to be: an exercise in self-formation. Mona Caird was branded as a New Woman, a threatening, disparaged, and occasionally celebrated stereotype through which to express in shorthand a sense that society was changing—and Caird can be taken as one of many figures from the period who in retrospect appear as founding mothers of an unfinished drive toward increasing political and social equality for women. But Arthur Benson does not fit so comfortably into such a teleological history. He is not an evident harbinger of battles to come, no New Man. Rather, his struggle with the idea of marriage seems part of his uncertain recognition of his own masculine ideals and a psychologically intense and personal revulsion before eroticized physicality. He is looking out of a college window at a scene in which he cannot feel at home.

When Arthur Benson came to read his mother's diaries and finally to realize the incompatibility of his parents—as he characteristically summarized decades of private tension and conflict—we might, then, recall how Minnie Benson wrote of her early married days that "Arthur only knows them as a child does" or how she had told him—to his evident dismay—that his views on marriage are "funny." He may have been struggling with what marriage implied for his identity, but to his mother his "transcendental ignorance" about marriage was all too apparent. Yet how should the marriage of Edward White Benson and Minnie Benson be understood? Fred destroyed much of the most "sacred" material, and what is left—her jolly early diaries and tormented later recollections—frames significant gaps in time and in our potential for comprehension. Even so, there are certain crisis moments that open a remarkable perspective on what marriage and its intimacies might mean, even and especially in a marriage at the very center of the British establishment.

In 1872, after Hugh, her sixth child, was born, Minnie Benson was unwell. She had had many a crush through her marriage so far, and at least one serious passion for Emily Edwardes (whom Arthur remembered as "devout and serious, loving tradition and antiquity," but not as his mother's obsession). Minnie was pregnant with Fred when this relationship had started, and Edward gently enjoined a return to the duties of mother and headmaster's wife. Four years and another birth later, she was physically crushed and visibly depressed; on the doctor's advice, backed up by Arthur Sidgwick's intervention, she was allowed to go to Wiesbaden in Germany to stay with Edward's brother Christopher, in order to recover. In the end she stayed away for six months.

She left behind her husband and her six children, who ranged from seven months to eleven years in age. The thought of return often brought on a relapse. Although there are some dutiful letters to the children, there is little sense of the distress one expectation of motherhood would require during such a separation. It was while she was in Wiesbaden that she fell in love with Miss Hall. Yet, despite the overwhelming nature of these feelings—which we will come back to—she could, at Christmas, write with what reads like a genuine emotion to her husband:

> Our first home—where we first <u>really</u> knew each other, and where our love, deep enough always, has grown old and deepened year by year, though each year it has seemed impossible to love you more— you have been very patient with me dearest—I was such a child when we married that I am afraid you must have had many sad moments—for it seems I have grown up of late years, and learnt the fullness and strength of married love, and what <u>unity</u> means and only of late years that I have really been a woman.

She talks of their first home because while she was in Wiesbaden, Edward was offered and accepted the job of chancellor at Lincoln Cathedral, leaving Wellington, the school he had established as headmaster, and moving into the career ladder of the church. When she returned, he duly went to Lincoln with the older boys and Hugh and Beth, while she went with the girls and Fred to her mother's. The family moved into the new house without her. Yet from Wiesbaden, she can write of their unity, their real knowledge of each other, his patience, and her gradual growth into true womanhood (she was thirty-two at the time). But when she did come home from Germany and Miss Hall visited, it is clear that things were grim. She recalls ignoring her children and Arthur crying. She also remembered how her volatile "tossings, doubts, indecisions, jealousies . . . grieved E to the heart." "The letter. Ah! my husband's pain," she wrote later, "what he bore, & how lovingly, how gently—<u>our talk</u>. My awful misery—my letter to her." What is clear from these shards of pained memory is that Edward was made well aware of Minnie's feelings and acted toward her—from her later perspective—with a generosity and even understanding, despite his pain, that she found remarkable.

It would seem that both the unity, patience, strength of married love, of which she writes from Wiesbaden, and her engrossed, overwhelming, erotic passion for Miss Hall—and other women—could co-exist within Minnie Benson, but not without depressive internal conflict and social disruption, which produced both her psychological misery abroad and at home in these years, and Edward's own "sickness of heart." Yet, with whatever accommodation of each other, they maintained an external face of happy dutifulness and managed their emotions in such a way that they continued in such an accommodation for the remaining years of their marriage. It is important to underline that we have no real knowledge of how this accommodation was brokered or even functioned: "our talk" is an evocative but silent emphasis of a deeply felt memory of intimate exchange—just as we cannot read either of the letters that marked the crisis.

For Ethel Smyth, the composer—and wonderfully rollicking personality of Edwardian Europe—Mrs. Benson, as she called her, was a savior. After an emotional crisis that threatened her whole sense of self, Smyth tells in her autobiography how her friendship and her conversations with Mrs. Benson extricated her "from the clutches of despair." Smyth had fallen in love with Lisl von Herzogenberg, the wife of her counterpoint teacher in Germany, a passion that was reciprocated. The family had intervened, and she was forced to leave Germany. Not long after she spent time with Julia and Harry Brewster. First, Harry fell in love with her, while she was infatuated with Julia (as she wrote to Lisl); gradually she responded to him. Julia was made aware of the situation, and a messy relationship of correspondence, forbidden, and stolen meetings unfolded over many years, until after Julia's death, when Ethel and Harry consummated their relationship in Paris. During this long-drawn out affair, she also formed a liaison with Lady Ponsonby, which lasted almost until Lady Ponsonby's death in her eighties. Lady Ponsonby was also married and had children. As Smyth put it, "If there is such a thing among human beings as a two-stringed instrument such as I once saw in an Arab band, for the next fifteen years I was that instrument and Harry and Lady Ponsonby were the two strings." Smyth describes the Benson family—after her falling out with Mrs. Benson—as Puritans and attributes their later disaffection to religious differences (Smyth was then a High Church Anglo-Catholic). As we will see, the collapse of their friendship was slightly more complicated than that. But it is striking that Smyth was forced not to see or communicate with Lisl von Herzogenberg, which caused the despair that led her to Mrs. Benson. Her epistolary relationship with Harry caused immense social difficulties, and her own family tried to prevent her from having any contact with him, and Mrs. Benson and others advised her to terminate the relationship totally. Her intimacy with Lady Ponsonby depended partly on her husband's absence—he died in 1895—and, of course, she never lived at Lady Ponsonby's house. Smyth, whom Edward White Benson hated, was self-consciously less conventional than any of the Bensons, yet for all the complexity of her paraded transgressions, the contrast with the Bensons also reveals just how extraordinary and how quietly ongoing *their* accommodation was.

What is perhaps most remarkable is that this accommodation lasted throughout their marriage. At Lincoln, from her own recollections, Minnie was brought out of her depressive state by a burgeoning relationship with Mrs. Mylne—Tan—an older, evangelical, theological student, whom Edward seems to have disliked and mistrusted. This encounter was described as a spiritual transformation, and there can be no doubt that from this period onward, Minnie did discover a faith in a personal God in a deeply felt and deeply committed manner—a transformation that was vividly embodied in her calmness at the death of her eldest son, and, as we have seen, in the outpouring of prayer and spiritual meditation at the death of her husband. At Truro, she had a passionate friendship with Charlotte Bassett—"Chat" (bizarrely, the same nickname as one of Cory's and

Lord Esher's most engaging male *amours*, Charles Williamson)—to whom she spoke a good deal about faith and spiritual healing, as Tan had done for her. In London, when Edward became the Archbishop of Canterbury, she met Lucy Tait, the daughter of the previous archbishop, with whom she formed a relationship that lasted until her death. Yet throughout this series of strong attachments to women—which we will return to, inevitably—she performed the role of mother to her children and wife of the archbishop, and did so in a way that was publicly and privately praised. Her intimate written response to Edward's death over many weeks—crushed, desperate, emotionally traumatized—reveals that her recognition of how gently and lovingly he had responded to her over Miss Hall was one part of an intricate, sensitive, caring, and deeply committed relationship, which is extremely hard to categorize—to name—according to the stereotypes of Victorian or modern marriage.

We can also catch from the family's censorship the occasional moments of Edward's reflections on the marriage's stormy progress. In 1879, visiting Wellington now as Bishop of Truro, he wrote back to Minnie in Cornwall:

> But oh! How I lament that I was so sour and clouded and so bitter and so hot, so incessantly that the sweetest place on earth has its scowling ghosts—and you, my dearest, know more of this than anyone. I hope you can forget. Lincoln would not be near so much so—in fact is quite different in this respect. Light not so bright but shadow not so dark, more glow and more softness. Kenwyn is all peace. Martin's sweet spirit that was pained as nothing but disunion, seems to have entered in there, and brought rest with power.

This is such a fascinating glimpse behind the curtain of their relationship. Edward knows how the early years of their marriage at Wellington were marred by his depression and his energy that turned into impatience and aggression, so that now, revisiting the place they started their married life together, its sweetness, he feels the need to remind them both of the "scowling ghosts" of the past—with the hope that she will forget what he is reminding her of and cannot repress for himself: her forgetting would be his absolution. Lincoln, slower, less extreme in its mood swings, turns now, for him, into the peace of Truro, but this peace is immediately given its darker coloring by his recollection of their shared loss of Martin (again to the fore of his mind)—the boy's sweetness that could be pained only by the disunion this letter is designed to overcome. As Edward looks back—and the imagery of light ("clouded," "bright," "shadow," "dark," "glow") is part of the struggle to see clearly—their intimacy is for him framed by his determining moods, and even in the performance of regret, he cajoles her into feeling what he wants. Yet it is also a letter that wants to reach out in intimacy toward Minnie, and which offers the apology of self-recognition and self-recrimination. The final phrase, however, is also telling. What he now has is "rest with power." As he marks the peace he longs for, he cannot help underlining that his career has also risen into a position of power. His public life again concludes and frames his private reflections.

At one level, it would be easy to tell the story in a familiar familial pattern: the idealized, though wholly asymmetric courtship, leading, after the honeymoon period, to a stormy early marriage, with bitter arguments and cantankerous, boring holidays. In an era when divorce or separation was a barely available option—and certainly not for a family in the Bensons' position in society—the father threw himself into work, and the mother into other friendships, establishing a pattern of increasingly separate lives, with a civilized veneer on public occasions, from either ends of the dinner table, as it were. Edward White Benson's fierce Christianity meant he could not take a lover, as many men in such a narrative would do; Minnie's feelings for women added a frisson and intensity to her friendships that finds fewer parallels—though some well-known ones—in such narrative expectations. The latter years of public probity and projected marital security depended on maintaining the daily separation and emotional disengagement.

Yet such a stereotyped story will not do. It suppresses first of all the black moods, brooding presence, and emotional neediness of Edward, and Minnie's emotional dependence on him, as her out-pouring at his death reveals, despite her retrospective distaste for their courtship and his bullying, and despite her love of women. Her passions for women *ran alongside* her religiously informed, dutiful, and intent commitment to her husband, and it is this combination, recognized—at least at some level by both of them—that makes the marriage so complex.

The complexity of the ongoing emotional interaction of Edward and Minnie certainly confused their children. A marriage is view-able from different perspectives, and children always have to nego-tiate between seeing their parents as individuals and as a couple in a relationship. The Benson marriage seemed to the children, however, to have a particularly polarized dynamic. Their father's depressions produced fear and helplessness. Arthur recalls Addington, the arch-bishop's official country residence, with misery, precisely because of his father's black periods: "I have scarcely a pleasant memory of Addington, and never went to see it again." Their mother provided the "precious balms [that] healed our heads," as Fred put it. Their father's love was manifested in strictness, a "love that hankered for ours"; their mother's was a love that was a "stern business, [with] never the faintest trace of sentimentality . . . [but] with a swift eager-ness." How, then, did they put their parents' differences together? After their parents' deaths, as we have seen, Fred rhetorically asked, "If her marriage was a mistake, what marriage since the world began was a success?"—while Arthur, who had read what Fred had pub-lished, could write that "her married life, though she would not have purchased her freedom at any price, had been a constant and urgent strain." The two unmarried boys saw the marriage differently.

This isn't just an Edwardian reticence or failure of comprehen-sion. Honor Moore in her biographical reminiscence, *The Bishop's Daughter*, tells a relentlessly modern story of her attempt to under-stand her father and mother (and herself), complete with shared therapy and lurid sexual details of the complex bisexuality of her father, the bishop (and her own). Her story of church life in a modern New York world echoes the Bensons', as she reads her parents' letters and diaries after their deaths and tries to manage her constantly anguished relationship with the dominating figure of her father. Yet, despite all the analysis, the self-exposure, the sexual knowingness, all she can trace, again and again, is the familiar baffled gap of incomprehension between a child and her parents' marriage. As Henry James captured so well, what a child knows is always a self-defining and frustrating exercise against the unknowability of those apparently closest to them.

As with Honor Moore's story, the Bensons' married life, too, took its shape in and against cultural and political shifts of particularly intense and lasting significance: the married women's property act, new rules on family law, the arguments for female suffrage were all flaring into public awareness through the years of their marriage. In their personal intimacies, however, there is barely a sign of any political framing of their accommodation. As the end of the century approached, the new ideal of "companionate marriage," with its fragile and uneven challenge to patriarchal authority, was redrafting the traditional insistence on a wife's obedience to her husband—to the degree that in H. C. G. Moule's book on St. Paul, the phrase that traditionalists loved to cite, "Wives, submit to your husbands," could now be polemically retranslated: "Wives, be loyal to your husbands"—and Moule was an evangelical bishop. . . . But this marriage of the Bensons looked inward; despite its very public aspect, it did not seek any validation in public political slogans or movements. For all the self-consciousness and obsessive recording of this family, there are also inevitable blind spots and gaps in its own knowing of just how much of its era it may be. Looking back makes it easier: Charles Ashbee, reminiscing about his own mother's extraordinarily brave decision to leave his father, could in old age reflect, "The Eighties saw a weakening of the *patria potestas* in the home; of Mr Pontifex, Samuel Butler's 'will-shaker.'" From a distance, his mother's story and Samuel Butler's novel can look of a piece; up close, even those who are historically self-conscious do not always see where they stand.

Minnie herself spent a good deal of time after Edward's death reflecting on her marriage. She found that his friends no longer wanted to see her with the regularity of their previous engagement, and this upset her: "I <u>toiled</u> to make myself agreeable to his friends! They did not want my 2d agreeableness—they wanted his massiveness—his large ideas—his power. <u>And I was never associated with these</u>. I wonder if they looked on me as a great trial to him also?" She is dismayed by the thought that she might have been regarded as a burden to her husband. This sense of her own unsatisfactory role is exacerbated by Lucy Tait's comments: Lucy "seems to think that with Edward, as with her, I didn't <u>enter into his life</u>, and that the want of sympathy which I know he continually felt was from my <u>not caring</u> for the things he loved. She says I have a way of disassociating people from their life and caring for them apart from it—she has often felt this and thinks he did." Once again she is upset by a perception of her lack of sympathy, not just with her husband but with all her intimates. Her style of caring is for people in and of themselves and not for what they find important or to be loved. Minnie's complex self-perception of her marriage, aided by intimate conversation with others, stands against the trite judgment of "unhappy" or "happy marriage." At the end of the marriage, she herself is still struggling to comprehend its emotional dynamics and to evaluate them.

Yet there is a further, even odder aspect of the marriage that the stereotyped story cannot really compass. For the last six years of Edward's primacy, Lucy Tait lived with the family at Lambeth Palace, at the invitation of Edward. She had lived there before with her father; she was already a close friend of Minnie; and Nellie, the Bensons' daughter, had just died. There was nothing to the outside eye that would look odd in such an arrangement, granted the normality of female companions and extended family arrangements: she was fifteen years younger than Minnie and without adequate means of financial support. Yet Lucy was already Minnie's love, the woman with whom she slept after Edward's death until her own. It is frustrating that there are so few comments on this living arrangement in all our papers from the family. Edward calmly notes in his diary the occasions when Lucy joins him on his early morning rides. There are laconic comments in Minnie's diary. "Lucy and I. Warum o warum!" ("Why oh Why!"). Minnie does tend to drop in German words at moments of passion (perhaps a memory of her time in Wiesbaden), but it is hard to make a story out of such an entry. There is a bare indication of a conversation later in the same week: "Finally talk with Lucy, 'Had I said that, had I done this,'" but in comparison with her feelings for Miss Hall or the others, there is a striking silence from these years. There is no suggestion, as some have hopefully imagined, that they shared a bed while Edward was alive. We are left with the oddity of Edward and Minnie Benson sharing Lambeth Palace with Lucy Tait, her love. It could be that Lucy's presence was the "high price" for an outwardly proper marriage for Edward's career; it could be that Edward was unaware or turned a blind eye to his wife's feelings or behavior. Neither seems a convincing picture; neither fits with what we know from earlier and later interactions. Yet we just don't know how the triangular relationship progressed or what accommodations were brokered. The children, as ever, seem to have noticed next to nothing at this time.

The marriage that started with that kiss turned out to be a very strange relationship indeed.

13

All London Is Agog

IN 1940, IN HIS LAST AUTOBIOGRAPHICAL VOLUME, FRED
Benson lovingly portrayed a day at Tremans, the house in Sussex
that provided the family's base since 1899, after the death of Edward
White Benson. After evening prayers, they "all went to their rooms.
Lucy slept with my mother in the vast Victorian bed where her six
children had been born in Wellington days. . . ." The ellipsis at the
end of the sentence is Fred's. He goes on: "Since morning, tides of
love had been flowing through the house, true and fervent religious
perceptions permeated it." So at one level, perhaps the only level,
the dot-dot-dots mark no more than the transition between everyone tucked up in bed, drifting off to sleep, and Fred's reflections at
the end of the day on how it had passed. But the drift into silence
also raises the question of how in 1940 he expected his readership
to understand the sleeping arrangements in his family. The bed, like
his mother, is firmly identified as Victorian, vast enough for two to
sleep in without touching, the place where her maternal role had
been fulfilled, six times. It is a description of continuity and a lost
past, not of overt eroticism.

Yet he had already explained that his "mother's intimacies and
emotional friendships had always been with women; no man, except
my father, had ever counted in her life, and this long love between
her and Lucy was the greatest of these attachments; it was impossible to think of them apart." This brief explanation of his mother's
relationship with Lucy is offered as one reason for the jealousy that

MISS GOURLAY. MAGGIE.

1906. [To face page 376.

FIGURE 4: Maggie and Nettie: the photograph of a relationship.

twisted Maggie's mind in her mental breakdown. Fifteen years earlier, in *Mother*, he had seen such relationships as absolutely normal
for a woman with a good mind: "My mother, throughout her life,
like all very intellectual women, formed strong emotional attachments to those of her own sex." In the 1930s Fred Benson was well
aware that things were changing: "A new female type, not a mere
variation of the old was evolving," he wrote in *As We Are*. "They
did not want men: their work and their friendships among themselves supplied them with means, with interests and with emotions."
But, he adds, lest you were getting worried, such women are "not
unfeminine at all." Fred's depiction of his mother, as one might
expect for an Edwardian gentleman's reticence, does not dwell on
her attachments to women with any prurience or even any imagination of impropriety. Arthur Benson's unpublished memoir allowed a
worry to emerge, but a worry expressed as no more than an excess of
involvement: "She formed a very close friendship with a Miss Hall,
so close indeed that she seems to have had scruples about the degree
to which it absorbed her." It is his mother herself, in Arthur's careful
prose, who is her own guardian of correctness, as if the issue were
merely a tension between close friendship and household duties.
The story of anguished letters, depression, passion, and his parents'
intense talk becomes no more than an example of his mother's scruples. How much is the reader invited to read between the lines? Is
this another example of writing for those who know?

The year in which E. F. Benson wrote *Mother* and A. C. Benson
started his biography of Minnie Benson falls in the middle of a
ten-year period after the end of the First World War, which for historians of sexuality has seemed fundamental in the public image of
female desire for females—fundamental, indeed, for the public recognition of the category of the lesbian as a pathology. Three events
in particular, each highly controversial and each widely discussed in
the press, were instrumental in this changing perception—much as
the celebrity of Oscar Wilde trial had the effect of fixing in the general imagination a particular cultural image of the man who desired
men as aesthetic, degenerate, appetite-led, over-sophisticated. . . .

In 1918 a small right-wing journal called, significantly enough, *Vigilante* published an article under the headline "Cult of the Clitoris." The very brief article noted that the dancer Maud Allan was giving private performances based on Oscar Wilde's play *Salomé* and suggested that if Scotland Yard collected the names of those who applied for tickets, it would provide a sample of those degenerates who were on a list, rumored to be held by the Germans, of British people whose sexuality left them open to corruption and betrayal. The piece was published by Noel Pemberton Billing, who had previously circulated an article in which he had asserted that the failing British war effort was because of a spreading moral degeneracy in the country, one cause of which was a cohort of German agents dedicated to the "propagation of evils which all decent men thought had perished in Sodom and Lesbia," evils that "hint at the extermination of the race." Some 47,000 citizens, it was claimed, were on the German list of potential sexual traitors. "Wives of men in supreme position were entangled. In Lesbian ecstasy the most sacred secrets of State were revealed." The audience of Maud Allan, declared Billing, included the first few thousand on that list.

It is unlikely that this brief splenetic piece would have attracted much attention beyond the usual readership for such paranoid extremist scapegoating, even though Billing wrote it partly at the suggestion of the famous author Marie Corelli (much-parodied friend of E. F. Benson); but Maud Allan decided to sue for libel. Billing defended himself in court, and the six-day sensational trial received increasingly over-excited press coverage, whose thrill was partly in contrasting response to the continuing horror of wartime news. The trial became such an iconic event because of a set of overlapping contexts: the threat of the enemy-within combined with anxieties about changing sexual moralities in wartime, to produce a fertile atmosphere for the conspiracy theories that Billing promoted. Maud Allan, who had danced for King Edward in Marienbad in Germany, was a fading star of erotic Eastern allure, thanks to her famous performances of *The Vision of Salomé*, and her reputation for living in a louche, Bohemian circle further made her open to easy accusations of impropriety. The fact that the play she was now dancing in had been written by the notorious Oscar Wilde allowed Billing to tap into negative images of male homosexuality associated with another famous trial. Maud Allan, a Canadian by birth, had lived abroad and spoke German—and the commonplace assumption of the foreignness of vice was exacerbated by the xenophobia of wartime. Yet it was Allan's own lawyer who produced the most striking images of female desire.

Ellis Hume-Williams, prosecuting counsel for Maud Allan, apologized flamboyantly for having to raise such a subject in a court where women were present, but insists on explaining how horrible a phrase "The Cult of the Clitoris" is. "You probably may have some idea," he allows, "but unless you have some physiological knowledge, you will not appreciate in its fullness what the gross obscenity of this phrase is." He goes òn to explain in what for the time is remarkably graphic exposition. "The fact is that this particular part of the female organization is open to treatment, let us say, other than by normal means which nature intended." Because of this physical potential, "there has come into this wicked world undoubtedly a practice . . . recognized as a vice which is supposed to have originated in the Island of Lesbos where there were women and no men—a vice by which the clitoris in the woman can be excited [*six words omitted*] and ways other than nature intended." The *Verbatim Report* of the trial explicitly omits the sixty-one words by which "*The learned Counsel explained in a very clear manner the precise situation and function of the clitoris,*" and, here, the six words in which he explained how the clitoris may be excited during lesbian sex. Counsel was, it seems, far too explicit for the official record, in the clarity with which he explained the "situation and function of the clitoris." Even to record such words challenges decency. The ignorance presupposed by such a need for and a hesitation around explicit description leads to a final ringing statement of how the world is: "There do exist in the world vicious practices where men are able to gratify their passions with men, and women with women—degrading, repulsive, contrary to nature, and consequently destructive of health—practices which, indulged in to any extent, sap and undermine the sanity and probity and self-respect . . . of those who indulge in them." Hume-Williams ringingly declares that corrupt practices exist—not lesbians, note—and, in terms with which the defense would agree, denigrates them as destructive of the mind, the decency, and sense of self of anyone who indulges in them. Prosecution and defense can agree on the horribleness of sexual activity between women.

If the prosecution insisted on educating the jury into the medical facts and the vices of the world—to give them the knowledge they may have lacked to evaluate the libel—the defense played a different game with knowingness. It brought in a medical expert who declared that "Clitoris is a Greek word, it is a medical term altogether; it has nothing to do with ordinary language; nobody but a medical man or people interested in that kind of thing would understand the term." On the one hand, the defense appears to claim that the article was not libel because no ordinary reader would have understood it; on the other hand, it slurs Maud Allan for bringing the case at all: if *she* could understand it, she must be one of those "interested in that kind of thing"—a degenerate. "Are you aware, Miss Allan," taunted Billing, "that out of twenty-four people who were shown that libel, including many professional men, only one of them, who happened to be a barrister, understood what it meant?" Billing went on to insist that Wilde's play, which had been banned in England already, was obscene and corrupting, and when Allan felt forced to defend the play's probity, Billing brought in Alfred Douglas, Wilde's former lover, who in different times had translated the play from its original French; he agreed that Wilde indeed "intended the play to be an exhibition of perverted sexual passion excited in a young girl." Billing insisted that the prosecution had misread the paragraph of libel, misread the play of Wilde, and did not therefore appreciate the corrupting influence of a figure like Wilde on the fabric of society.

This incoherent defense was successful, and Billing was acquitted. "It is safe to say," wrote the *Times*, "that no lawsuit of modern times has attracted such universal and painful interest as the deplorable libel action which terminated yesterday at the Central Criminal

Court. Not only in London, but even more in the provincial towns and countryside, the daily reports have been read with almost as deep anxiety as the news of the war itself." Yet, as the *Times* also noted, "any issue was on trial at most times except the one that was legally at stake." What excited the British public and what the defense utilized with rhetorical flair was a prurient mixture of the broad issues of public morality, suspicion of the sexual corruption of powerful people, the dangers of art's freedoms at a time of war. Whether Maud Allan was sexually immoral—the apparent libel—was buried in this swirl of arguments and was not discussed in the language of lesbianism at all.

The prosecution recognized the existence of vicious practices, and the defense challenged Maud Allan for knowing too much and yet for not knowing enough about the corrupting influence of Wilde's play—but there was no legal definition of lesbianism available and no legal provision to match the "gross indecency" charge against various forms of male activity with males. The defense offered no overt discussion of whether Miss Allan had actually committed any such vicious practice, even though a standard defense against libel is that the assertions under question are true; there was no statement by the prosecution or defense about whether Miss Allan herself did or did not exhibit sexual inversion, an intermediate sexuality, a morbid condition, or any other terminology that sexology had suggested to account for the vices that both prosecution and defense took for granted to exist in Britain. The trial is telling therefore not just because it focused a suspicious and prurient public attention on the potential for sexual activity between women, but also because its discussion of such activity remains so vague, veiled, and inconsistent. The act of silencing—the silencing of *clarity*, in the official transcript of the trial—is a sign and symptom of the struggle of an emerging but as yet inchoate language of transgression—and with it, an as yet unformed public repertoire of images of the woman who loved women.

Three years later in 1921, an attempt was made in Parliament to rectify the gap in the law concerning female sexual activity with other females. The Criminal Law Amendment Bill was introduced by Arthur Winnington-Ingram, the Bishop of London, who during the war had made quite a name for himself for his passionate patriotic support for the war effort, a xenophobic nationalism in the name of God; and who, after the war, had also been very active in campaigns for social purity, working to rescue prostitutes. The bill was concerned with the politics of consent and aimed to protect young women, especially those aged sixteen and seventeen, from seduction, brothel madams, and other forms of sexual lure and corruption. "I am asking you to extend the strong arm of the nation to care for the girls of the nation," Winnington-Ingram declared in Parliament with fervor. "We are trying to protect girls who are not able to take care of themselves." He did offer one final example of an older woman sending a letter to a younger woman, encouraging her to "a most unnatural sin"; the younger woman was persuaded by the plea that "there was no law against it." The law "educates the people," he concluded, so "the raising of the law" will raise "the moral standard of the nation." It was a bill designed to protect young women from predatory abuse.

A move was made, however, led by Frederick Macquisten, to add a clause, in effect to extend the Labouchère Amendment of 1885: he proposed that the criminalization of "acts of gross indecency" should be extended from activity between males to include activity between females. His motives were shady. The Criminal Law Amendment Bill had extensive feminist support and aimed to close the loophole whereby a man could claim that he had "reasonable cause to believe" that a minor was over the age of consent. Macquisten was opposed to the bill on both these counts and hoped that such an amendment would seriously hinder its passage. He was right, in that the Lords duly sent the bill back to Parliament because of it. The bill became law a couple of years later, with the compromise that men up to the age of twenty-three could claim the protection of "reasonable cause to believe"—but with any mention of sexual activity between women simply and silently dropped.

The language of the debate is no less remarkable than that of the libel trial three years earlier. Macquisten adopted the easy moral attack on the "beastly subject," which he called a "vice" and a "very real evil." But he also thought that Members of Parliament would know little of such things: "to many Members of this House the mere idea of the suggestion of such a thing is entirely novel; they have never heard of it." He was supported by Sir Ernest Wild (a name to conjure with in the context of trials of "gross indecency"), who argued that in 1885 it was hard for the public to imagine any gross activity except sodomy took place between men—with the implication that as then for men, so now for women. To be up-to-date is to recognize that vice is on the rise and is a female as well as male problem:

> [In 1885] people found it difficult to believe that such abominations took place. It was only in the course of years that juries could be induced to convict on evidence that such horrible acts between male persons, which it is unnecessary to specify, which fell short of, but were really morally worse than the complete act, which had been punishable for many years, had, in fact, taken place. This Amendment is simply an attempt to deal with a corresponding vice on the part of female persons.

His use of the word "simply" conceals a very complex legal and social set of problems, however (let alone his opportunistic homophobia). What acts will count with women? How will they be proved or witnessed? The Lord Chancellor, however, insisted that knowledge of such practices was lacking not just among the country's legislators but among its women: "The overwhelming majority of the women of this country have never heard of this thing at all. . . . I would be bold enough to say that of every thousand women, taken as a whole, 999 have never heard a whisper of these practices." The Lords were worried that the burden of proof, without the physical signs of penetration or emission, would prove impossible, and that blackmail would be the most obvious result of such poor legal drafting. The Lords duly voted the amendment and bill down, and sent it back to the Commons.

Yet this first attempt to legislate on female sexual activity with females also revealed how the language and conceptualization of such activity were changing. Wild informed the House that he had consulted medical experts as to how he should address Parliament. He was advised that he should go to Krafft-Ebing or Havelock Ellis for a full panoply of behavior and the technical language to describe it, but for clarity's sake, he was encouraged "simply to refer to the Lesbian love practices between women, which are common knowledge." The MP, ventriloquizing the medical expert, asserts that "Lesbian love practices" are "common knowledge" (despite the assertions of general ignorance by Macquisten and the Lord Chancellor). The term "Lesbian" is here entering the realm of legislation as the technical term (though the addition of "between women" suggests its reference was not as familiar as "common knowledge" would suggest), and, equally importantly, it enters with the *imprimatur* of the expert knowledge of the sciences of sexual behavior.

Wild cites Krafft-Ebing and Havelock Ellis together as authorities, although they took diametrically opposed lines on the issue of homosexuality. For Havelock Ellis, in terms that Arthur Benson significantly recalls, "The study of the abnormal is perfectly distinct from the study of the morbid"; that is, he argues, it is necessary to distinguish absolutely between that which does not conform to the norms of heterosexual desire and its institutions, and that which is sinful, corrupt, or degenerate. Those who desire their own sex may be a small percentage of the population and thus not normal, but they need not be thought for this reason to be diseased. The terms "abnormal" and "morbid" make up the matrix through which the boundaries of "sexual inversion" are formulated. So Edward Carpenter, whose books were far more easily available and far more influential with a broad public than either Krafft-Ebing or Havelock Ellis, writes:

> Formerly it was assumed as a matter of course, that the type [sexual inversion] was merely a result of disease and degeneration; but now with the examination of the actual facts, it appears that, on

the contrary[,] many are fine, healthy specimens of their sex . . .
with nothing abnormal or morbid of any kind observable in their
physical structure or constitution.

Carpenter pushes the argument further even than Havelock Ellis
by his very careful rhetoric here. There is nothing abnormal or morbid in such a "type," he argues, that can be seen in physical form or
constitution. He is rather shiftily manipulating some time-honored
stereotypes here to try to find a new, scientifically defended position.
The first stereotype concerns whether you can *see* a sexual pervert
in his or her body ("physical structure"): is there a sign in or on the
body that gives a material indication of abnormality? In antiquity,
according to physiognomic anecdotes, backed up by physiognomic
science, a sneeze or how you scratched your head with a finger might
reveal what your masculine body could otherwise conceal under a
hairy and muscular exterior, namely, that you were in fact a pathic,
someone who took pleasure in being used sexually by another man.
"The intermediate sex," argues Carpenter, is a type, but without
physical definition as a type. Second, there is no visible indication
of the type in "constitution," the same term Arthur Benson had
used for the makeup of proper masculinity. There are no behavioral
patterns, gestures, intellectual or social makeup by which the sexual invert can be visibly identified. From antiquity, the manner of
walk, the manner of talk, or the style of courtship marked out the
transgressive sexual subject. The need to make such signs visible is
traditionally because of suspicion of hidden corruption, the "worm
in the bud." But for Carpenter, the lack of observable signs is rather
because such people are "fine, healthy specimens." Where in the old
days, difference was explained as necessarily a sign of both disease
and of degeneration—that is, the overlapped social and physical
corruption of the sexual sinner—now science, thanks to its empirical "examination of actual facts," has rebutted such normative models. Indeed, for Carpenter, the "intermediate sex" could be lauded for
its special creativity, its hybrid vigor.

Havelock Ellis (let alone Edward Carpenter) did not necessarily persuade medical professionals. The *Lancet* in 1896 judged his work would fail "to convince medical men that homo-sexuality is anything else than an acquired and depraved manifestation of the sexual passion." Their worry was not merely that his theories were wrong, but also that his ideas might fall into the wrong hands. Ordinary readers would be "totally unable to derive benefit from [the book] as a work of science" and would even "draw evil lessons from its necessarily disgusting passages." Krafft-Ebing, like the *Lancet*, was equally clear in opposition to Havelock Ellis that sexual inversion was "incompatible with mental health," and he expressed a view that female sexual activity with other females was "practised now-a-days in the harem, in female prisons, brothels and young ladies' seminaries"—certainly not in proper homes. If Havelock Ellis encouraged recognition of "sexual inversion" as abnormal but possibly healthy, Krafft-Ebing offered scientific authority for the counterview that it remained a mental as well as a physical aberration—a view that found support in Freud also.

By 1921 Havelock Ellis, Carpenter, and Krafft-Ebing were familiar names in some circles at least as authorities on sexual psychology and behavior, though the details of their theories were hazy for many who dropped their names in discussion, as seems to be the case with Sir Ernest Wild. Yet it is clear enough that sexologists, even if they took a different moral perspective on the issue, were keen to see sexual inversion as a "type," as a pathology, and that the general vocabulary was beginning slowly to shift toward both "homosexuality" and "Lesbianism" as master terms.

The third public event was the banning in 1928 of *The Well of Loneliness*, Radclyffe Hall's serious, rather turgid novel that explores female sexual desire for other females. The book when first published was moderately well received, with a mix of decent reviews with some criticism, mainly in the higher-brow newspapers and journals. It was published, to mark its seriousness, with a preface by Havelock Ellis, by now the recognized doyen of sexology, and with a severe cover and high price. Barely a month after it was published, however, James Douglas, the editor of the *Sunday Express*, launched a bombastic and fervid attack on the book—carefully prepared by the paper's advertising—which became notorious for its outrageous pronouncement that he "would rather give a healthy boy or girl a phial of prussic acid than this novel. Poison kills the body, but moral poison kills the soul." His vitriolic article added many other terms of disease—"plague," "pestilence," "contagion," "leprosy"—to express his physical horror at the story.

The response to Douglas's article was very varied, with plenty of individuals prepared to dismiss its motives as well as its content. But it had the effect of goading Jonathan Cape, the publisher, into submitting it to the Home Secretary for a judgment on its decency. The Home Secretary, Sir William Joynson-Hicks, was, however, a polemical social reformer committed to the now old-fashioned campaigns for social purity; he consulted with the Deputy Director of Public Prosecutions, Sir George Stephenson, who within forty-eight hours of Douglas's editorial, consulted the Bow Street magistrate Sir Chartres Biron, who had already read the book and immediately counseled its banning. The Attorney General, Sir Thomas Inskip, was also consulted (and would go on to represent the Crown in the appeal), and he, too, agreed. Joynson-Hicks, Biron, and Inskip were all associated closely with highly conservative and by now marginal religious organizations that campaigned for social purity—the National Vigilance Campaign, the London Public Morality Council, and so forth. The prosecution of *The Well of Loneliness* for obscene libel was successful, but not because these four leaders of the legal institutions simply represented the voice of public opinion. Indeed Joynson-Hicks recalled that the government's actions "provoked a storm of comment—both well- and ill-informed—on the supposed literary censorship in this country, and I was attacked, at times in far from moderate language . . . [as a] narrow-minded Puritan zealot." Yet it was also "Sapphism" and "Lesbianism" that formed the basis of this storm of comment, since it was the subject matter of the book that had provoked its banning. As Virginia Woolf reflects with whatever wryness, "At this moment our thoughts centre on Sapphism. . . . All London is agog with it."

Both in Radclyffe Hall's book and in the commentary that swirled about it, the language of sexuality is still dizzyingly unstable. The description of the central character of the novel veers between "inversion," "Sapphism," "Lesbianism," "homo-sexual," "homosexuality." Some critics also used Carpenter's terminology of the "intermediate sex." The discourse mixed moral and psychological vectors, and played off "abnormality" and "unnatural" against the "corrupt," the "degenerate," or the "morbid." Scientific books were hidden from prying eyes and displayed with brazen idealism. Yet through this babble of normative descriptors, two crucial trends are clearly and finally emerging. The first is the increased agreement, based partly on sexology's theorizing, partly on attempts at legal definition, partly on self-identification in the postwar era, and partly on the classifying zeal of Victorian social science—not to mention Hall's own prose—that there exists a *type* that needs definition and naming. Although there was no agreement about the boundaries of definition or the authoritative scientific terminology, there was a general recognition that to discuss sexual activity between members of the same sex needed a psychological model of development that went beyond criminalized activity into the comprehension of a pathology.

Secondly, Radclyffe Hall's own photographic portrait, which circulated very widely at this time, emphasized the masculinity of her appearance and dress—with short-cropped hair and male clothes—and the *Sunday Express* chose a stridently manipulative image to illustrate their editorial. The postwar decade reveled in fashions that were made possible by the change of behavior for women during the war. The contrast between the bustles, dresses, and elaborate coiffure of the late Victorian and Edwardian period and the trousers, flat lines, and short hair of the roaring twenties resulted in a mass of journalistic flummery—cartoons, editorial comment, shocking photographs, amused articles—about the new New Woman and the confusion of masculine and feminine in dress and behavior. Radclyffe Hall's clothes and demeanor were in a line with such fashions but also became a defining characteristic of the "masculine woman" as the paradigm of sexual inversion. Much as Oscar Wilde's trial helped fix a stereotype of the homosexual, so Radclyffe Hall was instrumental in the establishment of the image of the lesbian as a masculine woman, short-haired, dressed in male clothes, adopting a male demeanor, even wearing a monocle and smoking a cigarette.

The 1920s represent a sea change in the public image of female sexual activity with females, and even of female desire for females. For the first time, the law tried to grapple with the subject, in trials about specific accusations, about particular books, and in Parliament's disingenuous and blustery discussion—all of which left London agog. In particular, the long and slow influence of sexology, which had already transformed thinking on male sexual activity with other males, allowed for a broader recognition of a pathology, a type of woman who loved women, though this pathology required increasingly more coherent and rigorous definition, as did the models of psychological development and moral understanding on which the scientific and medicalized vocabulary depended. The image of the lesbian as masculine woman became a particular paradigm, both of stereotypical abuse and appropriated celebration. One consequence of this new category of the lesbian woman or homosexual man is not just an increase of visibility or legibility or speakability, but also an increase of violence, scapegoating, and policing, both on the streets and through institutionalized structures. With the new image of the lesbian masculine woman also came a fear based, it seems likely, on familiar fears of male homosexuality, that a particular area of social danger is the seduction of young and vulnerable girls by older women into a corrupt world of transgressive sexuality. The continuing impact of such shifts in thinking and continuing conflicts around such imaging and their social consequences need hardly be underlined.

Anne Lister, the ultra-Tory Yorkshire landowner whose diaries are so revelatory of an exuberantly shocking private life at the beginning of the nineteenth century, could write in her diary: "I love, & only love, the fairer sex & and thus beloved by them in turn, my heart revolts from any other love than theirs"; she could revel in her "gentlemanly" ways as a masculine woman, and she certainly sought to understand her feelings through her study of Rousseau. Lister, we might say, recognizes her exclusive sexual orientation, self-fashions through masculine cross-dressing, and uses a scientific theorizing to understand her nature. Yet it remains important that there is for Lister no apparent requirement to see herself as a type or class of woman, no models of psychological development, no suggestion of degeneracy, even when criminality is worried about, no suggestion that women should be categorized according to a putative idea of sexual orientation. The self-awareness and social treatment of Anne Lister, for all the continuity of her sexual pleasure with women, serve to emphasize how different both from Radclyffe Hall and the subsequent conflicts of modern gender politics she seems. The 1920s are a turning point in the public recognition—and thus the social and psychological expectations—of lesbianism as a pathology.

Indeed, the influence of the science of sexology also tied the self-awareness of sexuality to the self-awareness of modernity. As E. F. Benson vividly articulated the sense of a gulf between his life in the Victorian era and the 1920s, so writer after writer on the three cases I have been discussing recognized the gulf between a then and a now. Vera Brittain paradigmatically thought that she and her friends were "sophisticated to an extent that was revolutionary compared with the romantic ignorance of 1914. . . . [W]e discussed sodomy and lesbianism . . . and were theoretically familiar with varieties of homosexuality and VD of which the very existence was unknown to our grandparents." Or as a self-help book put it to a future father, with greater anxiety than Vera Brittain's bravado: "You must realise, as a protector, that the early Victorian age is very early Victorian, and that the children of today are grown women in comparison with their sisters of the eighties." It could be said that the 1920s needed to construct the prewar generation, and the Victorians in particular, as ignorant, in order to emphasize their own status as those that now know.

Yet this sense of a specifically modern "being in the know" emerges out of an intricate dynamic of knowingness and scientific expertise, claims of authoritative knowledge and disavowals of any awareness. In Parliament, it could be stated both that 999 out of 1,000 women have "never heard a whisper" of lesbian practices, and, at the same time, that such practices and the vocabulary to describe them are "common knowledge." Science—misunderstood, appropriated, intently studied—was paraded, with competing declarations of authority; it was also locked away in private rooms, with the fear that in the wrong hands such knowledge would be corrupting. Maud Allan could be attacked in court for knowing even the word "clitoris," backed up by the assertion that twenty-three out of twenty-four professional men did not understand such vocabulary. It was assumed even by the prosecution that the jury needed to be provided with clear physiological knowledge to understand the libel of immorality. The self-defining performance of being in the know, of understanding about lesbianism, takes shape in and against such claims and disavowals of knowledge. It is because of the uncertainty about what constitutes common knowledge, as the category of lesbianism is under formation within public discourse, that "being in the know" can become such a charged style of self-representation.

So when E. F. Benson publishes *Mother* in 1925, and, as they discuss "the homo-sexual question," A. C. Benson also drafts his biography of his mother, it is against this background of London agog with discussion of Sapphism. In 1940, when E. F. Benson writes again of his mother sleeping with Lucy, there has been a further fifteen years of public discussion and psychological theorizing. Fred Benson was friends with Marie Corelli, who had been instrumental in the Maud Allan trial; he holidayed each summer at Capri, the Fire Island of its day, which he depicted in his novels as a place of "pagan gaiety"; he was fully embedded in the Henry James circle; he was, above all, a committed man about town, intimately connected in gossip and snobbishness with both grand homes and the artistic milieu. He had also read his mother's diaries, letters, and destroyed much of the most revealing correspondence. This makes his Sphinx-like smiling reticence all the more pointed. He places his mother's relationship firmly in the Victorian past: her portrait could not be further from any image of masculine femininity. He repeatedly asserts the normality of such a relationship for a highly intellectual woman—there is no suggestion of any morbidity; there is no imagination of impropriety. Fred Benson is undoubtedly in a position to be in the know; he undoubtedly does not wish to exhibit any such knowledge or flirt with any knowingness. It is this tension that makes his description of his mother with Lucy in a vast Victorian bed so inscrutable. What did he want his readership to know?

14

Carnal Affections

IN 1922 THE HIGHLY SUCCESSFUL INTERNATIONAL ACTOR
Seymour Hicks, already well on in age (famous then for creating the
role of Scrooge in Dickens's *A Christmas Carol* and now known also
as the first man to hire Alfred Hitchcock as a director), published
a celebrity self-help manual, *Difficulties: An Attempt to Help*, which
offered advice for younger men on "private and sacred" topics. One
of the more striking warnings concerns "the many strange types
of women abroad today who may desire" the young reader's wife.
This is a contemporary problem, he asserts with the by now familiar cliché of the modernity of homosexuality: "these wretches have
multiplied immoderately of late." You can always spot this sort of
woman, he continues, as "they are as easy of recognition as blights on
a rose"—and you should throw them out unceremoniously, because
"these kind are more dangerous than all the men who attack your
household put together." Hicks is aware, however, of the niceties in
such cases. "A woman who seeks your wife is difficult to demand an
explanation from, as her caresses may have an excuse of 'sympathetic
femininity,' and you may hesitate to call her a Lesbian." Nonetheless,
"if you are uneasy, better to be brutal and make a mistake than have
the innocent to whom you are devoted subjected to the advances of
a wretch of this kind, who, if she succeeds, will wreck your home
more thoroughly than you can imagine." Hicks's misogyny may be
painfully obvious and incoherent, but it is telling nonetheless. In
1922 the woman who desires your wife is a type, a kind, which is

instantly recognizable—even though you may not be sure ("easy" to recognize, but you remain "uneasy"—the paradox that defines paranoia). The revealing sign is to be seen in physical contact—and yet this could be "'sympathetic femininity'": so when two women touch, is this acceptable or dangerous? You may indeed "hesitate to call her a Lesbian"—a hesitation in 1922 not just of identification but also of vocabulary and implication. But it is taken for granted that your wife is an "innocent." She may be seduced or corrupted by another woman, but cannot be imagined to have any such desires in and of herself. What is at stake is the fragile security of home life: the threat to the household is the wreckage of your marriage. Thus it is better to be brutal—a self-justifying term designed to preempt any challenge to masculine certainty. As soon as female friendship has physical expression, it becomes a suspicious threat. Thus any woman who is a friend of your wife could potentially come between you and your wife. This smacks of the familiar double misogynistic fear, that a wife may learn more than she should, and that she may have emotional ties beyond her man: patriarchy never wants a woman to know more than her husband.

Seymour Hicks provides a precise contrast for the reaction of the Benson family to Lucy Tait. In a grumpy scene in 1910, as the family argues, Arthur sees Lucy as a disruptive force: "She is the evil genius of the family. I think it is she who has done most to disintegrate us. She doesn't assert herself, she just goes her own way." He goes on later to recognize her role for his mother, but nonetheless insists on her provocation to them all: "The fact really is that Lucy, who is very strong and unimaginative and good-humoured, has a subtle effect. She has been everything to Mama, and I am everlastingly grateful to her—but I think she has really rather broken us up as a family. She disapproves of us all. . . . It is she who is really the provocative element." Similarly, Fred saw that Maggie, as she descended into madness, "resented this intimacy" of her mother with Lucy, and he analyzed that Maggie felt "that [Lucy] occupied a position in her mother's house that was properly hers." The intimacy of Minnie and Lucy is resented by Minnie's children, but they also admit the positive value of the relationship for their mother. But the fear of "strange types of women," the anxiety about "caresses" or "sympathetic femininity," the perceived danger of female sexuality that structure Hicks's writing are wholly absent. The 1920s brought lesbian sex forward into the public eye and changed the horizon of expectation, but, as has been brilliantly observed for an earlier era, "because the Victorians saw Lesbian sex almost nowhere, they could embrace erotic desire between women almost everywhere." The biographical narratives of both E. F. Benson and A. C. Benson are fully Victorian, in outlook if not in date, in their willing—or even willful—description of their mother's intimate relationship with Lucy and their separation of it from any sexual urge, let alone sexual activity. Their descriptions are in this sense profoundly untimely, and such untimeliness is as much a part of the sexual discourse of the 1920s as the strident assertions of a new modernity.

Yet although Victorian public discourse may have "seen Lesbian sex almost nowhere," this did not mean that women in general, and Minnie Benson in particular, did not experience any carnal desires. Early in her marriage, Minnie was strongly attracted to a Dr. Ridding, who visited the house on clerical business, as she recalled many years later: "<u>how</u> I liked him—was even too excited—head easily upset—strange now to remember the feelings he stirred." But it was primarily with women that her erotic desires were felt. There was a pattern to these relationships. Ethel Smyth, the composer who was delighted to have been wickedly but fondly caricatured by E. F. Benson in *Dodo*, recalled in her autobiography that "Mrs Benson used to call the first stage, the 'My God, what a woman!' stage." This was followed by intimate conversation, walks together, and what she called "drawing together" and "fusing." "Annie and I drew together," Minnie wrote, "the ways she sat and kissed my hand—our walks— our sittings—and finally the beach—and all the while in an undercurrent I was knowing what love was growing in our hearts for each other . . . and so we spent the month, Annie and I, in the most complete fusing." She recalled these moments ecstatically: "Oh that sweet time with Emily! How we drew together! Lord, it was thou teaching me how to love—'friend of my married life'—how I loved her!" This affection for Emily Edwardes was sufficiently absorbing and intense that it provoked a rejoinder from her husband, whose surprisingly gentle piety in the face of such difficulties was nonetheless powerfully restrictive: "We went home—and my husband took me on his knee, and blessed God and prayed—and I remember my heart sank within me and became as a stone—for duties stared me in the face."

Wiesbaden and Miss Hall seem to have taken things to a further level. Again, the retrospective account is passed through the filter of her subsequent religious faith:

> Then I began to love Miss Hall—no wrong surely there—it was a complete fascination—partly my physical state, perhaps—partly the continuous seeing of her—our exquisite walks together. If I had loved God then <u>would</u> it have been so—could it be so now? I trust in God, NOT—yet not one whit the less sweet need it be—I have learnt the consecration of friendship—gradually the bonds drew round—fascination possessed me . . . then—the other fault—Thou knowest—I will not even write it—but, O God, forgive—<u>how</u> near we were to that!

There are few passages in her retrospect so reminiscent of St. Augustine's *Confessions*, with her interjections to God's omniscience, and prayer interleaved with recollection, shame with exposure of sweet pleasures. The narrative here is an extraordinary and riveting reflection. She begins with the onset of love, which she immediately declares to be "no wrong." It is telling of a different time from the later twentieth or twenty-first century, that she can see no problem with her feelings for another woman. "Love" is for her a Christian value, and even with its erotic dangers, with which her story ends, its positive value is upheld. Yet she terms her emotion for Miss Hall a "complete fascination"—a term that has not fully lost its sense of an uncanny and dangerous enthrallment. She tries to explain this connection by way of circumstance, her weakened state, their being pressed into each other's company, though the "exquisite walks" recall her previous *amours* rather too pointedly. But, perhaps prompted by the memory of this exquisiteness, she reverts to her new sense of propriety, and trusts that things really could not happen like that now. The emphatic, capitalized "NOT," in answer to her questions, seems a stark rebuttal, and yet she instantly finds recourse to the pleasures again: "yet not one whit less sweet need it be." She can still find the sweetness of such remembered romance in her new understanding of the "consecration of friendship," a religiously charged sense of intimacy, a Christian loving friendship. But if that seems like a point of achieved equilibrium, she immediately falls back into a searing recollection of a lost intensity of feeling. She recalls the bonds of desire growing around her, she is "possessed" by fascination—that is, its uncanny power, its bewitching—and finally she confesses to God, though she cannot bring herself to write it explicitly, how close they came to "the other fault." If her struggle over Miss Hall at the time was a struggle about how her erotic feelings ought to relate to her sense of decency and her sense of marital duty, now these feelings are reframed by a religious fervor and a heightened guilt. Her meditation is a vivid and sinuous journey that restructures memory and desire through guilt and grief, and through her new religious commitment. Whatever her regrets and shame, she cannot give up the truth of remembered sweetness.

Not long after she returned to England and to Lincoln, she met Mrs. Mylne and began her spiritual transformation. Thanks to Mrs. Mylne, when she felt "a fierceness, a tingling," she found new resources to resist: "The restless desire increased, and I knew, instinctively[,] it wasn't good." Her later relationship with Charlotte Bassett, her first serious encounter after her conversion, reflects this new sense of how the physical and the spiritual interrelate. She could write with gushing joy: "Did you possess me, or I you, my Heart's Beloved, as we sat there together on Thursday & Friday, as we held each other close, as we kissed." She signed the same letter with "Chat, my true lover, my true love, see, I am your lover, your true love, Robin" (Robin was her nickname in this relationship). Yet she also wrote to Chat, "When one's heart is fullest, when the physical side of Love asserts itself most, then one must <u>love in mind</u>, that things may be wholesome and well." To seek that everything should be wholesome and well is the aim, and for this state of affairs to pertain, then love must be an emotional but not a physical experience, even as the physical is elevated as an outpouring of the heart's fullness, and not as mere gratification. Yet, at least from this juxtaposition of passages, it would seem that the physical starts to become an issue well after kissing and embracing—which through the Victorian and Edwardian era are indeed standard expressions of "sympathetic femininity," as Seymour Hicks sniffily tried to dismiss. For Minnie Benson, when two women drew together, drawing the boundaries between them physically was an essential but precarious process, which required constant care and self-control. At stake was the elevation of love into a spiritual and satisfying value; or the collapse into a carnal aberration.

This was an especially precarious process with Lucy Tait. After Edward's death, she talks not just of "carnal affections" but also of "carnal stains"; "And I have been carnal today and backsliding. O Lord of Life, forgive and restore" (it is less likely that this refers to her constantly failing attempts to diet, though it may). Even a few days before Edward's death, she recorded a heartfelt prayer to raise herself away from the flesh:

> Once more, & with shame O Lord grant that all carnal affections may die in me & and that all things belonging to the Spirit may live and grow in me.—Lord look down on Lucy and me, and bring to pass the union we have both so entirely & so blindly, each in our own region of mistake, continuously desired.

She confesses that her carnal desires have led her away from the true desire for a union in and under God that they both, without enough success, it seems, have been longing for. The bed remained their "own region of mistake," as they repeatedly strove to sublimate their continuing physical yearnings into spiritual love. Minnie's marriage may be hard to fit comfortably into stereotypical models of married life; her relationship with Lucy across and after her marriage is no less difficult to accommodate in modern paradigms of erotic love or lesbian partnership. Her search for complete fusing both needed and repudiated the physical in the name of a fully religious spiritual longing, and this tension informs her serious passion for her female lovers, both during and after her marriage. Some years later, in 1930, Virginia Woolf had a correspondence with Ethel Smyth about such matters, where she wondered about the sense of labeling such complex relationships: "Where people mistake," she wrote, "is in perpetually narrowing and naming these immensely composite and wide flung passions—driving stakes through then, herding them between screens." Naming such queerness is like driving a stake through its heart. . . . So, she concluded pertinently, "what is the line between friendship and perversion?" It would, I suspect, have seemed a very rum thing to all concerned to insist that Minnie Benson and Radclyffe Hall were the same kind of woman.

During the late 1880s, when the Bensons were living at Lambeth and Addington, Ethel Smyth, desperate in her separation from Lisl von Herzogenberg, was emotionally tied to the supportive Mrs. Benson; Minnie called her "child" in their letters, and, in retrospect, Smyth snidely celebrated her "special genius" for "healing and directing of sick souls." "These cures," she wrote, "were pursued tirelessly, but on her own terms, and not without irritation . . . the quartersheets of notepaper, on which were inscribed in her clear scholarly script the words of counsel or comfort that kept the patients going, were nicknamed by me 'prescription paper.'" Smyth "bitterly resented," she later said, being treated as "a case." Toward the end of this time, however, Smyth, with her customary emotional promiscuity, started to have feelings for Nellie, Minnie's daughter. Mrs. Benson gave her permission at first: "I have always claimed both for myself and others, that when a new friendship began to blossom, there should be freedom given to form it. . . . I wanted and want you to understand how free I leave you about Nellie." Yet, just as her mother had manipulated and tried to regulate her own emotional life with Edward, so now Minnie found it impossible not to engage. She wrote to Smyth telling her an anecdote of how she had tried to read one of Smyth's letters to Nellie but had been prevented not only because Nellie had claimed it was private, but also because she had willingly confessed it would provoke feelings of indecency. She ends emphatically, "<u>Don't tell Nellie abt this letter of mine</u>." Mrs. Sidgwick had asked Minnie not to tell Edward about her reading his letters—and Minnie had refused. Now she is playing the same manipulative games with her own daughter.

Mrs. Benson remained confused about the situation. "Then there comes this new drawing of you and Nellie—I don't understand just at first." She is specifically in uncertain territory because she is Nellie's mother:

> <u>But</u>—and here we come to our present crux, your way out of it I cannot make mine. The play of nature between Nellie and me— The awful inner tie of mother and daughter—and if you will, <u>my own limitations</u> speak all together in clear tones, and a most deep inner instinct bids me be still—bids <u>me</u>, so to speak 'get out of the way' while this relation, which is evidently increasing more than either of you knew it would, developes [*sic*] itself.

To move into intimacy, and perhaps beyond, with first a mother and then her daughter brings images of incest too close for easy reflection. It puts too much weight on the name of "child." It makes Minnie Benson deeply uncomfortable. All her instinctive feelings demand that if Smyth is to have such a relationship with her daughter, Minnie cannot also have a relationship with her. It was not just religious or artistic differences that separated the two women (as Smyth repeatedly asserts in her autobiography), but her willful construction of an impossible eroticized family dynamic in the Benson household.

Within a few weeks of what was an emotional experiment too far for Mrs. Benson, Nellie died aged only twenty-seven from diphtheria, contracted while doing charitable work among the poor, and so the situation resolved itself, with unexpected and tragic finality. Smyth remained friends with Lucy Tait but saw the Bensons again only sporadically over the next years—though the space that her relationship with Minnie takes in the imaginative world of her autobiography reveals just how important, despite her snideness, the encounter had been.

The question of how a woman like Mrs. Benson, with her string of female friends and Lucy Tait installed in her vast bed, made a home with her daughters did not end there. Nellie certainly seems to have made no attempt to avoid Smyth—though we have only one side of the correspondence and no real insight into the range of her response. With Maggie, however, home life disturbingly overboiled. Maggie was the least in the know of the children. At age twenty-five, she wrote to Nellie to ask her to tell her about sex and sexuality, as her sister must know what's what by virtue of working among the poor. The other children found Maggie's relationships painfully awkward. She was a highly intellectual woman, passionate about philosophy (unlike the other Benson children), and, like Fred, seriously committed to archaeology. She became the first woman to dig and publish material from Egypt, following her three seasons excavating the Temple of Mut at Asher from 1895 to 1897. Yet like her mother, she found one quiet, determined, and caring female companion, Janet, always known as Nettie Gourlay.

Maggie and Nettie lived at Tremans with Mrs. Benson. Maggie had suffered from ill health since she had experienced scarlet fever as a young woman in 1885, arthritis a few years later, pleurisy, and a heart attack in 1900. In 1907 she had a complete mental breakdown and was hospitalized until her death in 1916. The descent into madness was finally marked by self-harm—she beat herself, shouting, "I am killing it"—and by threatening aggression toward her mother, but the months leading to the climactic scene of collapse are particularly revealing. She was working on her father's papers, and each of the children and Minnie noted how much she began to channel her father's gestures of disapproval and bad temper toward them. She was also especially upset by her mother's relationship with Lucy.

FIGURE 5: Mother and daughter, Minnie and Maggie: posed.

Maggie held forth "with great care on Lucy's influence on me," recalled Mrs. Benson, "being with me <u>day and night</u>—first thing in the morning, last thing at night—and she & I were growing apart." She asked her mother to take the family away on holiday without Lucy ("She was sure I wanted <u>my own kin</u>") and harped on how her mother's friendship with Lucy had changed since the archbishop's death. The violence that eventually erupted was the final explosion of the jealousy and indeed rage that Maggie experienced against her mother's lover. She remained convinced almost the entire period of her madness that Minnie and Lucy were plotting together against her. It is very tempting to see the channeling of the father and the jealousy of the mother as two sides of the same psychological deformation.

Both Nellie and Maggie had only female intimates and, living with their mother, found these relationships inextricably tied up with their mother's intimacies and way of conducting friendships. Neither travel nor work extricated them from the family web. Both girls found themselves in triangulated and invasive dynamics. Nellie's correspondence and "drawing together" with Ethel Smyth was overseen, discussed, and manipulated by her mother, and the triangulation led to an impossible and eventually fissured friendship. Maggie, although she had Nettie as her own companion, remained violently jealous of her mother's intimacy with another woman, who had, as it were, usurped her place in the family dynamics, at least as favored younger woman. The projected image of an idealized and self-controlled "friendship among women" reveals a much more frightening and unstable dynamic when it enters the immediate family. The scene of mother, daughters, and friends in the same home becomes a disturbing picture of dysfunctionality, where the vast Victorian bed echoes with the violence, despair, and breakdowns that finally left Minnie and Lucy alone at the center of the house.

15

Be a Man, My Boy

CHARLES KINGSLEY WAS A NEIGHBOR OF EDWARD WHITE Benson during Benson's time as the founding headmaster of Wellington; he often came over to walk and talk, and he became a favorite of the children. Like Benson, Kingsley moved between his role in the church and his role in education, acting at various points as Chaplain to Queen Victoria and, despite his lack of credentials as a card-carrying historian, as the Regius Professor of History at Cambridge. He also maintained a career as a hugely successful novelist and popularizer of natural science—he was a churchman who, unlike Philip Gosse, had no difficulties with Darwin, who happened to be another of the personal friends he walked with. More surprisingly, in the light of such an establishment career, he had also been a leading light of the Chartist movement, writing under the name of "Parson Lot," supporting the workingmen in their campaigns against poverty and oppression. Perhaps most famously, however, Kingsley became an icon of what was known first mockingly and then also with appropriated celebration as "muscular Christianity."

"Muscular Christianity" was not a term that Kingsley wanted to use of himself, but the title stuck to him and his friends (such as Thomas Hughes, author of *Tom Brown's School Days*), not least because he wrote in a passionate way both about the failures of masculinity in Christians he despised and about the benefits of a healthy, muscular, masculine embodiment of Christian virtue, especially in young men. Kingsley's strident public argument with John Henry

Newman galvanized a generation of churchmen. Kingsley attacked Newman, whose joining the Roman Catholic Church had scandalously fulfilled Broad Church anxieties about the tendencies of the Tractarians, on the grounds that he was not committed to truth. Newman's rejoinders finally took shape in his remarkable *Apologia Pro Vita Sua*, and for many, including the Bensons, even if Kingsley was thought to be on the side of the angels, the manner in which the argument was conducted left Newman on the higher ground, at least in terms of the ethics of decency. But Kingsley also attacked Newman and the Oxford Movement because of their insidious effeminacy, which he saw as a poisoning of national and religious values. The Oxford Movement's promotion of the beauty of holiness and the satisfaction of self-denial took shape in the renunciation of the love of women, the construction of all-male communities, where confession, the worship of saints or even the Mother of God, and earnest monk-like devotions not only appeared to mainstream Anglicans to be far too close to continental Catholic practice, but also seemed a sign of "unmanliness." Kingsley despised and distrusted such renunciations. Bishop Wilberforce—who founded the college at Cuddesdon, where curates were being trained in such ways—was also worried: "Our men," he wrote to a friend, "are too *peculiar*." Their affectations of dress and ritual stance implied to him "a want of vigour, virility and self-expressing vitality of the religious life in the young men." Lucy Tait's father, Archbishop Tait, was also frightened that the spreading practices of the Oxford Movement's young men "foster a womanly defence rather than a manly faith."

Kingsley met his future wife, Fanny, at Cambridge, and each told the story of their long courtship as a story of salvation, for him a salvation from vicious degeneracy, for her from a no less dangerous asceticism. He was a "most vehement, impulsive, stammering, shy, fiery young Cantab"; she was about to join a Puseyite nunnery. Against the snobbish opposition of her family, they eventually married. Kingsley anguished to Fanny about his physicality. "You cannot understand the excitement of animal exercise to a young man," he wrote, reveling in his muscular habits of riding, boxing, and vigorous walking. But he also confessed that he was not pure: "Darling, I must confess all. You, my unspotted, bring a virgin body to my arms. I alas do not to yours. Before our lips met, I had sinned and fallen. Oh, how low! If it is your wish, you shall be a wife only in name. No communion but that of mind shall pass between us." Yet it was clear enough that Fanny shared his view of the place of physical love within marriage. Separated during their courtship, they agreed to lie naked each in their own beds at the same time of day to think about each other; they discussed the wedding night some time before it took place and openly talked of the difficulties of abstinence. The strength of feeling between them during the marriage, as well as the pictures Kingsley drew, after they married, of Fanny and himself, naked, having sex in the fields, or sitting as a Greek shepherd and shepherdess in a pastoral bower, reveal how much his anti-Catholicism and his promotion of family life as a divine root of the church are easy to view as significantly intertwined with his own sexual life.

Kingsley's writing repeatedly stresses the spiritual corruption of celibacy as a driving force in the corruption that is the Catholic Church, a view expressed nowhere more forcibly than in his novel *Hypatia*. This historical novel is a thinly disguised polemic against contemporary religious asceticism, which is expressed in a horrified image of the degeneracy of the East:

> The races of Egypt and Syria were effeminate, over-civilized, exhausted by centuries during which no infusion of fresh blood had come to renew the stock. Morbid, self-conscious, physically indolent, incapable, then as now, of personal or political freedom, they afforded material out of which fanatics might easily be made, but not citizens of the kingdom of God.

This is a marvelous example of Kingsley's ideologically laden prose. His argument is, first of all, racialized in a fully nineteenth-century scientific manner. The "races" have found their vigor "exhausted," where an "infusion" of "fresh blood" would have "renewed the stock":

the new blood required, Kingsley later specifies, is the "great tide of those Gothic nations." The Teutons brought "an infusion of new and healthier blood into the veins of a world drained and tainted by the influence of Rome." Racial theory here depends on a mixture of world history and the medical model of pure and tainted blood, with an inevitable teleology leading up to the triumph of *"our race"* over the taint of Catholicism. The effect of such exhaustion of the bloodline is also gendered: the races are "effeminate." Such a stereotype has a long history, of course, applied to the East, which Kingsley happily manipulates and reframes in the contemporary charged language of degeneracy. The East is "over-civilized"—that is, hyper-sophisticated, corrupted by its own self-consciousness into a state of morbidity, a term we have already seen as the standard nineteenth-century marker of the combination of a sexual, psychological, and physiological sickness. This state of sickness has a political corollary. The East, since Herodotus's description of the Persian wars at least, has been associated with tyranny and a consequent lack of political freedom for its citizens; in the nineteenth century, the freedom allowed by the British constitution is routinely contrasted with the political restrictions of the continent and especially the Catholic states. But Kingsley also specifies a lack of personal freedom as a sign of Eastern life. His implicit opposition here is also between Protestant notions of free will and personal judgment, and Catholic commitment to authority and the rules of the church: personal freedom is a Protestant value. This combination of negative ecologies produces, consequently, fanatics—that is, extreme religious thinkers insistent on extreme religious practices, creating a "mere chaos of idolatrous sects, persecuting each other for metaphysical propositions. . . . They knew not God, because they knew not righteousness, nor love, nor peace."

This intense religious distaste for fanatical religious hostility, delivered in the name of a truly masculine, familial, national Christianity—Kingsley's Anglicanism—is further supported by his adventure stories such as *Westward Ho!*, where the hero slaughters Spanish Catholics on behalf of Elizabethan England; or *Hereward the Wake*, which shows the triumph of Englishness as a value over the Norman conquest, a triumph over the dangerously corrupt invasion of foreignness; or *Two Years Ago*, which offers a campaigning doctor as hero, who combines social reform with a pugilistic masculinity—"politics according to the kingdom of God," as Parson Lot demanded.

Kingsley's books, largely written in the years immediately before and during his regular visits to the Benson household at Wellington, promote and project an ideal of masculinity as a vigorous, honest, plucky directness linked to a Christian honesty and decency. It is this combination that makes him an icon of muscular Christianity— and muscular Christianity became a watchword of education, social development, and moral instruction in the last decades of the nineteenth century.

The public schools of England during the second half of the nineteenth century were one training ground for the sort of manliness that Kingsley demanded and that Thomas Hughes paradigmatically described through Thomas Arnold's Rugby. Across England from the 1860s onward, sports became compulsory and an archetypal arena of manliness. "Play up and play the game" became a rallying cry for young British men (echoed in Kipling's "Great Game," his term for the world of imperial spying and power). The ideal of godliness and good learning, epitomized in their shared school days by the earnest young Christians Edward White Benson, Joseph Lightfoot, and Brooke Foss Westcott, developed during the second half of the century into a model of godliness and manliness, which were epitomized by C. T. Studd, Cambridge and England cricketer, and Stanley Smith, stroke of the Cambridge rowing eight; both were leaders of the Cambridge Seven—seven young sporting and emphatically masculine students whose evangelical conversion and decision to go together as missionaries to China was a *cause célèbre* in the 1880s: a new and nineteenth-century understanding of the ancient idea of the "athletes of God." Thomas Hughes captures tellingly how these ideals of masculinity trumped more traditional Christian ideals of turning the other cheek: "As to fighting, keep out of it by all means . . . but don't say 'No,' because you fear a licking, and say and think it's because you fear God, for that's neither Christian nor honest. And if you do fight, see it out; and don't give in while you can stand and see." The famous scene in which Tom Brown stands up to Slogger Williams instantiates this male ideal of a plucky English, Christian hero, fists to the ready.

Popular fiction for boys and young men, particularly over the second half of the nineteenth century, was obsessed with manliness and the link between a schoolboy's training and his performance in the world of the empire. As Hughes again put it in *Tom Brown at Oxford*, "A man's body is given to him to be trained and brought into subjection, and then used for the protection of the weak, the advancement of all righteous causes and the subduing of the earth"—or, as William Tupper, friend of Kingsley and favorite of Queen Victoria, emphasizes, in case the political, racial, and imperial undertones of "righteous causes and subduing the earth" is not clear enough: "Break forth and spread over every place. / The world is a world for the Saxon race." Horace Vachell's novel about Harrow, *The Hill*, which Arthur Benson read with avid attention and some distaste, is subtitled *A Romance of Friendship. A fine, wholesome and thoroughly manly novel.* If "A Romance of Friendship" in a schoolboy story raises worrying images of sentiment, the second subtitle aims to crush such suspicions with a declaration of its "wholesome" and, above all, its "thoroughly manly" character. The beloved youth in the novel duly goes out and fights with immense bravery in the empire and dies. To Arthur Benson, this was "a poor, sentimental, snobbish romance . . . a sentimental friendship in the background, half-ashamed of itself and of a lumbering kind."

Edward White Benson was much concerned with educating the boys of Wellington into Christian propriety—honesty, duty, hard work—but it is striking that in his many weekly sermons to the boys, manliness is simply not a topic he explicitly reverts to with any emphasis or interest. Nor did he with his own children. In his letters to his son Martin, whom he wished so intently to be a model student; in his reminiscences of Martin after his death; and in the subsequent, often highly critical exchanges with his other children, he finds much to fault whenever there is a failing of academic seriousness, moral commitment, or social correctness; but there is no passion to maintain a fragile, threatened, or exalted masculinity as an ideal. It is striking, that is, first of all, that a friend of Kingsley—a headmaster in the model of Thomas Arnold, a man whose energy and physical activity was taken by his colleagues as the epitome of forceful manhood—seemed quite unconcerned by what was becoming such a term of art around him. To Edward White Benson—in his marriage, as a teacher, a churchman, a father—manliness, it seems, was not a pressing question.

It is also striking in comparison with Arthur Benson, who regularly expresses his opinions in terms of the difference between masculinity and femininity. Arthur Benson, like all the Bensons, repeatedly went on walking holidays, often in the Alps with the family and friends; in Cambridge he cycled ferociously, often for long distances; he went shooting often and was proud of his skill. Fred Benson wrote books on ice-skating and on golf, and practiced both very seriously. Fred's archaeological experience, like Maggie's, was physically tough. The cult of games and manly exercise played a significant role in their daily lives. In line with this pronounced manliness, for Arthur, femininity is a denigrated category. This can color his social judgements of men's loose talk: "It seemed feminine. I suppose flattery always does." It is often a way in which he expresses his distaste for women and their desire for him: "Indeed this afternoon I was conscious of her feminine <u>charm</u>, in a way of which I am very seldom conscious of it. Hugh expresses it by saying he does not feel safe if he is left alone in the room with Mrs. S." Femininity, when it enters his consciousness, is something that is slightly frightening. It thus defines disparaged desire: "He has no love for the feminine; and I think the same is true of me." He can use effeminacy to mock his colleagues: Charles Waldstein, archaeological fellow of King's, provoked him because he "is so tactless, so impatient, so girlish; his parade of manliness is the most effeminate thing about him." Such excessively emphatic masculinity is suspicious: "Does he really like games . . . or the pose of masculinity?"

Arthur is surprised by his brothers' relationships with women. Fred "understands women which I don't do," he wrote in 1898. When, after Hugh's death, he reads Hugh's letters as a priest to female congregants, he claims not to recognize his brother at all. He often expresses a sniffy distaste for women and what he sees as their emotional and demanding ways. In this, as in his all too easily dismissive rhetoric of effeminacy, he seems to conform to a conventional late Victorian and Edwardian set of polarizing, gendered social attitudes, with the language of evaluation to support them, which were and are especially prevalent in the all-male institutions in which he worked—what we would call today an unthinking sexism. Both Arthur and Fred moved in a circle of men who desired men, who talked about and recognized this desire, but there is—perhaps surprisingly in contrast with the historical evidence for other such circles—little sign of any special language or manipulation of gendered vocabulary. Arthur struggled to name his desire, but he did not seek to redefine or find transgressive or novel language for his own maleness. However we understand the queerness of this family, they seem resolutely conventional in their language and public performance of masculinity.

It is here where Fred makes, for him, a surprisingly outspoken contribution. For he describes what he wanted to achieve in his schoolboy story *David Blaize* in very precisely modulated and poised terms. In adolescence, he writes, a boy is "for a time, shy and impressionable and vastly sentimental," and "he belongs to neither of the two sexes, and does not melt into his own sex for a year or two yet." It is a transitional period. "Some boys, rather rare exceptions[,] are thoroughly male throughout this period, but most are of a strange third sex, lively but quite indeterminate." This may echo in near anagram Carpenter's language of an "intermediate sex," but it offers a different model of psychological development. "Just at that age everything is fiery; the proper human boy, who is on the way to become a man with stuff in him, whether for the building of empire or the amelioration of slums or the more ascetic devotion to art, touches life with a burning finger." Fred recognizes the standard tropes of manliness—on to empire, my boy, and so forth—but wants to offer a different narrative from the clichés of contemporary fiction: where a boy is "quite indeterminate" rather than simply and wholly male. So he compares girls' swifter development and lower commitment to games, and sidles toward describing "an adoration . . . a devotion wholly transcending the normal limits of friendships" as part of the story of a proper boy. It is crucial that these passions are located solely in adolescence: "In an adult they would rightly be termed abnormal, but at an earlier age they are so common that we must regard them as a stage in ordinary natural development." This sense of ordinariness is contrasted with what society and its fictions make of it: "the whole subject from the male point of view was somehow tainted with beastliness, or guttered with slosh"—either desecrated as degeneracy or swamped by sentimentality. This is typical of the postwar generation's particular anxiety about softness: as Quentin Crisp remembered, "The men of the twenties searched themselves for vestiges of effeminacy as though for lice." And Fred goes on thus to mock the conventions of the schoolboy book with its noble cricketers, dastardly cheats, beautiful singers—reserving a special scorn for *Tim*, the book of his brother's friend, Howard Sturgis, where the consumptive "younger boy . . . was carefully kissed by the elder shortly before he died." He wanted to write a book, he recalls, that captured "boyhood again before war was invented or sex manifested." Writing after the First World War and the new pathologizing of sex, Fred Benson recalls wanting to rediscover a world without either war or sex, where a young man's love of a young man could be recovered for the normal and the ordinary—and unmarked by the imminent violence of military conflict. It was in this book, he recalls with melancholy pride, that "at last I had written something which my mother hailed and rejoiced in," at last "with a thrill of amazed pleasure" he had won his mother's praise, at last he was a good boy— and, as we have seen, the book was a huge hit with the soldiers who shared some of his longing for another world.

<small>FIGURE 6:</small> Fred Benson at the age of so many of the characters in his novels.

For Fred Benson, a boy must, in his remarkable terminology, "melt into his own sex"; to be wholly male throughout one's life is abnormal, a rarity. A boy, he suggests, is actually not much of "a little man," and it is only the retrospective fictions and normative expectations of society that make adolescence a site of "beastliness"—sexual wrongdoing—or "slush"—the hypocritical sentimentalities of storytelling. Writing the story of *David Blaize* with its true version of adolescence was for him a way that he "locked out the war," with its brutal version of young and expendable masculinity. The narrative was, he declares, an "internal and subconscious clamouring of memories" . . . "so long forgotten by my conscious self"; not so much a fiction but a rediscovery of the experience of the self. It offered the thrilling pleasure of the real story of adolescence as an antidote to the compelling realities of adult, sexed social life.

Arthur, as one might expect, was wholly put off by Fred's all too vivid novel, let alone his later explanations. He wrote to his brother: "Of course, I think it would be <u>most</u> unadvisable to open the whole subject—it could only be done by a fanatical medical man, with a knowledge of nervous pathology." His desire for reticence is in equal and opposite intensity to Fred's desire to depict adolescence truthfully, and not only does he try to reserve such a subject for the decent obscurity of medicine, putting other people's sexuality as usual under the heading of "nervous pathology," but also he insists, with a certain desperation, that it could only be a "fanatical" man of medicine who would undertake such a task. The surprising adjective quietly screams out Arthur's anxiety.

The constant pull backward in the writing of Fred and Arthur—the obsessive retellings of the story of their childhood and youth; the memory of Martin's young death; the schoolboy stories published; the schoolboy crushes told, remembered, retold; the biographies of their parents, which always keep them as children; their novels of coming of age—all speak of the hankering desire that Fred recognizes as the motivation for *David Blaize*: the desire to be where it is not yet necessary to have melted into masculinity, into the restraints and strictures and fictions of society. Fred's constant mocking and playing with those fictions, as much as Arthur's melancholy and his anger, are ways of writing back against the melting into adult sexuality—hence compulsive, failing, and marked by longing; hence repeatedly expressive of distance and untimeliness. Writing thus is to escape the alienation of the present in a fantasy of remembered bliss. Or, as Fred Benson declares, he found in writing "so potent a Lethe for the current pains and pleasures of conscious existence." His once-forgotten memory of a lost time is the royal route to forgetting the here and now of his adult life, a writer's "escape from the boredom and the tragedy."

This description of how *David Blaize* was written out of the truth of male adolescence comes almost at the end of Fred Benson's biography of his mother, followed only by the death of his sister and then his mother. It is a story in a series of tales of loss. The writing and the story go forward as he looks back: the narrative, like the passage out of adolescence, goes in one direction, toward adulthood and death. It's as if while reading the story of *David Blaize*, we can indulge the fantasy of staying the progress (which may be one reason why it was so popular with the soldiers in the trenches): we can linger still on the playing field rather than the battlefield. *David Blaize* is a "genuine piece of self-expression" because it captures so vividly and directly what Fred Benson had long wanted to say about the sense of loss and dissatisfaction that fissures adult masculinity—the pathos in the injunction "Be a man, my boy."

16

"It's Not Unusual . . ."

IN THOMAS HARDY'S *JUDE THE OBSCURE*, SUE WRITES A LIT-
tle note of apology in which she says she "despised herself for being
so conventional." Patterns of social exchange are always marked by
the tacit and explicit conventions of society and, especially where
sexuality is involved, by the self-conscious playfulness that allows
and even demands that each person knows how such conventions
can be played with, without falling into transgression. Sue's apology
for being "so conventional," something she despises in herself, is a
thoroughly conventional indication that she knows where a stickler
for propriety would draw the line, and that she is prepared—with
suitable internal struggle—not to be such a stickler, and that such a
recognition indicates that she is certainly unwilling to cross the real
boundaries of propriety that they should share. Society demands
and enforces convention, but to be merely and simply conventional
is to reveal oneself to be incapable of enjoying the wit, fun, and
excitement of social engagement, just as not knowing where the real
limits of behavior lie will lead to social exclusion and accusations of
degeneracy, corruption, sin, or other forms of failure. Convention is
everywhere and everywhere necessary, but to be merely conventional
is a term of disregard. When Arthur Benson—former schoolteacher,
recent fellow of Magdalene College, successful author—pronounces
in 1905, "I don't think I am an entirely conventional person," he is
not so much declaring any queerness, as gently positioning himself

as someone in the social know, someone who understands how to play the social game.

From the courtship of Edward Benson and Minnie Sidgwick in the 1850s to the death of Fred Benson in 1940, the conventions of sexual life changed significantly. For historians of sexuality, this has proved fertile territory. It is always necessary not to lose sight of the deep continuities through this period, which are most easily summed up as the unchanging force of patriarchal ideology in institutional and personal interactions in British society. Marriage remained the cornerstone of social normality, and with it come constraints on non-marital sexuality, denigration of illegitimacy, and hierarchical domestic gender relations. However much the law changed and modes of representation altered, the life of the prostitute on the streets remained rough and humiliating and violent. But changes in convention did mark deep changes in social expectation, and these were represented in social and institutional norms: the vivid scene of Edward White Benson in Cambridge in the 1850s, earnestly nourishing his long courtship of Minnie Sidgwick, seems, as Fred Benson insisted, to shimmer on the far side of an abyss of time from the perspective of the decades after the First World War.

The criminalization and medicalization of the status of homosexuality—the invention of the pathology of sexuality as a definition of subjectivity—was a slow but defining process. Along with the violence and prejudice that this new status encouraged came new forms of repression, self-expression, and public recognition for types of sexual behavior and psychology: the homosexual and the lesbian became figures of the public imagination, and thus of law. At the same time, women were admitted to Parliament for the first time, after the First World War, and so, too, women were granted the vote. Socialism and feminism became genuinely transformative ideological apparatuses. The aftermath of the war was seen broadly as a period of release of social restriction, and subsequent increased mobility and privacy (as epitomized by the use of the car) provided different opportunities for personal contact outside the family or the closed community, in a way that took its fullest expression in the decades after the Second World War. Medical advances in contraception, constantly in tension with social and religious demands of marital propriety, were joined with advances in maternal care, which drastically lowered the rate of infant mortality and thus changed the dynamics of family life. Elite models of the economic and status requirements of marriage came under increasing pressure. Changing paradigms of psychological development, of which Freud has become the exemplary figurehead, recalibrated ideals of purity, desire, and personal growth, which gradually became part of the changing structures of education, medicine, and law. The hold of religion on the norms of sexuality was less dominantly broadcast and less explicitly effective.

This sea change was punctuated by a series of crises—moments that acted as nodes of public discussion, legal and political response, literary and cultural excitement. So from the Married Women's Property Acts of 1870, 1882, and 1893, which changed the legal status of women with regard to the ownership of money and property; to the notorious Contagious Diseases Acts from 1864 onward, which enshrined women as the dangerous transmitters of sexual disease in society, in need of drastic regulation; to the Labouchère Amendment, which first criminalized the idea of "gross indecency," thus extending the law's reach over a range of intimate activity; to the raising of the age of sexual consent for girls to sixteen in 1885; the law was instrumental in the construction of gender categories and in the social regulation of sexual behavior. Trials like the prosecution of Oscar Wilde or Radclyffe Hall or Boulton and Park, along with literary or cultural events like Bernard Shaw's production of *Mrs. Warren's Profession* or Ibsen's *A Doll's House*, produced page after page of commentary and, as scandals, changed public discourse. Above all, such moments of high social drama encouraged acute self-awareness of changing expectations and norms. As the Bensons and their friends repeatedly attested—and in this they are absolutely typical of the era—to recognize that there is something new going on in conventions of sexual interaction is a symptom itself of modernity, a sign of the times.

Yet even as these structures of convention were changing, the Benson family has a strikingly oblique engagement with them. On the one hand, it would be hard to deny that this family was at the center of things when it comes to the normativity and conventionality of social life. Edward White Benson was a headmaster of public presence, Queen Victoria's archbishop, and a dominant figure in defining what counted as the law of the church and the law of the land—and he acted out the role of the enforcer of moral regulation in his family circle with as much avidity and intensity as he reflected on the decisions he had to take as Prelate. Arthur Benson was a schoolmaster in a position of moral authority over generations of boys, who took his part as arbiter of taste and of cultural value with immense seriousness: he was fully a public intellectual. Fred, too, knew what he was up to: his bookplate, designed for him by George Plank, was a Pierrot bestriding the globe like a controlling archangel, with a quill instead of a sword—the comic writer as the unacknowledged legislator of social nicety. Fred Benson ended up as mayor of Rye, the small and very conventional Sussex town his novels parodied. Hugh Benson was a celebrated sermon giver, whose popular novels were weighed down by their profoundly authoritarian moral conclusions. Master of a Cambridge college, mayor and literary dignity, priest and public moralist—the children may well have lived through major shifts in English social expectation, but it would be hard not to see them as committed to certain strong models of conventionality.

Yet, on the other hand, Edward White Benson proposed to a twelve-year-old girl; his wife had passionate relationships with other women and ended up sleeping with the daughter of his predecessor in the archbishop's palace; he knew of his wife's feelings and somehow kept his marriage on its tracks; Nellie, his "good daughter," was courted by Ethel Smyth; Maggie, the daughter who went mad, had a long-term relationship with Nettie Gourlay and, channeling her father, was profoundly jealous and eventually psychotically violent toward her mother and her mother's lover. All three boys also resisted marriage. Hugh spent a couple of years intimate with Frederick Rolfe, who styled himself Baron Corvo, who was a thoroughly disreputable and avowed lover of men. Arthur and Fred were connected into the wide circle of men who loved men, from Henry James and Edmund Gosse to the island life of Capri, though each of the brothers appears to have maintained what might seem remarkable—unconventional—levels of personal chastity, or remarkable discretion, with regard to men and women, compared, say, with their friends such as Charles Ashbee, William Cory, or John Addington Symonds. There are few sexual relationships in this family that seem straightforwardly conventional.

The Benson family offers a remarkable insight into this formative period of modern sexuality, then, not just because they trace and comment on the exemplary transitions from the earnest 1850s through the gay 1890s into the roaring 1920s—though they remain fascinating guides to this history of change. Nor are they important just because they offer such a surprising gallery of possibilities within a society that also prided itself on the regulation of social and sexual propriety—though the picture of accommodation and exploration of relationships in and through the most privileged social institutions is a telling counterweight to current fascination with the more obviously and self-consciously outlandish groups of Bloomsbury or the aesthetes around Oscar Wilde or libertarians involved with Carpenter or Whitman. Indeed, one of the most remarkable features of the story I have been tracing is that it brings together men struggling with their desire for men, women experiencing desire for women, a marriage of conflicting desires, the interaction of widely different ages in erotic bonds, different generations responding to each other: a true family romance, as Freud would have it, which offers a very different and more intricate matrix from the usual more restricted focus historians offer—on, say, women's intimate relationships with women or men's sexual encounters with men. Rather, what is most telling about the Bensons is the way in which convention and queerness are in constant and dynamic interaction—which allows us to see a sexual discourse under constant and often laborious construction: it is the struggle—which they share and repeatedly mull over and write about—between religious values and sexual needs, between social rules and playful difference, between public life and intimate intensity, between desire, physical acts, and a man's constitution, between living at the very center of the establishment and feeling a decentering untimeliness and alienation from the present. What makes this family truly very queer indeed is not just their unconventional sexuality, but, more precisely, how that sexuality is accommodated, denied, negotiated within the tramlines and travails of a very conventional life. The Bensons are an exemplary case of why the language of homosexuality took so long to condense and solidify in British sexual discourse, and why it is so unsatisfactory a language of description for the generations in which it was being developed. The oddity of the Bensons, the ways in which they do not conform to conventional models of sexuality, provides a refractive, historical mirror for our contemporary drive toward labeling the pathologies of desire. True queerness is what is hard to name.

PART

III

THE
GOD
OF
OUR
FATHERS

17

It Will Be Worth Dying

PERHAPS IT IS BECAUSE I HAVE SPENT SO MANY YEARS AS an academic studying Greek tragedy that it feels to me inevitable that a man who committed so publicly to the values of a public Christian life should have been so crushed by personal, private religious anguish.

Although Edward White Benson was deeply distressed by the deaths of his mother, his sister, and his daughter Nellie, and was prey to depression throughout his life, and struggled with the emotional interactions of his family life continually, there can be no doubt that the single most terrible event in his life for him was the death of his eldest son, Martin. On his sixtieth birthday, some eleven years after the loss, he writes at length in his diary a reflection on his own life, a retrospective gesture of self-comprehension typical of this family, and produces almost in passing one of the most oddly moving sentences of all their many reticent self-exposures. "But Martin's death remains an inexplicable grief—every day—to see into it will be worth dying."

For the bereft father, daily grief is so painful and the event to him so inexplicable that it will be worth dying in the hope of gaining some insight into its meaning. The father's sentence is heartbreaking because of the awful combination of desperation and hope: desperation at the incomprehensible loss and its continuing pain; hope, expressed as clarity, that his own death will somehow produce an answer to the mystery, that after death he will learn what he needs to know. It is hard to tell whether it is the current misery or the comfort of a future promise that dominates his emotions. The oscillation between these feelings is the struggle of faith.

In the same diary entry, he also sums up his religious perspective in telling terms:

> I need not here write my sense of what are the greatest things of all—the intense sense, would it were much more intense, of the awfulness of sin and sinfulness in the inner spirit. There is an inner, higher, deeper *spirit* in each man which rules the soul, the mind, brain and all—as we know them. It is this spirit which is the man.

For Edward White Benson, sin and the inwardness of spiritual sin are the dominant forces in his comprehension of religion—and characteristically he only wishes that this sense of how terrible inward corruption is could be even more intense. He says that he need not write this truth here because he imagines that his children, the potential audience for his diary, will know it already—and indeed the heavy burden of their father's religious expectations on the children stems precisely from this fearful and certain sense of internalized awfulness—both the fear and the certainty were impressed unerringly on the children's minds.

This sense of spiritual sin helps us see Edward White Benson's particular religious position all the more clearly. An intense commitment to the necessary paradigm of sin and punishment is at the core of his Protestantism and might even seem to draw him toward an Evangelical tradition, which was always keen to balance the books of sin and punishment, but, for all his zealousness, he is no Evangelical; his interest and pleasure in ritual might fit more easily in a High Church group, but neither he nor they saw him as a member of any High Church faction. He was certainly orthodox, but, as we have seen, worked carefully but happily with the nonconformists in Cornwall. If it has become standard to see the grand obsession of Victorian theology to have shifted from an overriding concern in the midcentury with atonement to an overriding concern by the end of the century with the Incarnation, Benson here (no surprise for an archbishop?) seems old-fashioned—yet he led the church into its modern form and read widely in the critical history that focused on the life of Jesus. His forceful certainty sets him emotionally and politically at odds with the liberal Broad Church leaders such as Dean Stanley or—from his different, more evangelical perspective—Frederic Farrar; and, although he worked intently with workingmen especially at Lincoln and was close friends with Charles Kingsley, he did not follow Kingsley into the Christian Socialism associated with F. D. Maurice. In many ways, Benson could achieve what he achieved as archbishop—and annoyed whom he annoyed—precisely because he was not closely associated with any one of these dominant factions of Victorian Anglicanism.

Yet Martin's death challenged him to the core. He struggled to make sense of it *religiously*. It seemed, as he wrote in his diary, "inconceivable," when "so much past interest, skill, beauty, power, love were wrapped up in his growth and constant progress—so much hope for the future; such admirable preparation for good work, with such persuasive gentleness; such thoughtfulness and such reverence together," that Martin should die young and unfulfilled. It seemed to Edward White Benson that it was a break in what had appeared to be God's own will: "His path seemed to run on so completely in God's own way: we thought all <u>God's</u> plan for him was running on so sweetly towards some noble God's work." This, after all, is the promise of the teacher, the Christian, the politician— that doing what is right will lead to goodness and its own rewards. Benson knows what he has to think: "God's plan for him really <u>has</u> run on sweetly for him and for all." But he cannot manage it. "It has changed all my views of God's work," he writes. He feels "compelled to believe" that all is for the good: "and yet—he is dead." The brute fact of loss makes Benson rethink what he had thought he had understood: "'One's views of life change very quickly,' he said to me the last hour in which he spoke to me—my sweet boy, thou hast changed mine." Benson was, indeed, a changed man.

The mourning process was long, and the letters and diary entries show the effort of his struggle. Writing to his old friend Westcott during the month of the death, he stabs out half a dozen scratchy paragraphs, quite different from his usual fluid prose, which reveal the tensions he suffered. He opens with a bare but eloquent statement of his real fear: "If anything <u>ought</u> to strengthen one it is a life like Martin's: we can only pray that it <u>may</u>." He knows what comfort he should be drawing but cannot, and is, for once, uncertain that he will be able to do so. This leads to a more desperate expression of grief and incomprehension: "He and we <u>yearned</u> that he might have talked with us the last week. But God sealed his lips. Why?" The unbearable question "Why?"—which has no answer—is followed by an intense memory of the last hour of Martin's life, which lives out the hope for faith's comfort: "As surely as I see this paper he <u>saw</u> Jesus Christ—<u>through</u> if not with, his bodily eyes and while he was quite himself." He is desperate to find the consolation that Martin is with God, and the very desperation struggles against the surety.

Shortly after Martin's death, Edward White Benson sat down and wrote a long and moving account of his son's godly and learned life—a gesture programmatic of his children's future life-writing. He describes the last moment like this:

> He with a sudden momentary look of enquiry which instantly changed into an expression of both awe and pleasure—the most perfect look I ever beheld of satisfied adoration—gazed at <u>something</u>—some<u>one</u>—tried with his eyes to make us look at the same . . . but our eyes seeing saw not. . . . I knew it—but I was so fearful of deceiving myself that I said to the nurse—"Does he want something? He is pointing at something he wants, is he not?" She said, "No—no—He sees more than we see."

It is this scene that he is referring to in his letter to Westcott. This more confused story, where Edward thinks he knows what his son is experiencing but is afraid to deceive himself, and accepts confirmation from the nurse's consolation, becomes a bolder and more insistent assertion—"As surely as I see this paper . . ."—where the certainty is hard to disentangle from a process of self-convincing. But it is not only the nurse who teaches the archbishop. "My dearest wife understood it all more quickly—better—more sweetly than I." For Benson at the time and in retrospect—and this must play a crucial role in their continuing relationship—it is Minnie: Minnie with her recent conversion to a personal sense of God, Minnie who has in his eyes needed instruction from him all her life, Minnie who on his knee required reminding of duty—who now sees what must be seen and understands, who provides the rock of faith, who expresses the Christian truth that the archbishop can only grope toward.

So where Edward, on the one hand, writes: "It takes all my confidence in his present to keep me from murmuring" against faith; or "We are learning not to withhold him from God in our hearts"; or "I hope that I shall be able to win more faith"; he also writes, on the other hand, that it is Minnie who is "the mother's example"; or "my dear wife is wonderfully 'kept by the power of God'"; or, most touchingly of all:

> His mother's bearing of all seems to me as perfect as can be. A few hours after [his death] she knelt in our room and prayed aloud. "It is Thy will only that we will. He is Thine, Thou hast a right to him." I cannot reach this.

The archbishop records in his diary how her faith is beyond his grasp, her prayer beyond his ability to voice what should be voiced. The children, it will be recalled, were surprised and upset not just by Martin's death but also by their parents' reactions—their father's despair and their mother's calm. But for Edward, it was a remarkable and self-exposing moment of tension between her newfound religious strength and his own tottering sense of order.

Indeed the letter she wrote on the day after the death to Beth, her own and Martin's nurse, is an eloquent testimony of how her faith informed her response. "He is in perfect peace, in wonderful joy, far happier than we could ever have made him. And what did we desire in our hearts but to make him happy?" And in contrast to Edward's letter to a friend around the same time, where he wrote, "He is gone you know," Minnie adds to Beth, "Now he is ours and with us more than ever. Ours now in a way that nothing can take away." She goes so far as to suggest that any regret would be a mistake: "We cannot grudge him his happiness." It is against this that Edward's bare "Why?" echoes.

The disjunction was marked by Fred most vividly. He recalls that when he was a little older and could understand what his mother said to him, she explained that on the day of Martin's death, "she had . . . a couple of hours of the most wonderful happiness she had ever experienced . . . when she realised that though God had taken, yet she could give." This was no mere rhetoric: "Her innermost being knew that." And the result was "when she came back to us a few days later, there was no shadow on her." This was in contrast to the terrible sight of his father: his face "was the face of a most loving man stricken with the death of the boy he loved best, who had been nearest his heart, and was knit into his very soul." His mother told him, too, that however much his father accepted God's will, for the rest of his life "he could not . . . adapt himself to it." Fred grew up knowing that his father loved his brother best and could not adapt himself to the loss, and that his mother had turned loss into a sort of giving. For both mother and father—and for the children, too, as they internalized their parents' praise and blame—no one could live up to Martin adequately. However their mother had appeared that morning when she came back from Winchester, the shadow of Martin's death was certainly on all the Benson children as they grew up.

Every year father and mother went to Martin's grave at his school in Winchester, and for Edward White Benson the sense of his own deepest failure to adapt himself to God's will remained an undertow to his increasingly energetic and committed public Christian work. As Fred sadly noted more than thirty years later, his father "never . . . did . . . cease to wonder why his Martin was taken from him." For Edward White Benson, silencing the bitter "Why?" had become a constant failing labor of his life.

18

*The Deeper Self
That Can't Decide*

SO HOW DID THE MINNIE BENSON GET TO THE POINT—
which is hard not to be disturbed by—that she could find a couple
of hours of the most wonderful happiness on the day her oldest son
died?

Minnie Benson, when she was trying to recover from the emotional trauma of her convalescence and passion at Wiesbaden, met
a Mrs. Mylne at Lincoln. Minnie had arrived at the new city and
home, where her family had already moved without her, vulnerable
and deeply unsettled. Mrs. Mylne was an older woman, a committed Evangelical Christian and theology student. The two women
became swiftly close, described by Minnie in her diary with characteristic quick fervor: "my human love for her and hers for me—
felt it coming—felt how different places were when she was there."
Over two months, the friendship progressed: "and now I loved her
indeed—and she was getting <u>hold</u>, only humanly as yet." When
the family went on holiday that summer to Torquay—a trip when
Minnie and Edward were distant and nasty with each other—Mrs.
Mylne came too, a necessary prop. "So we went to Torquay. A most
lovely month! Such delicious memories, such hot talks, such exquisite loveliness—and yet E and I were more terribly apart, said more
hard, unloving things to each other than I remember for a long
time."

The emotional hold of intimacy became something else. Mrs.
Mylne and her husband were involved in Evangelical mission work

in Lincoln, and Mrs. Mylne took a strong moral and spiritual line with Minnie. She encouraged her to keep a spiritual diary; she discussed the nature of her marriage with her at length; she emphasized the misery of her current life; she placed the cause of the misery in her sinfulness; she directed her human feelings of love toward God. . . . It is a classic pattern of Evangelical conversion, and Minnie's recollections play out the growth of her new sense of sin. "Is it not really the same sin in my neglects and my loves?" she wondered—was not her neglect of household duties, her disaffection from her husband, her lust for other women all part of the same sinfulness? "Burn this out," she scratched in the margin of her diary. Her prayers seem to mimic a revivalist meeting: "Rouse, cleanse, fill"; "Possess and purify my heart." In 1876, when Minnie was thirty-five, she struggled out of depression, marital misery, and unfulfilled erotic feelings, into a profoundly held commitment to a personal God.

It was not easy. "I need <u>discipline, discipline, discipline</u>," she wrote to herself. "<u>I must guard myself against unnecessarily opposing</u>"— where the emphatic underlinings look like a form of self-punishment as well as self-strengthening. She never lost either her sexual desires or the fire that led her to long for "lawlessness as such." But she was encouraged to reflect deeply on her innermost being. She recognized what was at stake:

> I have come to this then . . . that within the source of all feeling, spring of all action, lies a self, <u>the</u> self. What remains undamaged through all the years, from childhood to youth, youth to middle life[,] is not the will, but something further back than that— something by which the will itself is set in motion . . . from this the will is agitated, stirred.

To change her will she would need, then, to change her self; and this started from an unsettling recognition that something was rotten in it. She returned from a trip to the circus with her children where the acrobats and dancers produced in her an uncomfortably

eroticized feeling, "an uneasy restlessness, a fierceness, a tingling."
She turned to Mrs. Mylne, who "helped me as she always does."
Minnie went into the oratory and turned to God, and "the consciousness of the *stain* came, more than ever before—and it seemed
as if the very <u>core</u>, the very <u>ich</u>, self citadel into which one retired
from God before . . . as if <u>this</u> was bad and rotten." The "*stain*"
expresses the sense of pollution that links her own wrongdoing to
the Christian notion of the fall, but here it is turned into a topography of the self. She imagines that inside her is a sort of citadel—
like Arthur's "carefully locked and guarded strong room"—where
she had in the past retreated to avoid God and the moral lessons
of religion. This is where she finds her self. Her self, not long after
Wiesbaden, also speaks in German at moments of passion and is
thus—in uncanny anticipation of Freud's topography of the self—
termed "the <u>ich</u>" (the ego). But when she now looks inside her safe
room, she finds that it was "bad and rotten." It was "the very <u>core</u>"
that needed to change.

More than twenty years later, in 1900, when she was discussing
with Hugh the nature of internal change, as he, too, was struggling
with religious conversion, she wrote him an extraordinary letter
that reveals a long thought-through sense of what it feels like to go
through a momentous shift in the self:

> Oh <u>don't</u> I understand! The heavy background of it doesn't the
> least interfere with vivid and proper life—since it can't as if you
> could <u>struggle</u> with what is going on deep down—as I gather, <u>it</u>
> is doing you, rather then you it. All your will power and deter-
> mination and action are of no avail with the deeper self which
> cant decide—which doesn't know—which <u>wont</u> move one way or
> another. Mercifully this underground self HAS its laws, and slowly
> but very surely makes up its mind—then it is as irresistible as the
> uncertainty was.

She offers her own experience and understanding to her son. She
knows that profound change cannot be willed (as she might have

hoped in earlier, more naïve days), as the self is subject to change, not the agent of it. Such changes are not part of the brittle certainties and doubts of mundane life. It is not a question of deciding. Rather, some subterranean tectonics may move, and the change will finally be felt. Much as uncertainty is overwhelming and feels uncontrollable (and prompts a longing for decisiveness), so change when it comes is irresistible. This is how Minnie Benson told the story of what happened to her, her self.

There were long-term consequences of her conversion. First of all, it led to a recalibration of her marriage. "I fancied most foolishly that when I became a Christian, [Edward] and I would be more in union," she wrote, but rather what happened was a longer, slower accommodation, as she felt more capable of taking part in his work and, above all, more committed to being a dutiful wife. This accommodation was not based on a shared religious outlook, but on her newfound sense of duty; but by the time of Edward's death, as we have seen, Minnie's emotional engagement with her husband was enduring and deeply felt. Second, it led to the constant struggle, which we have already mapped, between her religion and her sexual feelings. Her religion was—for the wife of the archbishop—an increasingly private affair, even and especially from her husband. She never lost the ability, however, which she shared with the earnest George Eliot, of giggling at the parade of clergymen she faced. Here's a typically sharp and funny letter she wrote to Hugh, at this point still an Anglican clergyman himself:

> O Lor! Hugh, why are there such men. He knows everything; he is a missionary in Africa (and that is scarcely large enough). He is Thoroughly Earnest; but he knows we must also be Cheerful—I met him walking in the garden with the Book, Psalms, and a cigarette. There is no Strength and no Weakness (innocent) of the Human Race with which he has not a large hearted Sympathy.

This is precisely and sharply focused satire, which captures nicely Minnie's ability to combine a witty, pleasure-seeking, intimate, worldly conversation with an inward dialogue of a quite different order of seriousness and struggle.

Her sense of sin and punishment, however, also led to the mutually enforcing conviction of heavenly reward and salvation, which grounded her hours of most wonderful happiness at Martin's death. The lack of shadow with which she greeted her children when she returned from Winchester is part and parcel of the same newly formed inward drive that leaves her struggling to repress her sexual feelings for Lucy Tait. It is one sign of how our contemporary understandings of religion and of psychology have changed that the image of the witty Minnie Benson's sexual anxieties in the bedroom has seemed to modern critics so much more comprehensible than her ability to rejoice at her son's transfiguration in death.

Edward White Benson, as one might expect for Queen Victoria's archbishop, is a central figure in any narrative of institutional religious development across the years from 1850 to 1890. It was an era that he, too, conceptualized as a period of change. He encapsulated this change, as we will see, in the marked difference he saw in religious services, as the fear of popery diminished to allow an increased ritualism. It was also an era, intently discussed as such at the time and since, when critical history as much as science seemed to threaten the narratives that grounded the institutions of the church, when novels of doubt or faithlessness jostled for public attention with young men's missionary zeal, and when the interrelations of church and state became the subject of energetic political argument. Churches were changing in their fabric, their place in society, and their intellectual purchase. Benson was part of all of this, and his understanding of history and of his place in an unfurling narrative of the church is integral to his self-understanding and his motivations. At the same time, like many Protestants who confessed their sins to their diaries, he repeatedly anguished over what his son's death meant, especially for his own faith, and, in the eyes of his family and to himself, his perspective on things changed. In her most generous mood—and she is trying to persuade Hugh to slow his impetuosity—Minnie saw this change as a tendency to "make larger and slower decisions." Arthur, in the official biography, saw the change as something perhaps more complex. Martin's death may have led him to "see the power and depth of love," but the death, followed by his elevation to the leadership of the church, also meant that "in the place of elation and self-confidence came the crushing sense of inadequacy, the tremendous weight of responsibility and the entire leaning on God." Consequently, his "later work was utterly different from the buoyant self-sufficiency of his early manhood." Benson's growth in power and influence was co-extensive with his lowering of self-confidence and self-sufficiency.

By contrast, Minnie Benson's early lack of confidence turned into a discovery of a private "self citadel," founded on a personal God—for all that, she still reveled in intimate, funny, intense, erotic conversations with women, and cajoled, encouraged, and criticized her children, and played hostess to a string of grand and cultivated visitors. She reframed her internal struggles. By the 1920s, however, when Fred and Arthur were writing their biographies of her, she seemed to be very much a figure of a past regime. Things had changed. When Fred pictured the scene of her and Lucy Tait in their big Victorian bed together, the chastity of this image is achieved in part by the religious framing. It is after "evening prayers" that the family retires—family prayers, a regular feature of Victorian life, including the staff, were already an oddity by 1940—and the day, he insists, had been permeated by "true and fervent religious perceptions," a phrase hard to translate into a mundane script. By the Second World War, the religiosity of a woman such as Minnie Benson was already becoming a difficult thing to portray in public discourse.

However else the Benson children understood religion, it was never without this frame of their parents' marriage. And in their different ways, the three boys, Fred, Arthur, and Hugh, not only spent a great deal of emotional energy responding to their parents' changing religious feelings, but also their own changing positions can stand as a paradigm for a more general shift in British society with regard to the church, as the last Victorian generation passed into the twentieth century.

19

Our Father

FRED BENSON COULD TELL A GOOD STORY ABOUT EVENTS in church, or religious men, or why music was a spiritual joy—he had the background, after all—but he seems to have found an extraordinarily calm disengagement from his parents' deepest concerns. He has left barely any writing that could be called religious even under a generous rubric; there are few reminiscences of any participation in organized institutional religion; and no signs of the ground-changing doubts or convictions of the rest of his family. To Arthur Benson, consequently, he was enragingly and bafflingly superficial. Fred "talked about religion in a way that astonished me," Arthur explodes in 1901. "He seems to accept the cardinal doctrines as a child of 8 might, without question and without enthusiasm. It is quite incredible to me: I don't <u>think</u> religion plays any part in his life. I don't think he is even interested in it. But who knows?" Alfred Lord Tennyson started a fuss among his critics with the thirty-third section of *In Memoriam* when he wrote:

> Leave thou thy sister when she prays
>   Her early Heaven, her happy views;
>   Nor thou with shadowed hint confuse
> A life that leads melodious days.

F. D. Maurice, too, could write a dialogue where a skeptical layman says, "I fancied that Christian mysteries belonged to the period of infancy." But there is none of such niceties in Arthur's disdain. The child of eight, for him, is not the child whose innocence leads to heaven, but merely his brother's extraordinary naïveté. His brother, he thinks, is not merely unaware—he doesn't even care. For Arthur, as the child of Edward and Minnie, it is absolutely amazing—and they are here both in their thirties—that a child of those parents could not register the necessary emotions of doubt and enthusiasm. A couple of years later, Fred's sheer ignorance amazes Arthur further: "He had no idea eg that the virgin birth of Xt had been questioned except by quite desperate infidels." Fred's response to growing up with his parents, it seems, was to produce a studied refusal of religious knowledge and feeling.

It is again in Fred's novels where the most cynical and difficult image of this dynamic emerges. In *Rex*, the grim and dying father asks Rex's mother, "'You believe in a future life, in our redemption and ultimate salvation, don't you?'" and, in reply, "the love that smouldered in her eyes, blazed out," and she declares with passion, "'My dear, I believe in it and know it as I know nothing else in the world. . . . Even you and Rex are less real to me than that.'" Fred has an ear for the certainty of evangelical conviction. It is this insider knowledge that makes the final scene so disturbing. Rex calmly observes of her religious belief "how absolutely real it was to his mother," but, "with a sense of estrangement and distance, how enormously little it was to himself." So when she asks her son to kneel and pray by his dead father's body, he is shocked by his own willingness to do what he does not believe and feels a certain repulsion. "For the moment he felt so utterly degraded that he almost cried out, 'It is all lies: I don't believe a word of what I have been saying.' And yet where was the harm? His assurance meant everything to her, and nothing to him. It hurt no one and it healed her." There is finally a dulled and unpleasant cynicism, a path of least resistance, as the boy agrees to conform silently to his mother's needy religious longing, while inwardly despising it and himself. Fred's fiction anatomizes a studied refusal of religious knowledge and feeling, as the product of a religious family's dysfunctional stresses. Arthur thought the book failed because it could not create sympathy for the figure of the father by understanding him from the inside. He does not say the same of the hero and his estrangement from his parents' religiosity.

Maggie and Nellie, who lived so much at home, had fewer opportunities to step outside the religious matrix of the archbishop's house. But the youngest son, Hugh, turned out to take the most shocking route of all the children away from their father.

Hugh Benson in his day was a celebrated personality, although his books and his cultural significance as a figure have passed into obscurity now. At his death, one appreciation set his novels at the same level as Dickens and H. G. Wells, and stated that his death left a hole in the cultural life of England, America, and Ireland that could scarcely be filled. He certainly packed halls and was in immense demand as a speaker. Yet there is undoubtedly one primary reason why he could have such an impact: he was the first son of an Archbishop of Canterbury since the height of the Reformation to go over to the Roman Catholic Church.

After Martin's death, which was put down in part to the pressure of excessive expectation, Hugh was allowed considerable leeway in his education. He did win a scholarship to Eton, but this success was regarded as a surprise almost immediately from the moment he arrived, such was the low level of his work. He went to Cambridge, to Trinity, his father's college, but appears to have done little there but play cards and run up bills. He tried for the Indian Civil Service and failed the examination. Despite some retrospective hagiography, especially from Catholic colleagues, he was no more than a rather charming, slightly feckless youth. Writing in retrospect, he talked with some consternation of the power of his father's influence on his religious life at that time, declaring that it would have seemed a blasphemy even to disagree with him. He had little time for the school Protestantism of Eton, and although he went to King's Chapel regularly enough while at Cambridge, his motivation seems to have been aesthetic and social rather than a deep calling. Hugh himself said he drifted into taking Orders as the path of least resistance (and it certainly made his father very happy), and he imagined no more for his future than a bachelor life, a good garden, and to be a country vicar with an exquisite choir. Like Arthur and Fred, he had no time for marriage or for the attendant business of courtship and desire.

Hugh was especially close to his mother. He read everything he wrote aloud to her, and she criticized it. He discussed each step of his life with her and spoke with the most freedom and intimacy of any of the children. He was the least organized and driven of the children, and it seemed typical that when Nellie died, Hugh decided he had to leave, and promptly went and stayed near St. Paul's in London, while the rest of the family stayed together to talk and walk and mourn. He studied to be a clergyman under Dean Vaughan at Llandaff in Wales, became a deacon in 1894, and immediately went to the Eton Mission in East London. He was busy, though he seems not to have made much of a show of working with the poor young men he was meant to bring to the Lord. He was ordained as a priest in 1895. The next year Archbishop Benson died, and Hugh's life made a sea change.

First he became ill, traveled for his health, and never returned to the slum parish of the Eton Mission. He took up a post as curate in a village in Kent, where he began to formulate for himself rather strong views on religious ceremonials and on abstinence and, to the initial consternation of his family, joined the House of the Resurrection at Mirfield in the north of England near Bradfield, an Anglican community but close to the Benedictines in practice, and as monkish as a Protestant order can be. He took his vows there in 1901 and loved the small community of like-minded men, where the rule was to spend six months in contemplation and work at the retreat and six months on mission work. The ritualism and robe-wearing of the Order attracted him, as did the intensely intimate masculinity of the closed group. He also traveled to the East, and in Jerusalem and elsewhere became vexed by the smallness of the Anglican community and attracted by the lure of the communion of the broader Catholic Church. By 1903 his struggles had become overwhelming. At his acceptance into the Order, he had been asked

FIGURE 7: Fred, Arthur, and Hugh, transitional days.

if he was tempted by Rome and had responded with a shocked denial. Now he felt that it was only in the Catholic Church that he could find his true spiritual home. He expressed his doubts and feelings to his mother and his Superior in the Order, he took advice from senior clerics and laymen of the Anglican Church, but by the end of the year, he made the final decision and went over to Rome.

Hugh wrote a book—he was a Benson through and through—about his experience; there are letters between him and his family; the recollections of Catholic friends; and there are the diaries of his brother Arthur, as well as the inevitable published biography of him by Arthur (along with the usual two-volume life and a book of a friend's gushing reminiscences). It is possible to trace the conversion almost week by week. Most of the writing is retrospective, apologetic, and public, with the inevitable rewriting and biases that such strategies involve. But there is surprising agreement about what the turning points in Hugh's mind were. There were two fundamental processes of thought—and both show how closely he was responding to his father in his rejection of his father's deepest held institutional values.

First of all, it was a question of discipline and authority. He felt, as he put it, that he "was an official of a church which did not seem to know her own mind even on matters directly connected with the salvation of the soul." He was increasingly vexed not so much by theological debates, which he knew could rumble on for centuries without resolution, but by the fact that, as he saw it, in the Anglican communion, "mutually exclusive views were . . . tolerated," even about "things that directly and practically affect souls." This led him "more and more to see the absolute need of a living authority who can speak as new interpretations of her former words contend for mastery." In the face of the swirl of differing opinions, Hugh was increasingly desperate for an authoritative view of what was right. For Arthur, this was a political and psychological clash between "liberty" and "discipline," and he recognized that "Hugh did not find in Anglicanism . . . a sense of united conviction, a world-policy, a faith in ultimate triumph, all of which he found in Catholicism."

As a good liberal, Arthur saw this need for "united conviction" as
akin to the nationalist fervor of the hated Germans and, in the name
of a beloved British compromise, comfortably offered the *bon mot*
that "the Catholic believes God is on his side; the Anglican hopes
he is on the side of God." But Arthur did perceive that the crucial factor was that "Hugh was fretted by having to find out how
much or how little each believed." Indeed, Hugh's descriptions of
Anglicans can be amusingly precise from this perspective. He captures the language of divided Anglican opinion brilliantly in his
description of Dr. Gore, who took him into the Mirfield community: "He was identified, rightly or wrongly, with the High Liberal School; he was supposed to be unsound on the doctrine of the
incarnation; his views on Higher Criticism were considered dangerous; he was thought a little extravagant on the subject of Christian
Socialism." Each of these phrases smartly echoes the judgments of
a high-minded, well-dressed tea party (especially the delicious "a
little extravagant . . ."). Hugh wanted a fresh—"living" would be
his term—engagement: "A church that appeals merely to ancient
written words can be no more at the best than an antiquarian society." And this led him finally to the rejection of scholarship and
the acceptance of humility: "Humility and singleness of motive, I
now saw, were far more important than patristic learning." When
his father, his earliest authority, had died, Hugh was at sea. Now he
sought actively to escape divisiveness in the authority of the Catholic Church. Where his father had talked repeatedly of unity as
the key principle of church politics, Hugh thought he had found
that unity in Catholicism's discipline. Where his father had worked
for more than twenty years on his patristic scholarship with his
life of Cyprian, Hugh sniffily throws specifically patristic learning
aside—a gesture he calls looking for humility. Hugh is also always
arguing with the father he could never challenge alive.

Secondly, for Hugh the turn to the Church of Rome was motivated by an understanding of history. It was partly that "her system
worked": it had lasted a long time across all regions of the world successfully, but, more tellingly, the argument of apostolic succession—

that the church was founded on the Rock that was St. Peter and had continued unbrokenly since—was, Hugh explained, "simplicity itself. 'I am in communion,' the Romanist could say with St. Jerome, 'with Thy Blessedness—that is, with the Chair of Peter. On this rock I know the Church is built.' The Roman theory worked, the Anglican did not." This led to his own study of Elizabethan religiosity, where he found that he "began to marvel more than ever how in the world I could have imagined that the Anglican Communion possessed an identity of life with the ancient Church in England." This was especially difficult for someone like Hugh, who so loved the ritual side of things: "in Elizabethan days were priests hunted to death for the crime of doing that which I claimed to do." The fragmented and contentious history of the Church in England itself led him to value the certainties and continuity of the Church of Rome. His conclusion was devastatingly robust: "To return from the Catholic Church to the Anglican would be the exchange of certitude for doubt, of faith for agnosticism, of substance for shadow, of brilliant light for sombre gloom, of historical, world-wide fact, for unhistorical provincial theory." Where the Lincoln Judgment of his father had been hailed as a historical decision precisely because of its strong reassertion of the long history of the Anglican Church and its continuity with the authorities of the early church, Hugh dismissed such talk as "unhistorical provincial theory." There was, for Hugh, real "world-wide" historical fact, then there is the sort of "unhistorical" argument his father made. He attacked the "identity of life" that his father had so vigorously and carefully promoted, as he underscored and justified the disjunction in his own religious life. His genial and firm case against Anglicanism knew its target all too well and hit precisely at it.

In his biography of Hugh, Arthur depicts himself as a kindly and supportive if dissenting brother. He tells the story, too, of Bishop Wilkinson, an old friend of the family, who came uninvited and unannounced to the railway station when Minnie went to see Hugh off to Rome. He took her by the arm and said, "If Hugh's father, when he was here on earth, would—and he would—have always wished him to follow his conscience, how much more in Paradise!" and left without another word. By contrast, in the course of a bitter exchange of letters, Wordsworth, the Bishop of Salisbury and an old friend of Hugh's father, wrote to say bluntly that "your father's and your mother's son should not do this." (Minnie, with characteristically more nuanced though equally unsuccessful persuasiveness, wrote to Hugh to say in explanation how much the bishop was suffering from Hugh's decision.) There was, for the family, a lot of public, recuperative work, and Hugh and the others were all too keen to declare that his conversion was not the rebuke to his father that it was so evidently taken to be. In his diary, Edward White Benson had celebrated Hugh's ordination as an Anglican priest: "I had the wonderful happiness of laying hands on my Hugh . . . my son whom I love." In retrospect, the echo here of the book of Genesis and the instruction to Abraham to sacrifice Isaac, "your son, your only son, the son whom you love," was perhaps ominous.

The keenness to find some accommodation between the archbishop and his son in public concealed much more dissension and unpleasantness in private. His mother invoked "the Vision of the Blessed Dead" to remind him of the weight of his duty to his father. In his diary, Arthur was less circumspect. He despised Hugh's defense of monasticism and celibacy, whatever his own feelings about marriage. And he railed repeatedly against Hugh's position: "His views I can only consider contemptible, second-hand and trivial," he wrote as Hugh was airing his doubts about his commitment to Anglicanism, "they are stubbornly held; but I fear that if he tipped over he w^d fall into absolute infidelity." Later the same year, he records his family debating the same issue: "We discussed with pain Hugh's intellectual position, and the position of the High Church party. . . . They think of God as a kind of Sunday School teacher in an organ loft, rubbing his hands at the smell of incense and delighted at Reservation. . . ." The arguments went on: "The moment I get inside the circle of Hugh's mind I feel cramped and unable to breathe. . . . I value <u>liberty</u> more than I value anything else: and these priests are foes to liberty. Everyone has to be submissive—but to whom? Who has got the truth. Hugh says . . ."—and on and on. When he reads Hugh's book *The Light Invisible*, he can admire its skill—but sees it as "hiding really abominable and perverted thoughts." Nor does he find Hugh simply the charming and thoughtful youth of the biography: rather he "is like a child, a transcendent egoist, and utterly unaware of it." When Hugh comes to the moment of conversion, Arthur is scathing: "I do feel that his absence of suffering and his indifference to the suffering of others in this matter are rather horrible. . . . It has cost him nothing to break with the old, I think. It is all just the jest and the pleasure of new experience. All this gives me a kind of shudder about the roots of the heart." Arthur thinks his brother should suffer much more to make such a break with the past, with family tradition. Nor is there any doubt for Arthur what is at stake: "The one thing Hugh wants is authority and the luxury of not having to make up a confused and not very profound mind. . . . I hate the thought of my father's son doing this." For Arthur, Hugh needs authority, and it is as their father's son that his actions are particularly horrifying. The arguments about history, truth, faith were always tied up with family dynamics.

Fred was no different. He understood that no sense of family duty would have held back Hugh in even a small matter, let alone one as important as his faith—but immediately tried to imagine what it would have meant for his father if he had been alive: "I cannot imagine what the effect on my father would have been," Fred wrote, some years after both had died. His mother had managed to "beat down her will" to her son's change and had managed even to support him. But Fred suspects Hugh's conversion would have seemed "as the death of Martin had been, an event unjustifiable, unbridgeable, unintelligible, a blow without reason, to be submitted to in a silence which, had it been broken, must have been resolved into bewildered protest." Fred's reflection on Hugh's conversion marvelously captures the image of his father's baffled horror, for whom, indeed, the turn of his boy to Rome could have appeared to be as brutal a rejection of reason and justice as a beloved son's untimely death. Hugh's religious journey was for the whole family about "our father."

Hugh Benson's conversion was announced in the newspapers, and it became something of an immediate scandal. Each day for some weeks, he received two weighty posts of letters from colleagues, acquaintances, friends, and strangers, mainly from Anglicans in annoyance or anguish at his move. He attempted to answer them all. He was already a published writer on religious matters and had been an active religious leader in Cambridge. There were many for whom this turn to Rome was a painful betrayal, though in his story of events it is the generosity of his friends he cares to record. His life as a Catholic apologist had begun, and Reginald Watt, the young priest who lived with him for the last two years of his life, describes him tellingly as a captain in God's army—a "soldier of the old fire-eating, 'longing for a fight' variety. The whole world was his battlefield; every non-Catholic either a foe to be fought and conquered, or a neutral to be won over." His first job—symbolically enough—was at Cambridge, where he joined the Catholic chaplaincy and preached to the students. Some dons were dismayed, not least by his success. Arthur was already resident. Hugh set out to retrace some steps and this, too, on his father's turf, as it were. There were many people at Cambridge who knew Hugh—knew him in his family context—and experienced his change. As Arthur recorded, "The painful thing was that his father's son should do it in his father's university." Hugh knew that his fight was with his own family and his family history, as well as with the religious world and its sense of the past. His decision to set up a small oratory in his mother's house so that he could say Mass when he visited and stayed was within this context. Each day, as he rang the bells in the upstairs oratory, he knew the sound echoed through his family's morning rituals.

20

Secret History

HUGH BENSON WROTE BOOKS AS FIERCELY AND AS FAST AS his older brothers—more than twenty volumes in twelve years—and in particular he wrote historical novels set in the Elizabethan period, where he exorcised his feelings about history and the Reformation; or in the Restoration, with its Catholic plots and intrigues. His heroes, fighting for the Catholic Church, strode into the sunset after deeds of derring-do, secure that they had done the right thing for the church and country. He also wrote modern novels with equally transparent agendas. In *Loneliness*, his last novel, a woman called Marion converts to Catholicism thanks to the influence of a quietly charismatic older woman. Marion is a musician, a singer—and as she accepts Catholic truth, her voice takes on a new dimension and she becomes the hit of the season in London, and a triumphant career beckons. She meets and falls in love with an upper-class man, and all seems set for a happy conclusion, when he confesses that he cannot join any church and cannot bring up their children as Catholic. She struggles desperately with her conscience, but her love wins out. She agrees to marry him anyway, and immediately she loses her voice, her Catholic friend dies, and her life crumbles around her. The plot is not simply a barely disguised morality play—a sermon in a frock—but also a rejoinder to Fred's stories, where the musically gifted child is forced to reject his religious parents but does not always end up with such immediate punishment. The novels flared in the public attention at the time, led by Hugh Benson's

notoriety, but they have not lasted well, despite some overheated celebration by his Catholic colleagues for his reinvention of the genre
of the "Catholic novel"—a genealogy headed by Newman's *Callista*
and Wiseman's *Fabiola*, books whose pious celibacy and celebratory
martyrdoms prompted Charles Kingsley, Edward White Benson's
close friend, to write *Hypatia*, his historical novel of early Christian
history, written to promote a counter-image of northern Anglican
virtue and full-blooded marital sexuality. As ever, there is an agenda
to Hugh's writing, where Catholic apologetics are also firmly located
within his own family history.

According to Reginald Watts, his companion at the end of his
life, Hugh "'saw red' over a certain popular type of sex novel, and his
criticisms of such were short and damning." He was dismayed even
by "those who tried to fight the vice portrayed in the sex novel by
writing highly moral books about it," not least because such tracts
inevitably "revel in true instances often filthier than the fictional
ones." Hugh Benson's advice, according to Watts at least, was just
"say your prayers, and think about something else." Despite his
extravagant preaching style and hyperactive public persona, Hugh
Benson was by all accounts deeply undemonstrative in his emotional
interactions, and there were fewer than six people in his packed
world whom he addressed by a first name. Just as Fred was unforth-
coming and inscrutable while writing witty and demonstrative novels; Arthur, reticent on personal matters and famous for continually writing—putting it out there—about his reticence; so, it seems,
Hugh, who had become one of the most charismatic preachers (he,
too, like Martin, stammered but was somehow overwhelmingly flu-
ent from the pulpit), was also deeply restrained when it came to
other people and, indeed, hated being touched.

It is something of a shock, then, that the one relationship of his
which blossomed suddenly into a thing of intimacy and obsession
was with the unreliable and unstable Frederick Rolfe. Rolfe, who
styled himself Baron Corvo, had written an novel called *Hadrian the
Seventh*, which Hugh read, loved, and typically dashed off a letter
of admiration to its author, which turned into a long and intense

and intimate exchange of letters, "exhaustingly charged with emotion," followed by their meeting. (Arthur, with his characteristic fear of exposure, destroyed the letters later.) Rolfe was also a convert from Protestantism and had wished to become a priest but had been expelled from the seminary. He had consequently developed a hatred of priests, whom he reviled in foul language, and a paranoid combination of bruised entitlement and anticipation of humiliation. He was said to wear a ring with a spike on it to defend himself against a feared kidnap by priests or their agents. *Hadrian the Seventh* is premised on the bizarre and painfully self-serving fiction that a person, not much unlike Rolfe, twenty years after he had been turned down for the priesthood, is recognized for what he truly is and is elected pope. A revenge fantasy of staggeringly egotistic proportions . . .

Rolfe and Benson became something of a Cambridge cult. One acquaintance remembers that the two men experimented with medieval magic recipes, and after two weeks of fasting and meditation, Hugh claimed he had seen a white knight on horseback enter his room and then after a few minutes fade away. "Father Benson had, I think, been delving a little too deeply into mysticism at the time," he added dryly. They loved bathing (and there are a large number of bathing scenes in Benson's novels) and spent a great deal of time together, not least on a walking holiday, and in planning a joint literary project on the life of Thomas à Becket. The project progressed to the point of planning out the book, but then his brother Arthur and Monsignor Barnes, the Catholic chaplain and Hugh's mentor, stepped in to stop the collaboration. Arthur had met Rolfe a couple of times at Tremans and despised him: he called him the "infernal exorcist" and noted with wry mockery that at Tremans Rolfe posed as a great author, on the strength of what Arthur judged to be a "quite appalling book (which Hugh thinks clever), called Hadrian VII." Boasting of being a published writer did not cut much ice in that household. Monsignor Barnes was worried about the implications for Hugh's reputation: Rolfe was sexually degenerate—he was knowingly homosexual and exchanged letters with a string of literary figures on the subject—and had failed entrance to the priesthood. But the withdrawal from the writing collaboration precipitated a total breakdown between Hugh Benson and Rolfe.

Rolfe unsurprisingly saw Hugh's decision as another priestly betrayal. He wrote a string of libelous letters to publishers and friends insulting Hugh, and in his book *Desire and the Pursuit of the Whole*—which was written not long after the breakup but not published until 1934—invented a character of a priest called "Bobugo Bonson"—Bob for Robert (Hugh's first name, by which he was never called in the family), Ugo for Hugh, and Bonson for Benson: "a stuttering little Chrysostom of a priest [who] did not aspire to control creation, but he certainly nourished the notion that several serious mistakes had resulted from his absence during the events described in the first chapter of Genesis." Indeed, Chatto and Windus, the publishers, originally turned the book down precisely because it was thought too libelous to be printed. Rolfe died, in penury in Venice, in 1913, the year before Hugh Benson, and Arthur reflected that he "must have been mad: he accused Hugh of all and sundry of nameless crimes and misdemeanours." Hugh, not long before Rolfe's death, however, had confided to Reginald Watts that as far as he was concerned, "The man's a genius and I love him. If he'll only apologize I'll ask him to come and live with me. He's quite destitute now, but is welcome to everything I've got." Both men were tetchy, self-absorbed, paranoid; both made fun of the priests of Rome, as much as they were passionate about the Catholic Church; both nourished the notion that their writing would change the world. They both returned to their tempestuous relationship throughout the rest of their lives, in angry distance as much as in intimate companionship.

Rolfe was thought remarkable by all those who cared to mention him, either remarkably interesting or remarkably unpleasant. His afterlife is also remarkable, for the story of this book at least. In 1906, for example, Benjamin Aelred Carlyle founded the "Anglican Congregation of the Primitive Observance of the Holy Rule of St Benedict" on Caldey Island off the coast of South Wales. He built a lavishly furnished monastery for thirty tonsured monks, who recited the daily offices in Latin. It became something of an ecclesiastical tourist attraction, as a rare experiment in Anglican monastic life. One practice that Carlyle introduced for his monks, which seems scarcely in line with St. Benedict's rule, was group nude bathing, during which Carlyle himself, as the self-styled Lord Abbott of Caldey, would read tales from Rolfe's *Stories Toto Told Me*. The combination of a monk's retreat, naked bathing, fake aristocratic titles, and reading stories about Italian peasants seems wholly inspired by a Rolfean vision. Rolfe, too, was rediscovered as the twentieth century progressed. *Hadrian the Seventh* was adapted successfully as a play for the West End and for Broadway in 1968, with Alec McCowen in the lead role; A. J. A. Symons's *The Quest for Corvo* was the first piece of life-writing that dramatized the author's own search for his subject and became a lasting success as the intellectual pursuit of a deceptive self-fashioner through his friends' and enemies' recollections. But above all, Rolfe—and always with Rolfe, Hugh Benson—has been reclaimed for the history of homosexuality. A few privately printed appreciations of Rolfe in midcentury became a handful of biographies and a regular if minor place in the history of modernism, where his homosexuality and self-fashioning have been productively intertwined. As the increasing openness about homosexuality became a biographical urge, Rolfe's rare explicit remarks and paraded passions and oppressions became a test case for the secret history of the vice that dare not name itself.

For Hugh Benson, marriage was not an option. His mother wrote to Maggie, his sister, on the day of his ordination into the Anglican clergy: "We had some dear talk—he can't at present conceive the possibility of giving his heart to a wife, it is so given to God, but he waits the call whatever it is, and is so sweet and kind and perfectly natural." Yet, like Arthur and Fred, he seems to have had a horror of physical contact and, further, to have been celibate by emotional and religious choice. He was taught at Llandaff by Dean Vaughan, the man in charge of training young priests, who had been the headmaster of Harrow forced to resign for sending love letters to a pupil. Vaughan was the schoolmaster about whom Arthur was congratulated for writing with such discretion that no one who did not know the story could tell what had happened. It was John Addington Symonds, the close friend of Arthur Sidgwick, Minnie's brother, who had been instrumental in the exposure of the affair. Hugh sought the exclusive and reclusive company of men: at Mirfield, in his house with Reginald Watts, on his walking holiday with Rolfe. His distaste for "sex novels," his withdrawal from physicality, not least in a paraded celibacy that deeply annoyed his family, his closeness with a very few men, meant that Hugh's religious life—as was the case for many men living on the contested border between High Anglicanism and the Roman Church—was constantly framed by what we could call the family dynamics of a struggle over sexuality. It was not merely that Hugh was celibate, but that he insisted on volubly promoting and celebrating its value in a family where reticence and discomfort about sexuality was *de rigueur*, and where their father's good friend Charles Kingsley was the spokesman of an Anglican horror of such practices of abstinence. Triumphantly displaying his celibacy was another way Hugh found to stand at odds with his family by his religious observance.

Yet perhaps the oddest sign of Hugh Benson's oddness was his fear of being buried alive. He specified that if possible his grave should be a mausoleum with an easily opened door and that the coffin had an easily lifted lid, and that if he died away from home, as in fact he did, then one of his arteries should be opened a day or so later in such a way as to confirm his death but not to kill him if still alive. In a ghoulish scene, Arthur Benson duly opened Hugh's artery according to his wishes. It is, I think, a strangely touching sign of Hugh Benson's still unfinished relationship with his father and his past that he should so openly dramatize his fearful sense of being conscious of dying before his time, of not being recognized as needing desperate help, of waking to an awful sense of dark oppressiveness and helplessness. Hugh's Catholic Christianity may have encouraged its believers to approach death with an assured confidence in salvation; he preached such salvation many times— yet he never managed to remove from his own mind a darker and ever-present terror.

21

Writing the History of the Church

WHILE MINNIE BENSON STRUGGLED WITH HER NEW FAITH, while the boys fought against their parents' commitments, while Edward White Benson himself suffered internal anguish over the death of Martin, in his public life the archbishop was intently and tensely engaged in the politics that would shape the Anglican Church for many years to come.

He was ever conscious that he lived in changing times. On March 8, 1891, Archbishop Benson went to church as usual, and on this Sunday to St. Jude's in Kensington. He was profoundly disconcerted by the experience and wrote afterward in his diary: "But how curious the change in the notion of Divine Service. Here is an <u>Evangelical</u> congregation and minister—cross on altar, and a white cloth with lace border always remaining on it and a piscine and a surplice choir—any one of these things would have been deadly popery (except in Cathedrals the choir)—<u>since I came of age</u>." Edward White Benson was baffled by the change he saw in the ritual of the service, as well he might be—though I suspect that few today, even those in the church, would appreciate either what upset him or the depth of his feelings. To see an Evangelical minister— Low Church, severely Protestant—happily officiating with a cross on an altar was a bizarre religious paradox in his eyes. Not only was an altar (rather than a communion table) a sign of High Church, Anglo-Catholic ritualism, with a dangerous assertion of a priestly status, but also to ornament the altar with a cross and a white cloth with a lacy border would in previous decades have been tantamount to displaying a Roman Catholic tendency—anathema to an Evangelical Protestant. A piscine is regularly used in Roman Catholic ritual for washing the ritual basins—but was scarcely familiar in Anglican worship, and a choir in surplices outside of a cathedral was reminiscent of the polyphonic sung masses on the Continent rather than the hymns and prayers of the Anglican service. In his lifetime, the threat of "deadly popery" had led to violence in churches and on the street, and to political mayhem, yet here was a calm acceptance of what would recently have been regarded as the most provocative of religious gestures. For Edward White Benson—as his emphatic underlinings make clear—it is not just the infiltration of such ritualism into an evangelical service that makes him so upset, but also the awareness that this change has taken place in his own adult life. Like Fred or Arthur in the 1920s, Edward White Benson is acutely aware of the abyss of time that separates his present and his past.

Who better to be aware of such a change? Archbishop Benson had in the previous year delivered the famous Lincoln Judgment, a decisive trial about ritualism in church worship whose reverberations are still felt. It is a story that encapsulates a moment of revolution in Victorian Britain and was the defining moment of Benson's era as Archbishop of Canterbury—a defining moment in his life's work. It is against this story that the family dynamics resound.

Edward King was appointed as Bishop of Lincoln, the successor to Christopher Wordsworth, Benson's old friend, and in many ways King epitomized values that Benson himself deeply respected. Indeed, it is one of the ironies of this tale that when Gladstone had sought to appoint to the bishopric a man who could represent a High Church perspective, it was Archbishop Benson himself who privately suggested the name of King as a more ameliorative option than the rather aggressive Henry Liddon, the leading High Church man of the day, to whom it was known that Queen Victoria was actively opposed. King was passionate about the pastoral training of his clergy and had been the chaplain at Cuddesdon, the training college with very High Church leanings that had led Archbishop

Tait, as we saw, to worry about its students' masculinity. King was also especially committed to care for the disadvantaged—"I shall try to be the bishop of the poor," he wrote to Gladstone on taking up the office. (Benson himself was celebrated for his commitment to workingmen in Lincoln itself.) It was widely known that King had personally stepped in to support a poor fisherman who had killed his girlfriend in a fit of jealousy and had been sentenced to death—campaigning unsuccessfully for a remission, earnestly talking and leading him toward prayer, and accompanying him right onto the scaffold. King was renowned and revered as a good and gentle man. Yet King had been influenced by the Tractarians of the Oxford Movement as a student in Oxford and was happy to embody their aims of increasing the ritual observances in church. And this gentle acceptance of a certain ritualism is what led to the trial of the Bishop of Lincoln.

Most of what we now recognize as the familiar old churches of the British cities and countryside were shaped by a Victorian vision. Nineteenth-century Britain witnessed a huge church-building program, initially kick-started by a large government grant, which had a lasting impact on the landscape of the country and on the cultural and economic structure of society. Not only were many new churches built, to cater for the new urban populations in the newly industrialized cities, and with them campaigns of missionary zeal among the urban poor, but also thousands of churches were restored—restored, that is, to the new architectural standards of the Gothic revival. Many churches in the name of restoration were completely redesigned to a projected model of medieval authenticity. (Much of what is taken to be the Olden Dayes is a Victorian fantasy . . .) The claims of the restorationists were vociferously promoted at an ideological level and were gradually opposed (and defended again) with even more strident voices in the name of preservation. It is in this arena that the modern arguments about heritage first took shape, along with the founding of the Society for the Preservation of Ancient Buildings, the National Trust, and other such agencies. It was a voluble, aggressive, and thoroughly Victorian controversy.

The restorationist ideology was not merely about the physical fabric of the buildings but also about the liturgical activities that such physical forms embodied. The restorationists who wished to remove closed pews and galleries also wished to introduce robes for preachers, altars, and ceremonies from the older church traditions. This aim was explicit: "It is obvious that in refitting churches we must have our own ritual and our own necessities in view," wrote Gilbert Scott, the leading restorationist architect. Charles Barry who designed the Gothic icon of the Houses of Parliament, agreed: restoration, he wrote, has "arisen from a great religious and social change. Revivals of form and ceremonies have much to do with architectural restoration of churches." In this light, it was proclaimed that church restoration was "holy work. It was a crusaded square, and trowel, and broadcloth"—doing God's work on earth, an architectural and ceremonial mission. And those who opposed such changes in liturgical practice were equally clear that these changes were worryingly, dangerously akin to Roman Catholicism. "The exact parallel growth of the Oxford Tracts and clerico-architectural Treatises, affords at least a very plausible reason for concluding that the seed from which they have both sprung is of like quality." Or more bluntly: "We want *Protestant Churches, not Popish Mass-houses*." The conflict of views was intense and battled out in pamphlets, books, law cases, and outbursts of street violence, especially around the years of the so-called papal aggression, when Cardinal Wiseman was appointed as the first Roman Catholic Bishop in England since the Reformation.

So when Edward White Benson was surprised to see an altar in the Kensington evangelical church, he was reflecting on the passing into obscurity of fifty years of intense arguments—which now no longer seemed to heat the blood. Back in the 1840s when he was an adolescent, the introduction of a stone altar into the Round Church in Cambridge had led to a bitter law case, questions in Parliament, outraged sermons, a string of heated pamphlets, and, finally, the removal and ceremonial destruction of the offending piece of furniture. Now, it seems, you could find an altar in the lowest of churches

WRITING THE HISTORY OF THE CHURCH **253**

without any anxiety. To see an altar implied that the officiant was a sacrificing priest, which not only evoked the specter of the Roman Catholic hierarchy, but also promoted a view of the true presence of the body and blood of Christ at the communion, which was at odds with Anglican orthodoxy. Or so it had seemed—and seemed of immense significance—only a few years previously. Now, apparently, the piscine and the cross aroused no suspicion.

The Lincoln Trial, for which Archbishop Benson was the sole judge, marks a watershed in this conflict over forms of worship. In 1874 the Public Worship Regulation Act had attempted to regulate the divisive conflict over ritualism but had succeeded only in exacerbating it. It was brought to Parliament by Archbishop Tait, Lucy Tait's father, and the debate stirred deep passions. At first sight, the law was a compromised but effective triumph against ritualism. Under it, now by the country's law, if a church officiant was accused of facing eastward during the sacramental service, mixing wine and water at the communion table, having candlesticks on the communion table (except for necessary light), using incense, wearing elaborate robes, kneeling during the communion service, or using wafer bread, his congregants could complain to the bishop, who could forward the complaint to a new court, headed by the retired judge of the divorce court, Lord Penzance, who could order the offending clergyman to desist from such activity, and then, if necessary, punish the miscreant with imprisonment if he continued to disobey the authorities in contempt of court. But the idea that the state should regulate religious practice, and through a judge rather than through the bishops—a divorce court judge at that—prompted an outcry from churchmen. The attempt to regulate ritualism, it seemed, opened a door on to a more profound argument about the role of the state in church matters—and thus the threat—or promise—of disestablishment.

The Public Worship Regulation Act led to a string of high-profile and shocking prosecutions where earnest, gentle, and much-liked clergymen were arrested for wearing robes or facing east during the service of communion. In 1881 Sidney Green was imprisoned for twenty months, and all his property was sold to support his destitute family, because he had followed his ritualist leanings. The widely circulated pictures of clergymen behind bars raised a good deal of sympathy for the newly criminalized and a good deal of suspicion about the law's common sense. Consequently, for some years afterward, there was a concerted attempt to avoid such prosecutions by bishops using their veto and not allowing trials to proceed. This only increased the venom of those frustrated by what they saw as the slide toward an acceptance of Roman Catholic forms in the Anglican Church. So the opportunity to prosecute a bishop also had the advantage that it could bypass the bishop's veto on prosecutions. In all ways, the prosecution of the Bishop of Lincoln greatly upped the stakes.

The leading organization behind such prosecutions was the Church Association, formed in 1865 to resist ritual innovation in the Anglican Church. In the Benson archive in the Bodleian Library in Oxford, the only piece of popular press preserved is a fly sheet produced by the Church Association in these years called "The Effect of Ritualism in a <u>Working Man's</u> Household." It's a garish, foolish thing but gives a good sense of the vehemence of feeling running through these arguments—and its very preservation in the Benson papers may be further testimony to the stress Edward White Benson was put under by the trial. The fly sheet tells of how a workingman's wife goes once to confession and early morning mass, and immediately the "husband found his influence completely gone." There is no breakfast for him as she dashes to church, and his children are left to run wild. He may find support through the courts, but "the Working Man's home [is] broken up and priestly domination established." The narrative ends with a call to battle: "Working Men, will you not help to stamp out this great social evil, by insisting on the purification of the Church from the Mass and the Confessional?" The Church Association was mightily displeased by the appointment of Edward King to the see of Lincoln.

There was an immediate publication by one J. Hanchard of a biographical portrait of King designed to demonstrate "the Romish tendencies of the Bishop's thoughts." The portrait is vitriolic in its insinuations and accusations:

> By his continued connection with the *English Church Union*, we have the link which connects him with the Ultra-Ritualistic faction. From the approbation his Lordship has bestowed upon persistent law-breakers, we cannot feel any confidence that he will exercise his authority to stem the tide of unreasoning sacerdotalism. By the work he maintained at Cuddesdon; by his apparently sincere regard for Romish playthings; by the display of gaudy gewgaws at his enthronement; and by his self-conscious vanity in sitting to be "taken" for the admiration of "the faithful" without even having sacrificed his whiskers to the Catholic razor, he is unquestionably assisting in "digging the grave of the Establishment."

The slide in Hanchard's rhetoric from ritualism through priestly cult and Roman Catholic materialism to the threat of disestablishment summarizes in one paranoid, aggressive paragraph all the standard moves of anti-ritualist fervor.

Edward King did not help himself, however. His friends may have regarded him as "happy, holy, serene, popular and harmless," but his public performances could not have been more provocative to the anti-ritualists. He had been presented with a miter by friends in Oxford; a second was also presented "so ornate" that, as the *Guardian* newspaper noted disingenuously, "the new mitre of the Archbishop of Cologne could not be compared with it." But since the Reformation, no bishop in the Anglican Church had worn a miter on his head. Other bishops may have gradually gone on to follow King's example, but for the overheated imagination of his opponents, it was an outrageous visual symbol—precisely designed to evoke the "gaudy gew-gaws" of the Catholic bishops of a foreign place like Cologne. What's more, in 1885 the bishop allowed himself to be photographed wearing vestments. Again, he was the first bishop since the Reformation to wear vestments. The photograph duly appeared in a shop window in the Strand in London, and the

Church Association used it as a centerpiece for a pamphlet with a nasty little poem about "Priestcraft stalking the land." King started his time as a bishop already placed within the battle lines. When he preached, churches were full to bursting. At the annual meeting of the Church Association in 1886—reported in the national press— King was decried as a lawbreaker and his prosecution was demanded. The intense publicity of a celebrity trial was set in motion.

The Bishop of Lincoln was accused in terms that were precisely gauged to the law that regulated public worship: that he had officiated at a service where there were lit candles on the altar; that he mixed water with the wine; that he had stood facing east; that his hands were hidden from the congregation; that he had caused the Agnus Dei to be sung after the Consecration prayer; that he had made the sign of the cross at the Absolution and the Blessing. The trial and its overheated discussion was a personal anguish for King and for Edward White Benson. Benson did not relish the public, legal jurisdiction over matters of spirituality and was acutely aware that any decision when matters were so vexed and divisive could not produce an agreed satisfaction. King's supporters attacked him publicly and personally for agreeing even to sit as judge in the case. George Russell, the journalist and Liberal politician, wrote a very long letter to the *Manchester Guardian*, in which he compared King—"his gentleness, his lovableness, his saintly life, his inexhaustible powers of sympathy"—with his judge, who was, he pronounced, "a good deal stronger in emotions than principles, and only too likely to set a higher stake on the showy and sentimental aspects of churchmanship than on its vital essence." Many years after the event, he still declared in his hagiographic memoir of King, "It is evident that the Archbishop, who loved pose and effect, longed to assert and exercise his jurisdiction, and to sit in judgment on the successor of St Hugh." Benson and his family, by contrast, recall this as a time of remarkable stress and difficulty, a very long way from reveling in the proud exercise of authority.

Indeed, like any serious churchman, Edward White Benson had been vexed for decades by what to think about the growing and changing ritualism in the Anglican Church. "In advanced ritual," according to Arthur's typically careful judgment, "he took a somewhat fearful joy." So, in 1883 Edward White Benson sent to Arthur, then an undergraduate at Cambridge, the longest letter the boy ever received from his father, precisely on the subject of ritual, in which he declared, "Now I own I have for years past looked on pleased but anxious to see our worship all over England getting ornamental." His pleasure was aesthetic; his anxiety was that ritualism could obscure the true spirit of worship. In short, Edward White Benson enjoyed ritualism, saw its value in increasing the dignity and aesthetic joy of the service, but thought that it had the dangerous potential to lead toward materialism, and to turn from true feelings of godliness into an obsession with the trivialities of observance. He wrote most directly and forcefully in his diary, as the arguments became more heated: "It is most wretched, since these litigations renewed themselves, to feel that every position or attitude or act is watched with rigour and more the more trivial it is. It is eating away the soul of public worship." Benson knew a huge amount about the history of ritual but "was almost ashamed of seeming to know so much about it." To be asked publicly to determine the church's views on such matters forced him uncomfortably to face how strongly he felt about something he thought was a distraction, and to do so with an emphasis that threatened to distort the issue.

Every step of the trial was contested and required careful political maneuvering. First, the Archbishop's right of jurisdiction was challenged; the Privy Council ruled that Benson could and should sit in judgment. Then he was put under immense pressure to exercise his right of discretion by dismissing the charges. He saw the need to treat them seriously and finally. There was no doubt about what had taken place. What was at stake was the significance of what had happened, the place of ritualism in the church, and, at the most abstract level, the relation between church practice and the authorities of church and state.

Benson gave his ruling in 120 pages of densely argued historical and theological justification to an intent and fervid courtroom of theologians and their multiform supporters and detractors. He ruled that it was indeed illegal to mix wine and water during the service, though not to use wine and water mixed before the service; he also ruled that during the Eucharist the hands of the celebrant must be visible to the congregants. Benson also declared that to make the sign of the cross in the air during the Absolution and the Blessing was "an innovation that must be discontinued." In all other matters, he dismissed the charges against King: the Agnus Dei was not to be distinguished from other hymns, clearly allowed; facing east had historical precedent, provided the hands were clearly visible; the candles were not lit by King and played no part in any ceremony and were therefore without doctrinal significance. The Bishop of Lincoln immediately declared his obedience to the ruling. King's supporters were delighted and relieved. King's detractors were dismayed but allowed that at least King had been restrained in two areas, which for them justified their action. Where there was no hope of complete agreement and joy on all sides, Benson's judgment may now in retrospect appear to have been a balancing act of some brilliance.

The result of the Lincoln Judgment, however, was defining of its time, "epoch-making," as Rowan Williams, the Archbishop of Canterbury at the end of the twentieth century, called it. For although there was an appeal immediately lodged and quickly rejected; and afterward there were still the occasional reprimand and even legal cases against clergymen who went too far too soon with ritual practice; and there were inevitably a few pompous letters of complaint immediately after the decision; nonetheless, Benson's judgment effectively closed the court established by the Regulation of Public Worship Act; allowed ritualism a gradual and historically defended growth in the church so that almost every aspect of the accusation made against King is now a familiar element of the regular Anglican liturgical practice; and it effectively blunted the ability of small groups of disaffected traditionalists to block the move toward allowable innovation. Figures such as John Kensit, who founded the Protestant Truth Society and went around the country interrupting the services that he thought had ritualist elements, were marginalized as annoying cranks; and Parliament, faced by sporadic attempts by the disaffected traditionalists to reopen the issue, was now resolutely uninterested. The trial effectively ended seventy years of increasingly bitter, personal, and divisive debate and laid the foundations for the liturgical norms of the modern Anglican Church. Benson is often celebrated as the inventor of the Festival of Nine Lessons and Carols, which particularly in its form from King's College, Cambridge, has become a familiar part of many people's Christmas celebrations. But it is in the Lincoln Judgment that his most profound impact on the church can be found.

There is one last bizarre irony to this tale. In 1886 Edward White Benson went on holiday in France, and, incognito, he had visited the church where the robes of Thomas à Becket were kept as a relic of his martyrdom. Becket, the archbishop of Canterbury in the twelfth century, was murdered by the knights of King Henry in the context of a struggle over the balance of power between the church and the state, and is revered as a martyr of the Catholic and Anglican churches. As Benson was shown the robes, the sacristan without warning dropped them over Benson's head. He found himself wearing a chasuble, which reached to the ground and enveloped his whole body—vestments not worn, he guessed, by an Archbishop of Canterbury since Becket's day, and the "first chasuble I had ever had on." Benson could see this moment as an omen—"like a bidding to do something or leave something undone." But, if we are to play the game of omens, it might be that his role in allowing such ritual robes to be part of the church again was presaged in this uncanny scene of dressing up. King found his image in vestments used in a propaganda war against him as "the first bishop since the reformation to wear vestments"; in this private scene, Benson had already found himself dressed in the full robes of the medieval martyr from whose seat he would pronounce on the rules of liturgical form.

The Lincoln Judgment relied on a historical vision of the church. The *Guardian* understood the significance of Benson's opinion and expressed it with exemplary clarity: "The Church of England of the present is historically one with the Church of England of the past. . . . She was not a creation of Henry VIII or Edward VI." That is, the Reformation did not mark the sole foundational moment of the Anglican Church, nor could it provide the sole sources of authority for practice or doctrine. There was a longer history that needed sifting, evaluating, understanding. Consequently, in delivering the justification for his opinions, Benson cited twenty-three authorities from the Council of Hatfield in 680 AD, and, along with Reformers like Cranmer and Tyndale, fathers of the church such as Basil and Chrysostom, as well as the Clementine liturgy. The Ritualist claim of a restored continuity with the past as a justification for innovations in contemporary practice was upheld. The Lincoln Judgment proved a foundation for the modern church by asserting the continuing significance of the long history of the church.

So when Edward White Benson went to church that Sunday in 1891 and recorded his startled awareness of how there had been such a sea change in liturgical practice that now even in an Evangelical service a surplice choir sang, and an altar had its ornaments of cross and piscine, his recognition of change is not just an older man reflecting on the passing of the days or a shift in fashion. He is also reflecting on his own understanding of the deep time of the church and the role this understanding had played in changing the current church's attitude toward its own history. He was considering his own prime role in such a story of change. Archbishop Benson, with the characteristic historical self-consciousness of the day, was marking his own place in history.

Two years later, in 1893, and in the shadow of such a dramatic institutional and political story, Fred Benson, the archbishop's son, with equally characteristic insouciance, published *Dodo*.

22

Building History

SO, EDWARD WHITE BENSON KNEW HOW TO MAKE HISTORY.
He also built a monument to make his history real, physical, and
permanent. Truro Cathedral is Benson's church building for Victorian Britain.

When he was appointed Bishop of Truro in 1877, and the family
moved to Cornwall from Lincoln, part of the excitement for him
was the challenge of founding a new see. For the family, it marked
a fundamental shift in their communal life, and they wrote about
it repeatedly as a key transition in their emotional narrative as a
family. Truro was the first cathedral to be founded in Britain since
Salisbury in 1220. It brought for Benson not merely an opportunity to live out his evangelical zeal, bringing a new region into the
Anglican fold, like an apostle, but also the opportunity to create a
new institution of the church. Lincoln had been there for over eight
hundred years; Truro was a foundation in the present for a history to
come. He threw himself into the job with characteristic energy and
ambition—a stirring image of Victorian imperial thrustingness and
progress. It was, typically enough, taken as a sign of the new era of
Victorian Britain that a new cathedral, a project so bold and at such
a grand scale, could be established. Benson himself dismissed grum-
bling accusations against the project's extravagance with a telling
turn to ancient Greece: "The one man whom the ancients describe
to us as . . . the very author and model of domestic economy is he
who built the Parthenon—Pericles, the Athenian." History justifies

and will justify the grand builders, who, building for God, had the right combination of domestic restraint and public, divine glorification (even when for a pagan god). The see was established in 1876, the bishop consecrated in 1877, and the building, after the necessary fund-raising and design discussions, was started in 1880. The service of consecration took place in 1887, by which time Edward White Benson had become Archbishop of Canterbury and was shortly to face the Lincoln Trial.

Benson wanted to be involved in every aspect of the design of the cathedral. The architect of the building was John Loughborough Pearson, already a renowned figure in the Gothic revival movement, and the design was formed resolutely in the tradition of the movement's understanding of Gothic principles. Pearson had been the architect for the restoration of Lincoln Cathedral, where Benson had been canon chancellor, and there are clear resemblances between Truro and Lincoln, as well as the great cathedrals of northern France. For the first time, an architect from the restoration movement could create in England a cathedral from scratch according to his idealization of the past.

Unlike all the great cathedrals, which were its models, Truro could be of a piece, a single, synchronous design (although this has not stopped subsequent extensions and restorations). Integral to this design was the stained glass. The glass of Truro is a truly remarkable piece of work by Clayton and Bell, the leading firm for the Gothic Revival. It is in this glass that we see Benson making history and writing himself into it.

The sequence of images in the stained glass tells the history of the church from its foundations right up to the establishment of Truro Cathedral itself—and ends with a stirring image of Benson and the cathedral's foundation, dressed in medieval guise, as if their modernity was indeed of a piece with the great medieval foundations it imitated in its Gothic form. The cathedral glass embodies its own deep history and culminates with Edward White Benson.

The glass was completed after Benson's elevation to Canterbury, and a committee saw the installation through to its conclusion, with the inevitable push and shove of pious argument and tinkering alterations. But the design at its heart was Benson's, and it encapsulates a vision of the past that exemplifies how religious history—ideologically manipulated, theologically slanted, nationally triumphant—played a foundational role in the public self-representation of Victorian Britain. Bishop Westcott, Benson's lifelong friend, saw Truro Cathedral as "a splendid monument of his never-failing conviction that the life of our fathers is one with our life"—history as a living force in the present—and recognized that the Lincoln Judgment was equally "defined by these enquiries." For Westcott, the public, material proclamation of history in the cathedral's design was of a piece with the historical justification of church liturgy enacted in the Lincoln Judgment.

Immediately and vividly, in the images emphatically situated either side of the west door, you are faced by Benson's precise and particular construction of the past he wants you to see. On the north side, there is an extraordinary trio of images of John Keble, F. D. Maurice, and Henry Martyn. This is a triptych to make the churchgoing viewer stop and wonder. Keble was Benson's favorite poet—he learned much of it off by heart—as Keble was for the hundreds of thousands of Christians who bought and read *The Christian Year*, which from its publication in 1827 was one of the best-loved and widest selling books of poetry in the nineteenth century; but he was also the founding father of the Oxford Movement, which by the 1880s in the minds of many mainstream Anglicans was still suspiciously tainted by Newman's conversion to Roman Catholicism. F. D. Maurice was an icon to many Christian intellectuals, Charles Kingsley among them, both as a Christian Socialist and as a personally inspirational preacher and friend; but he had been sacked from King's College, London, because of his heterodox views on eternal punishment and remained a rebellious figure in the view of many evangelicals in particular, for whom eternal punishment was a central plank of divine justice. Keble and Maurice come from precisely opposite ends of the Anglican spectrum, and it is probably only in the world of stained glass—and in

Edward White Benson's personal pantheon—that they would sit down together in this way. Henry Martyn is less well known today but is a hero of the Christians of Truro. He was born in 1781, and his father was a mine captain at Gwennap (a few miles west of Truro). He became a convinced evangelical, missionary Christian, after encountering the charismatic evangelical Charles Simeon at Cambridge—when Simeon was still regarded as rather shocking and had not yet become the saintly figure who attracted thousands to his funeral—and he not only went to the East to proselytize, leaving his one true love behind unfulfilled, but also translated the gospels into Urdu, Persian, and Judeo-Persian, and the Psalms and the Book of Common Prayer into Urdu. He died from a fever in Tokat in Turkey on his way home in 1812. Below the three men is a further image of Martyn debating points of translation with turbaned Persians. In the baptistery there is an extraordinary and beautiful further sequence of images of the life of Martyn, portrayed as if he were a saint, complete with a thoroughly medievalizing climactic representation of his burial. Martyn's epitaph was composed by Macaulay and his life and letters edited by Samuel Wilberforce: he was a paradigm of the pioneering missionary for a period besotted with the idea of the Christian mission. The name Martyn itself was bound to echo for Benson. So the combination of these three figures by the west door make up a fascinating snapshot: a Tractarian, a Christian Socialist, and a philological missionary, each exemplary of a strand of Christian life in the nineteenth century, each a remarkable figure, but together offering a surprisingly ecumenical picture of inspirational counter-trends to mainstream Anglican religiosity.

The imagery on the south side of the door gives an equally surprising trio of modern religious figures. It shows John Wesley, his brother Charles Wesley, and Samuel Walker. The Wesleys, founders of Methodism, are the archetypal heroes of non-conformism, and so something of an oddity to see in an Anglican cathedral—although A. P. Stanley, the liberal Dean of Westminster, and always one to bring lost sheep into the fold, had unveiled a marble memorial to them in Westminster Abbey in 1876. Samuel Walker, not much remembered these days, is an eighteenth-century local hero in the dissenting tradition, from the generation before John Martyn. He was the curate of St. Mary's, the church on whose site the cathedral was built. Walker had an archetypal Damascene conversion and became a close friend of John Wesley. Walker was a controversial and polemical figure, but he seems to have been a remarkably successful preacher and just about stayed within the Anglican Church, despite his Methodist sympathies and the sometimes bitter resistance to him from within the church itself. Wesley was a frequent visitor to Cornwall and had particular success with the miners and other workmen: a striking image below the three men, parallel to Martyn discussing with the Persians, shows Wesley preaching to the miners at Gwennap, where Martyn's father worked. Benson himself acknowledged the strength of Methodism in the region: "He always recognized quite fairly that Methodism had kept religion alive in Cornwall when the Church had almost lost the sacred flame, and he treated Nonconformity as an enthusiastic friend." Martyn, however, had not been welcome in his home church because he returned from Cambridge "tainted" with "Methodism." Here, too, then, we see represented both a strong sense of local Christian activity and a willingness to include figures often seen as resistant to or at least in a combative relation with mainstream Anglican orthodoxy. The images not only give a remarkably untraditional snapshot of the variety of Christian leaders from the last century or so, but also offer a picture of Cornish Christianity in relation to the trends of modernity. This combination of these particular local and international figures by the west door of Truro Cathedral constitutes a particularly self-aware positioning within Christian history, a narrative of how the nineteenth century has unfolded.

From the west door stretching back along the nave, there is a sequence of images, each of them with trios of figures, which march back through the history of England, the Anglican Church, and Cornwall's part in it. Queen Victoria, an inevitable presence, is squired by General Gordon, devout Christian, imperialist, and military hero, and Alfred Lord Tennyson, poet laureate: the divine right, supported by military might and soft power. The eighteenth century is represented by Bishop Joseph Butler, a celebrated theologian, whose *Analogies* defended orthodox Anglicanism against deism; Isaac Newton, the scientist who was also a serious theological writer; and George Frederick Handel, who provided so much of the musical score for Victorian public life, not least in his biblical oratorios: theology, science, and the arts. The seventeenth century has a more directly Cornish coloring with Margaret Godolphin, a saintly woman from the court of Charles II who was married to a Cornish statesman; Sir Bevil Grenville, who led the Cornish Royalists during the Civil War; and Sir Jonathan Trelawny, Bishop of Winchester and a Cornishman, who was one of the Anglican leaders of opposition to the declaration of indulgence by James II, which would have introduced a religious tolerance into Britain. Indeed, the trial of the seven bishops who opposed the king is a set piece of Thomas Babington Macaulay's history of Britain, a best-seller that for mid-Victorian readers created a narrative of national and imperial self-formation (the same Macaulay who wrote Martyn's epitaph). This window combines piety against the corruption of royal power, the defense of the divine right of kings, and opposition to a royal interference with the religious autonomy and the monopoly of the Anglican Church over public worship: an extended gloss on *noblesse oblige* in its grandest political and moral form. This is matched by the next window, which shows Charles I (described in the guide today with a full-blooded rhetoric as "saint and martyr . . . who might have saved his crown and his life had he abandoned the Church. . . . His suffering and death made the causes of Monarchy and Anglicanism sacred to the English people"). He is joined by George Herbert, Anglican priest and poet; and Sir John Eliot, leader of the House of Commons, which had opposed the king. The imagery and its modern commentary are of a piece in its construction of a one-sided account of what was, after all, a civil war. Thomas Cranmer, John Wycliffe, and Thomas Coverdale are linked in their commitment to the Bible and Book of Common Prayer in

English translation, the cornerstones of the Anglican liturgy; John Colet and Thomas More, the only pair rather than a trio, are key figures of the English Reformation. Thomas à Kempis, Girolamo Savonarola, and John Huss take us back to the fifteenth century and its turmoil—these last two were burnt as heretics—and to the foundational crisis of the Anglican Church.

The story of each one of these figures was told by Victorian historians in a very particular way, to capture how the English nation developed as a Protestant country. The sequence is a material embodiment of the history of the nation as a history of the church. It is easy to imagine Benson lecturing his children in front of each window and, for good measure, on the sequence. At one level, it is typical of Victorian historical self-consciousness that the construction of a sequence of images in this newly conceived and built cathedral turns to a representation of the history of the Anglican Church itself, culminating self-reflexively with the very construction in which the viewer is standing. It is a history told through great men (and two women), across the centuries, each expected to stand for a turning point in the ecclesiastical narrative. But, at a further level, it is quite unique: there is no other sequence of glass like this. There are great sequences of glass that set the images of the Hebrew Bible against the images of the New Testament as a typological fulfilment. King's College, Cambridge, where the Bensons spent many hours in services, is the greatest of such sequences. The glass of King's College also expresses a religious view of the world—but it is wholly focused on the Bible as the model and quite different from Truro's historical characters over the centuries of modernity. But the glass of Truro is also unique because it embodies Edward White Benson's very particular vision of what counts in the past and how the past leads to the present—and thus how the modern church embodies its own history. The polemical trio of Keble, Maurice, and Martyn is designed to bring together what might be thought to be incompatible perspectives in a willed, historically layered ideal of the church's progress through conflict toward a more peaceful establishment, toward unity. That is why Westcott could see the construction of Truro Cathedral and the Lincoln Judgment to be of a piece. Both embodied Benson's sense of history.

The Victorian practical imagination was ever willing to alter the shape of things according to a historical agenda. Cityscapes, landscapes, individual buildings were molded by human agency to express a sense of national and religious history. If the railways, reservoirs, and the industrial city became the signs of modernity's impact on the environment, to clear away the buildings of centuries in order to leave the Parthenon in Athens as a newly stark and idealized image of the classical past, or to rebuild St. Alban's cathedral to match a projected model of a never-existent Gothic original, or to bring an Anglican cathedral and bishopric to a colonial city such as Jerusalem, or to rebuild one's own Elizabethan house to look more like a fantasy of an Elizabethan house, as Edward Bulwer-Lytton did at Knebworth—all were exemplary ways to make the physical world fully express a sense of history, and a place for the modern citizen within it. Truro Cathedral is a grand example of this historicized world building.

The Lincoln Judgment and the building of Truro Cathedral are the culminating triumphs of Edward White Benson's career as a very public figure of a very institutionalized Christianity. As the founding headmaster of Wellington, he had already designed its chapel, together with services and instructional stained glass to inform the boys' incipient religious feelings. There was also a string of legislative measures with which as archbishop he was intensely involved in intricate discussions and political exchanges—clerical benefices, the disestablishment of the Welsh Church, the Deceased Wife's Sister bill, the Sunday Observance bill, and many others—as well as the daily, engrossing, vexing infighting of a central institution of Victorian society. For Benson, the Anglican Church was "co-extensive with the nation." Although he did not "underestimate the great influence which the church possessed," he also "felt bitterly how small that influence was compared to what it might have been, had the sense of religion grown in proportion to the secular and commercial prosperity of the land." His task, he saw, was to extend the influence of the church in and against such material prosperity, and to this purpose his diaries are full of his meetings and discussions with the great and good of Victorian society and the constant march down the corridors of power. He was fully a churchman, committed to the betterment of the world through institutional work. His understanding of the institutional history of the church was formulated in service of this ideal. Benson's life was woven into the fabric of the church.

Edward White Benson also spent more than twenty years writing his historical study of Cyprian, the third-century Carthaginian bishop, a book that was published posthumously shortly after Benson had died. Cyprian emerges from this long analysis rather like Benson himself, as someone who was primarily worried that "many contemporary institutions which were the life of society were working powerfully for degradation and destruction"; by contrast, Cyprian sought to demonstrate that "God had . . . provided other institutions" to lead humans to a better life. Benson supported this argument with a quotation about the need for the "positive institutions" of "the settlement of a Visible Church," taken from Bishop Butler, another hero of the past whose image he also inserted into the windows of Truro Cathedral. Benson saw in Cyprian and Butler a continuing model of the need to fight for correct institutional Christianity and constantly to search for the true unity of the church. Benson's sense of history and sense of the present were mutually defining. For him, Cyprian "seemed to be among us." As he said in his last sermon at Truro, "The little particles, you and I, pass away to holier worlds, but the work goes on: the change is small, the continuity long." Benson's historical work was, for him, the continuation of an unfinished history. Life, a life's work, made sense only within such history making.

From the time of Edward White Benson's marriage to the time of his death, England moved from the wealthiest industrial country to the most extensive imperial power. The church was fully part of the imperial project. When Benson was a student with Westcott, it was a time "full . . . of warnings of changes political, social, intellectual, religious." Such turmoil "could not but stir us deeply," recalled Westcott. Their shared response was to move through teaching into the church, to rise through the ranks toward power, and to use that power in the expression of a social and religious vision. Benson's religion was significantly formed in response not just to the earnest religiosity of his mentors in the midcentury but also to the sense of political potential and danger of that revolutionary era. It was for him a mission to make a world in this idealized image. Religious politics was an act of constructing the city of God. Benson, in all senses, wanted to make history.

When Edward White Benson's children turned away from the institutional religion of the Anglican Church, then, it was a rejection of the vision of the world their father fought to build, the history in which he wished them to find their place, the very structuring of their own childhood. It was the ripping of an embracing fabric, a refusal to stand in the monument their father built.

23

Forms of Worship

FORM MEANT A GREAT DEAL TO ARTHUR BENSON.
For many years, his form and form-room at school provided a
structure of engagement with the development of the boys in his
charge. He talks a good deal in his diaries not just about individuals
but about a form as a group and their moral fiber and work habits.
He thought with some care also about literary form and discussed
such matters with Henry James, Thomas Hardy, Edmund Gosse,
and other literary lions of the day: "If I were a great writer," he wrote,
"I would try to overthrow this tyranny of form." He was pernickety
about social interactions and worried about good form. He talks
of his form in shooting and being on good form. But he also was
much concerned with forms of religious worship. It is not surprising that there are thousands of comments about religious services
and churches and ecclesiastical matters in the Benson diaries—he
is his father's son—nor that he should have argued with Hugh as
his brother turned to Rome and celibacy, nor that he should have
been amazed and horrified at Fred's insouciance in religious matters. Rather, what is odd is how little those who have written about
Arthur Benson have seen religion as an integral element of his life
(it is as if their absorption with sex has made them blind . . .). Yet
just as Arthur Benson's reticent struggle to name his own sexuality
is a paradigm of how complex it was to express a life of male desire
at a time when homosexuality had not yet taken full shape as a legal
and social category, so, too, is Arthur Benson's lifelong struggle with

religious feeling a paradigm of a different sort of cultural shift—a shift epitomized in a new indifference to forms of religious service. For Arthur Benson, as for so many others, "form" marks the significant interconnections between his teaching life, his writing life, his sense of social propriety, and his religious experience.

When Edward White Benson went to university, attendance at chapel was still compulsory for students, and religion was the arena where students competed to express their identity and argued over the future; until 1871 dons had to subscribe to the Thirty-Nine Articles. The schooldays of Edward White Benson, Westcott, and Lightfoot, all future bishops and major intellectual figures of the second half of the century, arguing together about religious ideals, is a potent image of midcentury earnestness and fervor. In those days, a sermon could cause a riot; people went to church to engage in such polemics and overheated responses; so many of the books that were thought to be turning points in the century's development were icons to fight over precisely because they caused intense religious upheaval—Robert Chambers's *Vestiges of the Natural History of Creation*; Henry Hart Milman's *History of the Jews*; John Colenso's *Pentateuch*; *Essays and Reviews*; or novels such as James Anthony Froude's *Nemesis of Faith* or Mrs. Humphry Ward's *Robert Elsmere*; the church, in sum, provided a social and moral structure that was fully interleaved through British society. The early years of Edward White Benson's marriage were a time when religious excitement could seem to be one of dominant elements of Victorian culture. Yet by the time Fred Benson died in 1940, things looked very different. The First World War, the Russian Revolution, the Great Depression of the 1930s made political debate increasingly definitional and increasingly separate from religion. Discourses of race and nationality overlaid religious thinking in the drive toward the Second World War, so that in Germany Jesus could emerge as an Aryan. Psychology, medicine, the rise of science made the pervasive religious earnestness of mid-Victorian Britain seem desperately old-fashioned. This general and familiar narrative of a sea change has often been told, sometimes in misleadingly simple terms as the triumph of secularism. Yet what is harder to trace, and what Arthur Benson paradigmatically offers through his diary, is the expression of a daily engagement with such change over the course of many years. So how did the son of the passionately evangelical Victorian Archbishop of Canterbury become modern?

In 1901 Arthur Benson, still teaching at Eton, was aware that things were on the move. In his diary, which rather charmingly has a tiger's whisker from Durham Zoo labeled and stuck to its frontispiece, he wrote: "I think in religious matters, we are awkwardly situated in this decade, we schoolmasters, I mean. Criticism of the Bible is advancing so rapidly, but we are still in a state of mild orthodoxy. Yet the other day I looked over a Genesis paper set by H. Bowlby [another master at Eton]; and thought the book from which it was set too advanced. I don't believe we meet the inroads of scepticism by prematurely introducing boys to it." This shows precisely why Arthur Benson is so telling and so vexing a guide. First of all, with the historical self-consciousness we have come to expect, he recognizes that this decade, the first decade of a new century, has left schoolmasters "awkwardly situated." It is both wholly characteristic of Benson to focus on feelings of awkwardness in his highly localized arena, and for this awkwardness to be a sign of what elsewhere marks the seismic changes of social expectation. Arthur Benson's historical self-consciousness is always overlapped with more trivial personal feelings of not quite fitting in. The reasons he gives for his feelings, however, are equally fascinating. When he states that biblical criticism is advancing rapidly, it is as if he is fifty years or more out-of-date. The inroads of German rational critique were already available and outraging decent people in the 1830s; *Essays and Reviews* was a scandal in the 1860s; Darwin had been around for more than forty years. It is almost as if Arthur is channeling his father's anxieties or, at least, trying to explain his awkwardness through a very old set of issues. What does it mean to be "of one's time"? Arthur Benson underlines the precise awkwardness of "this decade," but his worries conceal a time lag of many years. He also sets such critical advances against his—our—"state of mild orthodoxy." This is a perfect, almost parodic phrase for Arthur's religion at this time: it is a state, a condition, something you live in and with—and it is a state of "mild orthodoxy": traditional, but not aggressively so; certainly not evangelical or high; feelings warm, but not heated. If there was any phrase designed to enrage his father, it would be "mild orthodoxy." So he worries that a paper set by a colleague on Genesis might be too advanced for boys, who should not be introduced to skepticism before the proper time. This, nearly three generations after David Strauss's rationalist critique, *The Life of Jesus*, was translated by George Eliot for the British public. Benson here strikes the pose of a deeply conservative schoolmaster, worried that modern ideas might frighten the boys.

Yet in the same passage in his diary, Benson also recognizes a "really strong anti-<u>clerical</u> feeling" among the boys. He recalls how the school had been visited by a bishop who said that "a wave of infidelity <u>had</u> been passing over the nation, but it had practically subsided." Benson can't wholly agree. "I think it has," he allows, "but it has subsided into indifference. People are not interested enough to discuss religious questions." Now, in contrast to the schoolmaster worrying about his boys encountering trendy skepticism, he worries about a general lack of concern for any religious question—the loss of the intensity of feeling that motivated his father's generation. If indifference is the expected stance now, why worry about the introduction of skepticism?

This awkwardness of Arthur Benson is performed repeatedly, where he both regrets the apparent indifference of people to religious questions—Fred's problem—and wants himself to display a superior engagement, which to his equal regret he can never feel with the directness and intensity of his parents. He is suspicious of enthusiasm—especially when it takes Hugh's shape—and anxious that he has no enthusiasm himself: enthusiasm "makes Englishmen sheepish." As with desire, then, so with religion: reticence fighting with interest; commitment undone by anxious self-reflection; concern for good form fighting with sarcastic dismissiveness.

So—to take a few comments from a few days in June 1902, his

last year at Eton—Benson's struggle with religion is articulated at multiple levels. When he goes to church, he felt the sermon was "being addressed straight to me. But then he didn't tell me <u>how</u> to do it—<u>how</u> can one change oneself—<u>how</u> revive the energy that flags, the faith that grows dim. How recapture the old joy." Here he sounds like a man struggling with his loss of faith and going to church to test his grounding, without relief. His response to the church itself and its work, however, is also more robustly dismissive: "It is really monstrous that the Ch of England should be in these aged hands," he rants about the hierarchy, and of a cleric, "The fact is that he wanted to push missionary work and proselytize and was thoroughly tactless too." Tactlessness is unpardonable in Benson's scheme of things, an aggressive awkwardness always to be avoided. Perhaps most interesting is his response to Ernest Renan, whose *Life of Jesus* was a rationalizing, provocative best-seller from the 1860s onward and, it seems, still a name to conjure with. Renan threatens Benson because he says that anyone who writes a personal diary "in the sight of the stars, nature and humanity, has no faith and must be a paltry thing." So, continues the miffed Arthur Benson in his personal diary, "He ought, he goes on, to want to help, to alter, to uphold, to amend. A fine idea; and the finest people do it. But Renan did not—he wrote his diary and called it the Life of Jesus." When criticism gets close to Arthur Benson, he can be pretty snippy, and it is clear that the idealism of Renan provokes him to sharp sarcasm. Religious questions here are subordinate to his challenged personal identity as a diarist. Next Sunday, however, he "skipped chapel to write letters . . . but did not begin." And he ends, "I close these troubled pages. This has been a bad, overweighted time—very restless—troubled."

Benson's troubled time is partly tied up with religious uncertainty and its overlap with his social and intellectual life. On Christmas day that year, he reflected that "the only strength of Christianity is to take all the old wholesome emotions of simple life—the family, the house and so on—and to make them new again and holy." He seems to reject any questions of theology or institutions or organized religion, and to revert to some complacent, comfortable ideas of the family and the house—a watered-down version of Charles Kingsley's ardent vision of a Christianity based on marriage, climate, and race. But I wonder whether the dominant emotion here isn't rather a nostalgia for the "old wholesome emotions" that he no longer has—since his family has become dispersed and his house is the schoolhouse he is about to leave rather than his ancestral home. Benson here seems to be longing for a lost time, before his troubled restlessness, when things were simple, or so he fantasizes. His threatened faith is always bound up with these losses of the passing of time. Like Fred, ever aware in his family history of the abyss that separates him from his father's days, Arthur's uneasy rejection of the institution of the church is not just a sign of the abyss of loss, but also and more specifically an inability to repeat the words of Genesis with sincerity, "the god of my father." The strength of Christianity may be the revival of "old wholesome emotions," but the weakness of Benson is his inability to reach such feelings, a simple life he cannot experience.

Arthur Benson continues his sniping at the church throughout his time at Cambridge too: "We had an interesting talk today about the condition of the church—the debased quality of the men who enter it; the Roman tendency; the difficulty of checking it; the want of discipline . . ."; but he also begins to think in a much darker fashion, anticipating the despair of his breakdown: "Religion, what is it? I sometimes think it is like tobacco, chewed by hungry men to stay the famished stomach. And perhaps the real food for which they starve is death." He finds the sharpness to express himself in ways which would have horrified his father: "I can hardly say I am a Xtian; I really believe the Church is anti-Christ." Yet he fusses away at a Christian belief in thoroughly nineteenth-century terms, not far from the polemic of Renan and other writers of Lives of Jesus: "If I could be <u>sure</u> that the miraculous elements of the Gospels were false, I should be able to have a far nobler conception of Christ because I could then feel him <u>truly</u> human, instead of only masquerading in human guise." Arthur Benson lives in the constant repetition of "If I could be sure . . .": as in his sexual life and in his writing, reticence—the awareness that he might not be sure and must not give himself away—is the watchword of his religious engagement. Such reticence is the antithesis of his father, who not only always knew that his redeemer liveth, but also was all too ready to tell anyone and everyone, loudly and clearly. The move away from the church and religion in these years is all too often not so much the triumph of secularism as a group of men reacting nervously or violently against their fathers: Benson, Gosse, Butler, Froude . . .

When Arthur Benson had his first breakdown in 1908, however, it is marked not just by suicidal despair but also by a sudden intensity of feelings about God. "I was feeling the fire of the wrath of God," he writes in November 1907, as the onset of depression takes hold. In the nursing home, he records, "I feel utterly and entirely deserted by God. My fault, no doubt." And in the darkest time, he scrawls, "I do indeed <u>desire</u> God to do [unreadable] for me. I will try to submit to and to welcome his chastisement, and to hope he will yet lead me out of the darkness." As he begins to feel a little less oppressed, he expresses his gratitude to God: "I do thank God with all my heart and soul for withdrawing the dreadful cloud from my brain, and letting me live again for a little . . ."—although it took more than a year for him to recover enough to take up his life again. In his misery, Arthur Benson can talk of God's agency with all the direct fervor of his parents.

Yet when he has recovered and returned to Cambridge, it is as if those religious feelings have disappeared with his other symptoms. When he reads Benjamin Jowett's biography, he is as distanced and reflective as ever: "My principal interest in Jowett's Life . . . is to see how utterly religious feeling had changed, and how free comparatively we now are." Now, back at Cambridge, the "we" of the elite educated generation of the Edwardian era can testify to a separation from their Victorian parents, a feeling of liberation. In terms to shock his father, again, he blithely records: "I think I am an almost pure agnostic," although he adds immediately with typical ameliorative demurral, "though I believe in Christian principles." So, with the standard rationalism of critical history, he notes, "I wondered about the Resurrection. It seems to me that there is simply no historical evidence as to what did happen." And, as before, he can be extremely hostile to clerics, dead or alive—"Pusey seems to me a perfect monster of iniquity"—and to the organized factionalism of the Anglican establishment: "If Christ could come again to visit the earth, and could have our Xtianity explained to him, what would he think? What would he say to the ritualists?" He still argues with Renan; he reads and enjoys, apparently for the first time, David Strauss's *Life of Jesus* ("on the whole, I agree with that view of the Gospel"); and, above all, he emphasizes that his real love of Christianity is through the aesthetic effect of form. It is the beauty of the music, the light in a chapel, the architecture of a country church, the associations of an "old" way in which he finds his sense of religious feeling: "The best kind of Xtianity seems to me unconscious Xtianity, the sort of grace that expatiates and spreads of itself, by sheer force of beauty." This aestheticism is not just a weak version of Ruskin or Pater. It is the strongest redefinition of his father's Christianity—and the drive and forcefulness he embodied. In sharp distinction from Edward White Benson, Arthur Benson wants an "unconscious" Christianity, where debate, polemic, and realized history are silenced, a "grace" that does not require agency, and the sort of directed, evangelical action his father specialized in. Arthur's grace is passive, unevangelical, it spreads "*of itself.*" His love of beauty is also a way of performing in reticence a rejection of his father's religious principles and religious life.

Arthur Benson does not experience a loss of faith in the way that a character like Robert Elsmere does in Mrs. Humphry Ward's novel. There is no moment on a Damascus road, no reverse of the standard conversion narrative when a blinding flash convinces him of a new truth. He never stops going to church. He follows good form. And he is inevitably and intricately connected with the business of the church. He was recommended to edit the letters of Queen Victoria by a future archbishop of Canterbury; he reads books of theology and critical history; he worries about church dis-

cipline and evaluates the character of the clerical leaders of a previous generation with a sharp disdain; he attends major events at
Westminster Abbey; he meets and evaluates tersely the current crop
of clerics in the church hierarchy; he preaches in chapel as master
of Magdalene; and when he is at his lowest, he turns to God for the
consolation he denies is possible in happier times. But in his diary,
he records a long process of distantiation from everything that was
central to his father's life. Arthur Benson is agnostic, critical of the
biblical narrative as historical truth, dismissive of the church as an
institution and of organized religion as a spiritual form. His long
descriptions of the churches he visits on his vacation trips are both
typical of what Victorians wrote in their diaries and also a way of
finding in aestheticism a passive rejection of the vibrant missionary
activity and engaged institutional commitment of his father and his
father's friends.

Arthur Benson wrote regularly for the *Church Family Newspaper*,
a rather conservative periodical of the Church of England, and
he collected a good number of his little essays in *Along the Road*,
which he published in 1912. They are pious, reflective, sentimental squibs, and the audience for them would no doubt have been
deeply shocked to be faced by the sharp cynicism and doubts of the
diary. The first essay in the collection is entitled "Old England,"
an encomium of the "incomparable treasure of old and beautiful
things . . . hidden in our land." His example, inevitably for this publishing milieu, is a "tiny belfried church, in a wide meadow," where
he found a jumble of signs of the past, a Georgian pew, a Jacobean
pulpit, stretching back to a Roman mosaic. "What a mystery hangs
over it all!" he exclaims; how did a Roman ruin eventually become
"a tiny Christian church, who knows by what hands, or how many
dim years ago!" His brothers found the gap between Arthur's public
and private prose remarkable, and it would be easy to dismiss such a
nostalgic evocation of England's Christian past as the hypocrisy of
the journalist. But to bring together a hankering for the old and a
love of beauty is precisely the sort of religious feeling Arthur Benson could express, not only as a soft focus comfort for his readers,

but also as a way in which he could contribute to the Church of England in which he was brought up, while still strategically repositioning himself against his father's sense of religious history and directed religious fervor.

The penultimate essay of the collection is called "The Younger Generation." Here he celebrates the modern education of children against the Victorian past, "a hazardous experiment; but . . . the results have been, as far as one can see, wholly good." He praises the simple idea of bringing up children to be happy and contrasts his own experience with a more liberal contemporary attitude. "One of my own terrors as a child and a schoolboy was the fear of some penalty falling on me out of the blue for some transgression that I had not understood nor intended." This is connected to the expression of affection. Children should know that they are loved: "That concealment of affection which used to be considered wholesome is a mistake." The essay ends pregnantly with a memory of his father and how later in life he had deplored that he had educated through strictness and through "driving" rather than "leading." His father gets the last word—but only to take back his treatment of Arthur. With characteristic restraint—tact and reticence—Arthur explains how he was deprived of affection and terrified as a child, and uses this experience as a springboard to look back in pain to the Victorian past, with a hope for the future. He is poised here as his father's child and as the teacher of the modern generation, reflecting on the transitions of contemporary history. For all the comfy, bourgeois Anglicanism of the genre, Arthur Benson still finds a way to bring the shadows of the past into view. "The old idea was that children were to be taught their place," he writes, "and the result was that they were not taught their place at all." Arthur Benson knows that his awkwardness, his failure to find his place, is a result of his dysfunctional past.

The last essay of his collection *From a College Window*, originally written for the *Cornhill Magazine* in 1906, is entitled simply "Religion." This is a heated article closer to the sentiments of the diary, though it reserves its waspishness for the pope. Without any reference to Renan or other arguments about the humanity of Jesus, it rehearses the familiar contrast of the simple truths of the moral educator Jesus with the institutions of the church, culminating in a specific dislike of papal grandeur (sentences he wrote no doubt with Hugh in mind): "Could there, to any impartial observer, be anything in the world more incredible than that the Pope, surrounded by ritual and pomp, and hierarchies, and policies should be held to be the representative on earth of the peasant-teacher of Galilee?" Yet here, too, the essay ends with the narrator at night looking out over the college courtyard and aspiring toward God: "Oh, that I knew where I might find Him! That I might come into His presence!"—and the narrator retires satisfied that he had "been for a moment nearer God" in his melancholy thoughts. A. C. Benson as public essayist here reflects his harder, private rejections of institutional religion and Christianity as form, but, at the end, pulls back into an expected aspirational longing for religious insight.

It is a balancing act that his readers clearly found attractive, as they bought and read his books in their tens and even hundreds of thousands. A. C. Benson, indeed, may be thought in this way to speak for his generation—in his shifting lack of commitment, his growing distaste for the institutions of the church, while maintaining his grumpy and pious sentimental public engagement with forms of worship and publishing a string of essays that allowed his readership to absorb a more critical stance by ameliorating such a negative position with a pose of longing for a more spiritual grasp. It in these tensions of reticence and disdain, critical dismissiveness and social form, recollection of fear and longing for love, that A. C. Benson finds a religious expressiveness that is both his own response to a particular family dynamic and a sign of the shifting culture of religion in Edwardian and post-Edwardian England. It may well be that Arthur's havering is the more telling instrumental force at this turning point in the history of the Anglican Church than either Fred's insouciance or Hugh's rebellion.

Arthur Benson's havering is instrumental because it is public and, indeed, spoke to such a large public—much as did Hugh's writing and preaching on religion, or, for that matter, Fred's wry reflections on the passing of time. It is in this sort of personal politics that the Benson brothers spoke for a generation. Although each moved in literary circles that stretched from Walter Pater through to Henry James and Virginia Woolf, and in sexual circles that abutted the world of Thomas Carpenter and Oscar Wilde, their life, public or private, seems never to have engaged seriously with "the brilliant sunrise" that Olive Schreiner recalled in the socialism of the 1880s, nor with the literary feminism of Amy Levy, nor with the institutional politics of Keir Hardie. Retrospective, teleological history has made heroes of such political figures, and the modern portrait of the fin de siècle has placed them center stage, at least in one dominant academic perspective. The politics of the personal was a burning issue for these nascent socialist elites too, for sure, amid the broad theorizing. The clash between accusations of faddishness (à la Bernard Shaw) and thoroughgoing reconstructions of a way of life (à la Thomas Carpenter) was enacted in constant debates in small cabals about free love, the duties of comradeship, vegetarianism, Jaeger clothes, or the means of production: a parallel, as it were, to the common-room and drawing-room discussions that took up the Bensons' evenings. But, for very many more middle-class people than were touched by such elite, theoretical, socialist political debates, it was the space epitomized by A. C. Benson's writings on religion and the turmoil of self-understanding that allowed a developing personal politics over these transformational years. (The Bensons themselves repeatedly talked, slightly regretfully, about how middle class they were.) Even for Fred, it was easy to dismiss London's socialist aesthetics out of hand: "A band of April-eyed young brothers singing revolutionary ditties and bent on iconoclasm is disastrous to any clear conception of what was actually going on." It is a telling insight into the barriers that continued to be erected within networks of social interaction in this period that the Bensons could come so close to so many politically active groups and so many politically committed individuals, and yet maintain their absolutely discrete distance.

Yet it is even more telling that their *aesthetics* of reticence has thus also a *political* vector of disengagement: a detour around commitment. E. F. Benson's *As We Are* includes a chapter called "The Shadow Falls on the Parable House," where the effects on a stately home of postwar economics and the consequent social upheavals are asked to stand as a microcosmic index for major social shifts in the country, but where, perhaps inevitably for a Benson, the real focus of his narrative turns out to be the indifference of children to the concerns of their parents. Disengagement is both the style and the matter of his story; a helpless recognition of a new social division, over dinner: "But all the evening these two generations, typical of those in a thousand other homes, had been ill at ease and ill-fitting." If the impact of the socialism of the 1880s in Britain is to be fully appreciated—especially when set in contrast with the violent revolutions, say, of Germany or Russia—then it needs to be seen against the pervasive, reticent politics of personal anxiety exemplified in the work of Arthur Benson. Conversion, change, the abyss of social transformation run through the Benson narratives—but, for Arthur above all, this awareness of the trajectory of modernity leads to introspection and even mental breakdown before it broaches the possibility of committed and concerted political activity. The paradigmatic modernist obsessions with artistic self-expression, sexuality, the inheritance of religion, self-understanding, for the Bensons lead to a politics of the personal that constantly turns away from grand, historical gestures toward the lonely stare across the college courtyard, across the dark losses of time and memory, in search for some grounding for belief.

24

Capturing the Bensons

HUGH'S CONVERSION WAS THE DEFINING POINT OF HIS LIFE in his own mind and in the representations of him that others essayed. He practiced conversion: he remained "a man of single purpose. His objects were the conversion of Anglicans and the salvation of Catholics." Conversion is both a narrative of internal change and a cognitive experience, whereby a subject's knowledge or perception of the world is transformed—sometimes by external imposition. (The *Bildungsroman*, the novel of a growth into identity, is one nineteenth-century model for telling such stories, which both mimics and feeds into contemporary narratives of religious change, as the writing of the era traces the transitions of the era.) Edward White Benson was a staunch and fervent Christian whose life was changed, he said, by the death of his oldest son. Minnie Benson's evangelical conversion to a personal God realigned her sense of the world, to the extent that she could rejoice at the death of her son—but she spent many years of conflict over her desire for women and her faith. Arthur Benson was riven between public and private expressions of doubt and had nothing but anger for either Fred's lack of concern or Hugh's excessive concern for certainty and authority. All three boys found ways to stand out against their parents' religiosity and against each other—in strident or more subtle forms of conversion.

My story in this book has been how a narrative of change across the period from 1850 to 1940—in writing, sexuality, and religion—can be traced through the Benson family's history, not because they are normal and thus exemplary but because they are queer and yet paradigmatic.

Writing, sexuality, and religion are in this story intertwined as practices of self-formation: they are three practices in and through which the self articulates a place in society, develops a psychological narrative, finds a location within history and within the family. Of course, as with so many histories, we approach the Bensons today primarily through the writing they left behind, but it is the historically specific technologies and sociology of writing—all those letters, diaries, books—that make up the particularity of their shared cultural world of the word: to write down the self, as Edward White Benson put it, is the constant aim and struggle of such expressivity. And so much of what they write about is tied up with shifting engagements with sexuality and religion, against an especially fraught sense of change in both spheres: for each of them, writing down the self inevitably requires a narrative of desire and an expression of personal and institutional commitment to the inwardness of their spiritual life. In each sphere, and in their interrelations, the transition from strategies of earnestness, directness, commitment to those of reticence, indirection, and morbid self-consciousness marks this family history—as society itself, in the eyes of its citizens, from the 1860s to the 1890s to the 1920s recognized new possibilities of openness, relaxation of rigid norms, loosening of social form.

Patterns of conversion are thus integral to this history of change, both as a narrative form and as a mode of knowing. The peculiarity of this family and their personal stories of change are also a history of a culture's development. But the relation between the story of a culture and the story of a family is fraught and hard to disentangle. At one level, all the Bensons were acutely aware of their potential as agents within society, from the archbishop and his contribution to policy at the highest levels of state, to his wife and her "cases," to Hugh as a preacher, Arthur as a teacher and essayist, and Fred as a novelist and commentator. Maggie, too, wrote, excavated, and produced a new account of the Egyptian past; and Nellie's brief life of charitable social work was supported by a posthumous book. Each, in their own way, strove to make for themselves a place in history—often by writing history—and to change the world they were in.

Yet the potential for action and self-understanding is only articulated within a particular social framework, as well as within a particular family dynamic. Arthur's or Minnie's experience of sexuality is not only a personal story but formed in and through the legal, medical, religious, psychological, and social expectations of a generation. It is not enough, however, to say—though it always trivially true to say it—that the Bensons were "of their time." Each was increasingly aware and articulate about the chasm that separated themselves from their own family's past; each felt the weight of modernity and often felt "untimely" or out of their own time—though feeling untimely might also be a sign of the times, when historical self-consciousness is made a defining stance of the period. Indeed, most tellingly, each was aware and expressed their awareness strongly of how they were out of place—not usual, normal, typical—in psychological state, in sexuality, in writing, in religious responses—even as a family. Each talks repeatedly of how things are changing, and how conscious they are of the change around them, and the changes within themselves. The Benson family is a test case for the self-awareness of change in an era of rapid social change.

The Bensons are a very queer family indeed, then, not because they are sexually, intellectually, socially transgressive—though there are many ways in which they are so, just as there are many ways in which they are as establishment as it is possible to be. Rather they are queer because they embody the sheer difficulty of self-understanding within such overlapping narratives of conversion or change. Queerness is what makes naming, and the understanding that comes with naming, uncertain. (One should always hear the query in queerness.) The three boys—Arthur with his constant hesitations, Hugh with his brash certainties but from an aggressively other place, Fred with his studied refusal to engage—are each responding to their father's and mother's religiosity, but in so doing also encapsulate something emblematic about the multiple self-positionings that made the transition between the high Victorian world and first decades of the twentieth century possible and conflicted.

PART
IV

NOT
I . . .

25

Not I . . .

I LIKE TO TEACH OUTSIDE IN THE SUMMER, TO SIT ON THE grass by the river with my students and talk about the ancient Greek plays that I have spent so much of my life studying. Each summer, for several years, as we sat discussing in the sun, I would see one of the college porters amble purposively toward me, reach our small group, and then say, "Oh sorry, Dr. Goldhill. Mr. Rylands phoned to say that there were some tourists on the grass. He can't have known it was you." I understood that Dadie Rylands had looked out from his rooms above the Old Lodge in King's, seen a bunch of young, hairy people sitting on the hallowed college grass, and sent the porters to clear them off and leave his view of the river undisturbed. Dadie was by then in his nineties, the oldest fellow of the college, and could still be seen trotting elegantly across the front court back toward his rooms—he always seemed to be about to break into a run. I couldn't really expect that he would recognize me: it was a goodly distance and anyway I was a new, young fellow. We hadn't been introduced.

The porter's embarrassed interruption of my class gave me the chance to explain to my students that up there—I could point to it—was the room where Virginia Woolf had had that lunch with a fellow of King's, which she describes in *A Room of One's Own*, and that very fellow was now looking at them. Some of the classics students had no idea what I was talking about, and a brief education followed; others were thrilled that a moment of their imaginary life, cherished from reading about the Bloomsbury Group in Cambridge, or from early forays into feminist writing, had suddenly become real. I also told them that it was fascinating that Virginia Woolf, when she described her lunch with a college fellow, did not mention that he was a stunningly beautiful young man.

Back in the 1920s, Dadie Rylands had blond, floppy hair, high cheekbones, and blue eyes, and turned heads everywhere he went. After his undergraduate time at Cambridge, when he was hanging around Bloomsbury and its publishing business, his face was on the side of London buses advertising cigarettes. He had also been the last crush of Arthur Benson, and there are some striking photographs of the old, walrus-like Benson walking arm in arm with the dapper young Dadie in his double-breasted suit. When Dadie complained to the porters about the group sitting on the grass, I had no interest in the Bensons. By the time I had started work on this project, Dadie had died, and I had lost the wonderful opportunity of asking him what it was like to hang out with Arthur Benson after the First World War. While I taught my students by the river, I did not know what I was going to want to know.

It can be an uncanny experience to work on the Bensons while living and working in Cambridge. I cycle to work every day past where Llandaff House stood, the building where Hugh Benson lived when he returned as a Catholic to Cambridge; and then past the Granary on Silver Street where Arthur lived. H1 in King's, where Arthur had his life-changing experience of possibly sexual horror, is the office where Stephen Cleobury, the director of King's Choir, played through the piano transcription of Mendelssohn's *Antigone* for me when I was researching German Idealism and tragedy. I spent a long and painful summer reading through the 180 volumes of A. C. Benson's diary in Magdalene College library. "I thought I would go to dine at King's," he would write, and I would put down my pencil and walk back down to King's for lunch. The more he wrote about his depression, the more gloomy I became (though I had other reasons to feel miserable, too, that summer). When "Land of Hope and Glory" is blasted out every year at the last night of the Proms, for

me its image of unreflective triumphalist patriotism is now pleas-
ingly undermined with the thought of its author's, Arthur Benson's,
tortured sense of reticent selfhood. Every year the famous service of
Nine Lessons and Carols is broadcast from King's College Chapel
around the world, a service my grandfather, a Jew from Liverpool,
loved to listen to, religiously, as it were: for me, now, it will always
be a service invented—as it was—by Edward White Benson, patriarch of a queer family. Now, as the service unfurls its order, starting
with the solo boy treble singing "Once in Royal David's City," I
can't help but hear inside my head the Benson boys' anxieties about
their father; Edward himself turning his gaze on the eleven-year-
old Minnie; and the archbishop's lifelong attempt to keep order in
the church and his family. The whole family, with their continuing
love of the aesthetics of the Anglican Church, had sat so often in
King's Chapel. The service now has very paradoxical and disturbing
echoes. It has been strange to work on the Bensons in Cambridge.

But I can see my friends Mary Beard and Helen Morales rolling
their eyes at any such romanticism of "the very place where," and
the narcissism of the male world of the colleges (or worse). And in
reality such feelings played almost no role in the motivation or production of this book. I saw no reason to go to Rye to see where Fred
lived, and, although I have stood where Edward White Benson died,
it came as a real shock at the time, because I was in Gladstone's private chapel at Harwarden for quite other reasons and found myself
by chance reading the mournful little plaque that marks the spot: I
had simply forgotten that this was where Edward had keeled over.
I was quite excited when I found in a secondhand bookshop Minnie Benson's copy of Mrs. Oliphant's autobiography with Maggie's
dedication and Arthur's essay written into it, and I did buy the volume, which the seller had not opened and consequently sold for a
pittance. But the other volume I found with Maggie's signature was
interesting only because it had Maggie's signature, and I couldn't see
the point of owning it. The actual starting point for the research for
this book was first coming across Minnie Benson and being trans-
fixed by her story as a Victorian woman—as others have been. She

FIGURE 8: Arthur and Dadie Rylands, his last crush, striding forth.

opened for me an idea of another Victorian world. I had already read some E. F. Benson, *David of King's* in particular (of course), and seen an occasional episode of the first TV adaptation of *Mapp and Lucia*, but without much excitement. It was really only when I bought a secondhand copy of Fred's book *Mother*—in Los Angeles of all places, after lunch with a fellow of Newnham—that I became hooked: not just on Minnie Benson but on the son's compulsive retelling of the story of his mother—and from there the idea of this book came into shape. That was more than ten years ago, and it has taken a very long time, amid other work, to gain a working knowledge of the vast Benson archive. For a classicist, trained to read everything relevant, it has been a daunting task to get to the point of writing. It was no doubt because the story that emerged from the sources spoke so clearly to my long-term scholarly interests in writing, sexuality, and religion that it has kept my attention for so long.

These interests in writing, sexuality, and religion were honed in my professional career teaching and working on Greek tragedy. But there is no doubt in my mind that the environment in which I worked also played a formative role in my attention to the Bensons. When I came to King's College in 1975 as an undergraduate— and I have worked there ever since—it was an instantly revelatory place. Coming from an argumentative North London family and a school that was both seriously committed to intellectualism in a way which the modern educational czars would find baffling, and seriously committed to theater, jazz, and art in a way which few schools cherish now or cherished then, I found the febrile intellectual atmosphere of the college at that time immediately embracing. I had not yet the political nous to recognize how privileged this life was, nor the historical experience to recognize how rare it was, nor the self-awareness to see that this might not be true for everyone there. I just thought this was what academic life was.

It was revelatory also in a social and sexual way that I would later recognize in the reminiscences of the Bensons and Charlie Ashbee and Goldsworthy Lowes Dickinson. King's then was the first place I had been—and my experience was pitifully thin in such matters—

where a significant variety of sexual self-expression was on show and accepted not just without demurral but with joyful panache. Now, of course, coming of age is coming of age and is always troped as revelatory, however banal and clichéd. And, of course, one of the great potentials of a university is to throw together people of different backgrounds and ages. But nonetheless a combination of different factors did make this time—even with a more mature perspective—a particular juncture, a now passed moment of transition in British society.

The 1970s were an era of profound change across Britain. It was in this decade that the divorce rate started to rise exponentially; the so-called sexual liberation of the 1960s had finally reached the Home Counties; alternative modes of living were being tested with a confidence that violent social upheavals and political unrest did not yet undermine. And Cambridge had its own particular version of this cultural moment. Colleges had just begun to become mixed—in King's, the first previously all-male college to accept women, the first female students had arrived only three years before I started there. There was still a sense of the experimental. The politics of the personal dominated conversation and the possibilities of social transformation seemed inspirational. If you were researching this era, you would find not only that the government report on obscenity and film censorship was written by the Provost of King's, Bernard Williams, but also that the *Sunday Times* sent a young journalist, Tina Brown, to write a long and prurient magazine piece about King's and the new college life: a handful of self-appointed beautiful students, arm in arm, stared out from the cover of the color supplement. The self-obsessed, elitist bubble seemed to the newspaper to be the sign of something new in English life. In the newspaper's portrayal, a different world was erupting for the students, or at least the students they chose to write about. Flamboyantly camp gay men screamed and kissed in the bar; relationships of all sorts were public, explicit, physical, and gossiped about. The atmosphere of sheer reveling in such freedom was palpable. It was an image many cared to live up to.

Yet there was still also a predominant older culture that had been formed when homosexual acts were illegal and when the social pressures against public expressions of homosexuality were intense. As a young man I was invited to garden parties by older dons, to stand around in white trousers and a blazer and to drink champagne. Late nights of conversations with older men were fenced around, without any direct indication of sexuality. Twenty years later in a restaurant in Texas, a retired expatriate classicist reminisced to me about the old days—older than mine—when after many weeks of intimacy, a single kiss outside the college gate would feed the imagination and the heart for months to come. There were men, too, who had been steadily drinking themselves into oblivion over the years, in self-loathing or buried despair. King's College itself had a long tradition of a supportive gay life—as Arthur Benson himself had observed with shocked confusion. I was told the college stories: how Boris Ord, the organist, had been arrested and imprisoned for cottaging—picking up men in a public lavatory—and when he returned to King's and dined shamefacedly at High Table for the first time, the icy silence was broken by another don who said loudly, "Don't worry, Boris, old chap, it could have happened to any one of us." The college's annual report contained—and still does—the most wonderful short obituaries of its members. One read: "He was distinguished among his contemporaries not only for his great height but also for his pronounced heterosexuality." There was a constructed genealogy of sexual liberalism, a story the college told itself of itself, proudly. What I now regard as traces of the social world that the Bensons knew, were still visible, and the connections back into that time embodied in the expectations and the lives of people around me.

So it is very likely that my writing of the Bensons in the way that I have is very much the product of living through that juncture, a particular time and place and story: conditions of possibility do determine what can be seen and said. One of the biggest changes in my lifetime in Britain has been the growing public acceptance, legally and culturally, of being gay—for all the shocking and horrific violence and disdain that still mar individual experience. I have lived for most of my adult life in a place where queerness has been self-consciously nourished—where an Anglican Chaplain's farewell speech to the college could be a rousing clarion call for "more dykes" on the college's fellowship. It would be crass to turn one's eyes away from the conservative thrust of the media, the Hollywood film or newspaper morality to which so much of public discourse plays lip service, but meanwhile, meanwhile, nothing less than a social revolution has been taking place. And such is one determinative context for writing this book.

At its grandest, then, this book claims to be about how modern society took shape in and against a nineteenth-century heritage. But it will also be immediately obvious that it has had little to say about economic history, high political narratives, the upheavals of class conflict, and many other aspects of what would properly play a role in the history of how modern society came to be what it is. It has, in this respect, followed the trajectory of the Benson children themselves, at least, who, despite or because of their father's position at the heart of British power in a way not now accorded to archbishops, resolutely avoided political thought and political engagement—despite the potential for forming the relationships that would have led to such engagement, not least through Arthur's and Fred's connections in the Cambridge and London literary scenes. So it would be better to say that this book is really about how modern identity finds some of its major lineaments: how is a life story told, what role does sexuality play in an understanding of the self, and what place is there for religion in personal and social formation? The agenda here has been first and foremost a plea for the value of complexity—standing out, on the one hand, against the silencing of historical depth in such areas, the forgetting of the richness of the nineteenth-century past and the intricacy of the processes of transition away from it; and, on the other, standing out against the trivialities that so easily dominate the language and narratives of sexual identity, life stories, and religious commitment in our contemporary public discourse. Revolutions flourish on slogans; but this account has tried to offer a case for a more nuanced sense of how distorting and uncomprehending such slogans can be.

With any story based on a family, there is an evident danger of parochialism, even with an archbishop's family, even when he is the head of the Anglican communion at the height of the British Empire—and the danger is especially insistent when the story has so often roamed around Cambridge, where the story's author lives. But the value of taking a single family as a route into such large questions stems not just from the extraordinary detail and nuance of its records; nor just from the sharply vivid perspective it gives on the politics of the personal; nor just from its ability to reveal how changes in sexual discourse, psychological theorizing, religious belief, strategies of self-representation, take shape over time and as a process of change—on the ground, as it were. Rather, the single family also establishes a fascinating question of exemplarity, which lies at the heart of this book—and in two ways.

First, it asks how much a family can speak for history, to what degree the story of a family encapsulates the history of a time. This is a family that is both decisively odd, and yet expresses so much of what is distinctive about the transitions from the later nineteenth century to the interwar years. How paradigmatic—and of what— should the Benson family be thought to be? Second, the family also sets up a reflective and self-exposing mirror for contemporary readers. It was for me a continuing problem not to assimilate the Bensons to my modern expectations. It was hard, for example, not simply to call Minnie or Arthur gay; not to talk about Hugh with an eye on recent lurid accounts of repressed and not so repressed homosexual drives in the Catholic Church; not to frame their expectations of elitism as a failure of modern ideals of gender awareness or political equality. Yet this practice of attentiveness to historical specificity did not only reveal something about turn-of-the-century models of psychological self-understanding, but also about my own formation within contemporary paradigms of expectation and the particular intellectual and social environment in which I have been lucky enough to work. To talk of one family may seem parochial, but as most people grow up within some form of family life, it is a parochialism that speaks to a more general condition, and understanding another family's oddities is always also a process of self-definition. I take it that such self-awareness is a necessary condition for the understanding of complexity that is at the core of the historical aims of this book.

When enough people had asked me how I had come to study the Bensons to make me feel that such a coda as this would be appropriate, I began with Beckett's *Not I* in my mind as a working title. The illuminated autobiographical mouth with its transfixing voice, which seems to echo with trauma but which is so hard to turn into a single coherent narrative, resonated powerfully with the stories I had been tracing and seemed to capture a tellingly different modernist aesthetic of fragmentation, indirection, and revelation. But the expression "Not I" quickly seemed like a gesture of withdrawal from what was all too clearly a self-implicating narrative, however academic in formation. How families tell, retell, and remold stories, how a life is expressed, how sexuality finds expression, what a religious commitment involves, are all questions that demand a place and a position from which they are explored. How could "Not I" be any starting point for such a project, even with an ironic nod to the aesthetics of reticence? Or, if you like, when you sound out such questions, they also sound out you.

This, then, has been a long journey to try to understand the story of a kiss. Which was not just a kiss, at least in the minds of a growing circle of people, from Minnie's mother at the time to Fred, sixty years later—let alone for the girl and her future husband, a pious man of twenty-three, a girl of twelve . . . The effort to understand this story is also—for everyone involved—an exercise in sexual, religious, and narrative self-understanding.

Bibliography and Notes

IT SHOULD BY NOW BE CLEAR THAT I MADE A DECISION not to engage directly or by name with the secondary scholarship in the body of my text, though I hope these notes give a guide, for those who want one, to where I have benefited most from others' research and where I see the thrust of my argument making a contribution to more delimited and focused scholarly debates. The book, I hope, will speak not just to those who want to think about writing, sexuality, and religion—which includes most of us, I suppose—but also scholars engaged in contemporary discussions of queer theory, life-writing, religious history, theories of conversion, and so forth. But I have not entered the usual academic cut and thrust of "he says," "she says," but "I think . . . ," nor have I offered another doxography of queer theory or the like, because it would have made the book much longer and been distracting from the argument: it is designedly not that sort of book. I have not, even in these notes, engaged in correcting others' transcriptions from the manuscripts where they are wrong, or other such mistakes; nor have I indulged myself in criticizing others' arguments when they have seemed to me hopelessly misguided, bread and butter though such disagreements are to my philological bent. Scholars who wish to see dues paid and where exactly in the contemporary debate my work lies will be able to get that from these endnotes.

For each chapter I have provided first a highly selective general bibliography, with necessary cross-references to other chapters; and second a running set of references for specific quotations, specific titles cited, and some specific references where particular books are specially relevant. I have tried to keep things to a minimum rather than aiming at exhaustiveness. Works in a chapter's opening bibliography are given a short title in the notes; others are given are a full reference in the notes.

ABBREVIATIONS:

ACB = Arthur Benson's diary, by volume number and folio from the Pepys Library Magdalene College, Cambridge.
BFP = Benson Family papers, by class number, from the Bodleian Library, Oxford.

Part I: The Family That Wrote Itself

CHAPTER 1: SENSATION!

For the major modern biographies of the Bensons, see the following:

Askwith, B. *Two Victorian Families*. London, 1971.
Bolt, R. *As Good as God, As Clever as the Devil: The Impossible Life of Mary Benson*. London, 2011.
Grayson, J. *Robert Hugh Benson: Life and Works*. Lanham, MD, 1988.
Lubbock, P. *The Diary of Arthur Christopher Benson, a Selection*. London, 1927.
Martindale, C. *The Life of Monsignor Robert Hugh Benson*, 2 vols. London, 1916.
Masters. B. *The Life of E. F. Benson*. London, 1991.
Newsome, D. *Godliness and Good Learning: Four Studies on a Victorian Ideal*. London, 1961.
Newsome, D. *On the Edge of Paradise: A. C. Benson, the Diarist*. London, 1980.
Newsome, D. *Edwardian Excursions: From the Diaries of A. C. Benson*. London, 1981.

Palmer, G., and N. Lloyd. *The Father of the Bensons: The Life of Edward White Benson, Sometime Archbishop of Canterbury*. Harpenden, 1998.

Ryle, E. H., ed. *Arthur Christopher Benson, as Seen by Some Friends*. London, 1925.

Watt. R. *Robert Hugh Benson: Captain in God's Army*. London, 1918.

Williams. D. *Genesis and Exodus: A Portrait of the Benson Family*. London, 1979.

Bolt, *As Good as God*; Newsome, *On the Edge of Paradise*; and Masters, *E. F. Benson* are especially useful and readable. There are also dozens of contemporary obituaries and memoirs.

For the Bensons' own biographical writing on their own family and selves, see the following:

Benson, A. C. *Mary Eleanor Benson: A Memoir*. London, 1891.

Benson, A. C. *The Life of Edward White Benson, Sometime Archbishop of Canterbury*. 2 vols. London, 1899.

Benson, A. C. *Life of Edward White Benson*. 1 volume. London, 1901.

Benson, A. C. *Hugh: Memoirs of a Brother*. London, 1915.

Benson, A. C. *Life and Letters of Maggie Benson*. London, 1917.

Benson, A. C. *The Trefoil: Wellington College, Lincoln and Truro*. London, 1923.

Benson, A. C. *Memories and Friends*. London, 1924.

Benson, A. C. *Mary Benson: A Memoir*. Rye, 2010.

Benson, E. F. *Our Family Affairs, 1867–1896*. London, 1920.

Benson, E. F. *Mother*. London, 1925.

Benson, E. F. *As We Were: A Victorian Peep-Show*. London, 1930.

Benson, E. F. *Final Edition: Informal Autobiography*. London, 1940.

Benson, M. E. *Streets and Lanes of the City, with a Brief Memoir by Her Father*. Privately printed, 1891.

Benson, R. H. *Confessions of a Convert*. London, 1913.

Essays by the Bensons that pertain to their own experience and lives include the following:

Benson, A. C. *From a College Window*. London, 1906.
Benson, A. C. *Along the Road*. London, 1912.
Benson, R. H. *Papers of a Pariah*. London, 1907.

A.C. Benson's diary is in the Pepys Library, Magdalene College, Cambridge; Edward White Benson's diary is in the Wren Library, Trinity College, Cambridge; the Benson Family Papers, including Minnie Benson's diaries, are in the Bodleian Library, Oxford.

Notes

For the history of Victorian biography, see below, pp. 310–11.
For the place of Minnie in lesbian historiography, see below, pp. 315–17, especially Vicinius.
"Treated him with a half lover-like, half paternal adoration": E. F. Benson, *As We Were*, 59; a "Romantic and devoted affection," 58.
Life of Thomas Arnold, see A. P. Stanley, *Life and Correspondence of Thomas Arnold* (London, 1845).
Story of Crummel of Queen's: A. C. Benson, *Edward White Benson*, 109.
"No gesture in the world has ever seemed so formidable": A. C. Benson, *Mary Benson*, 61.
"She did not often walk with us . . . ," A. C. Benson, *Mary Benson*, 31, 32.
"A nightmare of grief and dismay": A. C. Benson, *Mary Benson*, 115.
"Her married life . . .": A. C. Benson, *Mary Benson*, 116.
"Her friendships were seldom leisurely . . .": A. C. Benson, *Maggie Benson*, 46, 122.
"Remorseless": A. C. Benson, *Maggie Benson*, 52.
Adam Phillips, *Becoming Freud: The Making of a Psychoanalyst* (New Haven, CT, 2014).
"Wholly unrecognisable": A. C. Benson, *Mary Benson*, 77.
"The bright, clever, superficial self . . .": E. F. Benson, *Mother*, 174.
"To set me on my guard against impure temptation . . .": A. C. Benson, *Mary Benson*, 45.
"It was thought that a denial of Christianity . . .": Sir Alfred Denning, *Freedom Under the Law* (London, 1949), 46.
Bruno Latour, *We Have Never Been Modern* (Cambridge, MA, 1993).

CHAPTER 2: WOOING MOTHER

Gay, P. *Bourgeois Experience: Victoria to Freud*. 3 vols. New York, 1985–93.
Michie, H. *Victorian Honeymoons: Journeys to the Conjugal*. Cambridge, 2006

Rose, P. *Parallel Lives: Five Victorian Marriages*. London, 1983.

Rowbotham, J. *Good Girls Make Good Wives: Guidance for Girls in Victorian Fiction*. Oxford, 1989.

Notes

"The old order of secure prosperity . . .": E. F. Benson, *As We Were*, 344.

"Real gulf, vastly sundering . . .": E. F. Benson, *As We Were*, 22.

"Men and women now discuss . . .": E. F. Benson, *As We Were*, 22.

"Frankness and freedom . . .": E. F. Benson, *As We Were*, 23.

"Smiling oasis . . .": E. F. Benson, *As We Were*, 25.

"Outward form of dignity and politeness": E. F. Benson, *As We Were*, 85.

"The true spirit of Victorian reticence . . .": E. F. Benson, *As We Were*, 224.

"Reads like some extraordinary . . .": E. F. Benson, *Mother*, 8.

"There was he . . .": E. F. Benson, *Mother*, 8.

"Seemed to have been . . .": E. F. Benson, *Mother*, 9.

"An earnest, young Victorian wooer": E. F. Benson, *As We Were*, 62.

"I have always been very fond . . .": E. F. Benson, *As We Were*, 60–64. The reading of Tennyson's *The Princess* is a typically layered moment: Tennyson used this poem in wooing his wife—and then it was used for the children as an educational text: both elements of which are poignant for Edward's choice of reading with Minnie: see E. Jones and P. Weliver, "*The Princess* and the Tennysons' Performance of Childhood," in *The Edinburgh Companion to Literature and Music*, ed. D. da Sousa Correa (forthcoming).

"And then this little authentic . . .": E. F. Benson, *As We Were*, 64.

"From that time onwards . . .": E. F. Benson, *As We Were*, 66.

"She looked out on to an inconceivable emptiness": E. F. Benson, *Mother*, 34.

"It was as if some earthquake . . .": E. F. Benson, *Mother*, 38.

"All the beauty of our past life . . .": E. F. Benson, *Mother*, 40–43.

"Mother rather feared . . .": BFP 1/71–80: March 17, 1898.

"I remember my mother saying . . .": A. C. Benson, *Mary Benson*, 16.

"A terrible time . . .": BFP 1/71–80: March 17, 1898.

"Edward Benson's child-bride . . .": A. C. Benson, *Mary Benson*, 18.

"Misery . . .": BFP 1/71–80: March 17, 1898.

"He restrained his passionate nature . . .": BFP 1/71–80: March 17, 1898.

"A triumph of surrender . . .": E. F. Benson, *Mother*, 18.

"She obliterates herself completely . . .": E. F. Benson, *Mother*, 19.

"No doubt at the behest of my father . . .": A. C. Benson, *Mary Benson*, 23.

"You must not measure . . .": BFP 1/71–80: Minnie Benson to Edward White Benson, 1858.

"Ah mine own love . . .": BFP 1/71–80: Minnie Benson to Edward White Benson, June 3, 1859.

"I wd have died rather than anyone . . .": BFP 1/71–80: March 17, 1898.

"Good Lord, give me a personality . . .": E. F. Benson, *Mother*, 40–41.

"I have fallen to pieces . . .": E. F. Benson, *Mother*, 42.

"I have never had time . . .": E. F. Benson, *Mother*, 42.

"She always seemed so secure . . .": ACB, CLXXI, 16.

"Not one touch of self-pity . . .": E. F. Benson, *Mother*, 43.

"Appeared to suffer no loss . . .": E. F. Benson, *Mother*, 43.

"72.73", "4th period . . .": BFP 1/71–80.

"Morbid and self-scrutinizing mood . . .": A. C. Benson, *Mary Benson*, 87.

"From the time when . . .": A. C. Benson, *Edward White Benson*, 143–44.

"I need not define the strains . . .": ACB, III, 70.

"At present he has said nothing . . .": BFP 3/73: Minnie Benson to Hugh Benson September 14, 1900.

"My mother, I gather . . .": A. C. Benson, *Mary Benson*, 17.

"But her diary is very painful . . .": cited in Palmer and Lloyd, *Father of the Bensons*, 203–4.

Eliza Lynn Linton: G. S. Layard, *Mrs Lynn Linton: Her Life Letters and Opinions* (London, 1901); N. F. Anderson, *Woman Against Women in Victorian England: A Life of Eliza Lynn Linton* (London, 1987) (the title indicates her take); A. L. Broomfield, "Eliza Lynn Linton, Sarah Grand and the Spectacle of the Victorian Woman Question: Catch Phrases, Buzz Words and Sound Bites," *English Literature in Transition 1880–1920* 47 (2004): 251–72; On Sarah Grand: A. Richardson, *Love and Eugenics in the Late Nineteenth Century: Rational Reproduction and the New Woman* (Oxford, 2003), 95–126; G. Kersley, *Darling Madam: Sarah Grand and Devoted Friend* (London, 1983), with the useful collection of Grand's writings: A. Heilman and S. Forward, eds., *Sex, Social Purity and Sarah Grand*, 4 vols. (London, 2001).

"She said it was rather romantic . . .": BFP 3/4–5: Mary Benson to Edward White Benson, December 1, 1852.

Social Purity Campaigns: P. Levine, *Prostitution, Race and Politics: Policing Venereal Disease in the British Empire* (New York, 2003); J. Walkowitz, *Prostitution and Victorian Society: Women, Class and the State* (Cambridge, 1980); J. Weeks, *Sex, Politics and Society: The Regulation of Sexuality since 1800* (London, 1980); E. Bristow, *Vice and Vigilance: Purity Movements in Britain since 1700* (Dublin, 1977).

Sabine Baring-Gould: S. Goldhill, *Victorian Culture and Classical Antiquity: Art, Opera, Fiction and the Proclamation of Modernity* (Princeton, NJ, 2011), 213–15; W. Purcell, *Onward Christian Soldier: A Life of Sabine Baring-Gould, Parson, Squire, Novelist, Antiquary* (London, 1957).

Ruskin and Gray continue to fascinate critics: T. Hilton, *John Ruskin: The Early Years* (New Haven, CT, 1985) has not stopped the prurience most influentially inaugurated by M. Lutyens, *Millais and the Ruskins* (London, 1957); see from different angles, S. Cooper, *The Model Wife: Effie, Ruskin and Millais* (London, 2010); R. Brownell, *Marriage of Inconvenience: John Ruskin and Euphemia Gray* (London, 2013).

CHAPTER 3: BRINGING UP THE SUBJECT

Chase, K., and M. Levenson. *The Spectacle of Intimacy: A Public Life for the Victorian Family*. Princeton, NJ, 2000.

Notes

On Henry Sidgwick, see the magisterial B. Schultz, *Henry Sidgwick: Eye of the Universe: An Intellectual Biography* (Cambridge, 2004)—particularly good on his relationship to Edward White Benson.

"I wish I could just come . . .": cited in Bolt, *As Good as God*, 27.

"This desire was formulated . . .": A. C. Benson, *Edward White Benson*, 144.

"I earnestly hope . . .": this and the following quotations come from BFP 3/4–5: Mary Benson's Letters to Edward White Benson.

"M let <u>me</u> . . .": BFP 3/4–5: Mary Benson's Letters to Edward White Benson, August 28, 1852.

"Mama wanted me . . .": BFP 1/71–80.

"<u>I wasn't true</u>": BFP 1/71–80.

"Dear Minnie . . .": BFP 3/4–5: Mary Benson to Edward White Benson, March 2, 1853.

"Minnie is a most affectionate . . .": BFP 3/6: Edward White Benson to Mary Benson, July 30, 1858.

"You don't think . . .": BFP 3/6: Edward White Benson to Mary Benson, August 18, 1858.

"Believe me though . . .": BFP 3/15: Edward White Benson to Minnie Benson, n.d. (probably 1859).

On letters, see C. Golden, *Posting It: The Victorian Revolution in Letter Writing* (Gainesville, FL, 2009). For the formational earlier period, see (with further bibliography) David Vincent *I Hope I Don't Intrude: Privacy and Its Dilemmas in Nineteenth-Century Britain* (Oxford, 2015), 190–228.

CHAPTER 4: FIFTY WAYS TO SAY I HATE MY FATHER

Broughton, T. *Men of Letters, Writing Lives: Masculinity and Literary Auto/biography in the Late Victorian Period.* London, 1999.

Broughton, T., and H. Rogers, eds., *Gender and Fatherhood in the Nineteenth Century.* Basingstoke, 2007.

Nelson, C. *Invisible Men: Fatherhood in Victorian Periodicals, 1850–1910.* Athens, GA, 1995.

Sanders, V. *The Tragi-Comedy of Victorian Fatherhood.* Cambridge, 2009.

Tosh, J. *A Man's Place: Masculinity and the Middle-Class Home in Victorian Britain.* New Haven, CT, 1999.

Notes

Oedipus as master plot, see Roland Barthes, *S/Z*, trans. R. Miller (London, 1991).

On Gosse, A. Thwaite, *Edmund Gosse: A Literary Landscape, 1849–1928* (London, 1983), is head and shoulders above other treatments.

"As touchy as a housemaid . . .": Virginia Woolf reviewing Sir Evan Charteris's

Life and Letters of Sir Edmund Gosse (London 1931), reprinted in Virginia Woolf, *Collected Essays* (London, 1966), vol. IV, 81–87.

"At the present hour . . .": E. Gosse, *Father and Son: A Study of Two Temperaments* (London, 1907), preface.

"It seems to me now profoundly strange . . .": E. Gosse, *Father and Son*, 332.

"Like an old divine": E. Gosse, *Father and Son*, 335.

"Beautiful . . ." ACB, LXXXI, 22; "A book I should have liked . . .": ACB, XCVII, 54.

"Unique and noble . . .": E. Gosse, *Father and Son*, 338.

"Kept the spiritual cord . . .": E. Gosse, *Father and Son*, 338.

"The letter . . .": E. Gosse, *Father and Son*, 330.

"Not ashamed": E. Gosse, *Father and Son*, 331–32.

"Hints, he qualifies . . .": Virginia Woolf, *Collected Essays* (London, 1966), vol. IV, 86.

"When I was a small boy . . .": S. Butler, *The Way of All Flesh* (London, 1916), 1.

"Bitter pill . . .": S. Butler, *The Way of All Flesh*, 414.

"Because he . . .": S. Butler, *The Way of All Flesh*, 456.

"His father's instincts . . .": S. Butler, *The Way of All Flesh*, 456.

"Of your inner life . . .": S. Butler, *The Way of All Flesh*, 194.

"Every man's work . . .": S. Butler, *The Way of All Flesh*, 70.

Anthropology too as a discipline was formed in scholars' rejections of their parents' religiosity: see T. Larsen, *The Slain God: Anthropologists and the Christian Faith* (Oxford, 2014).

"I do not think . . .": A. C. Benson, *Edward White Benson*, 206.

"In spite of the fact that . . .": A. C. Benson, *The Trefoil*, 253.

"Extracted from . . .": A. C. Benson, *Arthur Hamilton*, title page.

"A very religious man . . .": A. C. Benson, *Arthur Hamilton*, 1.

"Asked him rather sharply . . .": A. C. Benson, *Arthur Hamilton*, 4.

"He had suspected all along . . .": A. C. Benson, *Arthur Hamilton*, 28.

"He disliked his father . . .": A. C. Benson, *Arthur Hamilton*, 4.

"Mr Challoner—though drawn . . .": ACB, LVII, 40.

"I never got a true perspective of him": E. F. Benson, *Our Family Affairs*, 105.

"I deplore . . .": E. F. Benson, *Challoners*, 23.

"He was so intensely serious . . .": E. F. Benson, *Challoners*, 14.

"Herein lay the secret tragedy . . .": E. F. Benson, *Challoners*, 15.

"His passion springing . . .": E. F. Benson, *Challoners*, 14.

"As wanton and wicked . . .": E. F. Benson, *Challoners*, 279.

"You get angry . . .": E. F. Benson, *Challoners*, 56.

"He felt and felt truly . . .": E. F. Benson, *Challoners*, 56.

"There was Rex's mother . . .": E. F. Benson, *Rex*, 60.

"Why, he's got your father's name . . .": E. F. Benson, *Rex*, 62.

On *Dodo*, see E. F. Benson, *Our Family Affairs*, 297–311.

"He was aware . . .": E. F. Benson, *Rex*, 8.

"Never from his earliest days . . .": E. F. Benson, *Rex*, 28.

"If only Sinai . . .": E. F. Benson, *Rex*, 32.

"You're no son of mine . . .": E. F. Benson, *Rex*, 148.

"Would the mouth open . . .": E. F. Benson, *Rex*, 181.

"Had not, it would seem, been in love . . .": E. F. Benson, *Rex*, 15.

CHAPTER 5: TELL THE TRUTH, MY BOY

Notes

"The awful sight": A. C. Benson, *Edward White Benson*, 203.

"Sadly addicted to lying" (and story of being whipped): A. C. Benson, *Edward White Benson*, 22.

"Returned to find hideously bad lying . . .": A. C. Benson, *Edward White Benson*, 213.

"Real candour . . .": A. C. Benson, *Edward White Benson*, 204. Edward Lyttelton, close friend and colleague of Edward White Benson, became headmaster of Eton and continued such concerns well into the 1880s: see E. Lyttelton, *Causes and Prevention of Immorality in Schools* (London, 1883).

"I never, his mother never . . .": Edward White Benson, biography of Martin Benson, Trinity College. See Newsome, *Godliness and Good Learning*, 158.

"I can never be sure . . .": ACB, LI, 42–43.

"I know less of what Fred . . .": ACB, CXI, 11.

"Freddian": BFP 3/60.

"Little writing . . .": ACB, IV, 35.

"I write to my friends . . .": ACB, LXXXIX, 11.

"I don't think that many families . . .": ACB, LXXII, 62–63.

"One thing I claim . . .": ACB, XVIII, 74.

"Makes no claim to be complete . . .": A. C. Benson, *Memories and Friends*, vii.

"If I am posing all the time": ACB in 1905, cited by Newsome, *On the Edge of Paradise*, 6.

"What an odd book . . .": ACB, LXI, 60.

"I can't speak or write . . .": ACB, III, 259.

"I reflect that . . .": ACB, XXV, 59. I wonder if A. C. B. was thinking here of the famous lines toward the beginning of Dickens's *Tale of Two Cities*: "A wonderful fact to reflect . . . that every one of those darkly clustered houses encloses its own secret; that every room in every one of them encloses its own secret; that every beating heart in the hundreds and thousands of breasts there, is, in some of its imaginings, a secret to the heart nearest it!" (10).

"So near to my heart . . .": A. C. Benson, *Thread of Gold*, 13.

"Percy says I make . . .": ACB, CXLVII, 44.

"In fact, he never knew himself . . .": Percy Lubbock, ed., *Diary of Arthur Christopher Benson*, 18.

"Intime style . . .": ACB, LXIV, 54.

"But the sticking of the autobiographical . . .": ACB, LX, 36.

"Sayle dined . . .": ACB, CXVI, 19.

"Sayle rather horrified me . . .": Newsome, *On the Edge of Paradise*, 247; on ACB's reaction to Sayle's death, see the evocative description in Newsome, *On the Edge of Paradise*, 371–73.

"He committed no indiscretions . . .": ACB, LXXXVII, 3.

"The most terrible thing . . .": ACB, LXXXIII, 73.

"A genuine piece of self-expression": E. F. Benson to Mr. Manson, January 23, 1936, UCLA Library 177/129, quoted in Masters, *E. F. Benson*, 215. The surprising success of *David Blaize* among the soldiers is not as surprising as the success of the play *Pinkie and the Fairies*, a sentimental children's story of the loss of fairyland, starring Ellen Terry, which night after night reduced soldiers to tears in 1908: see T. Dixon, *Weeping Britannia: Portrait of a Nation in Tears* (Oxford, 2015), 209–11.

"The three ladies most perceptive": ACB, LXIII, 26.

"It distresses me . . .": ACB, CLXXIX, 30–31.

"I did intuitively regard it . . .": Henry James, *Collected Letters*, vol. II, November 15–18, 1913.

CHAPTER 6: A MAP OF BIOGRAPHICAL URGES

Amigoni, D. *Victorian Biography: Intellectuals and the Ordering of Discourse*. Hemel Hempstead, 1993.

Amigoni, D., ed. *Life Writing and Victorian Culture*. Aldershot, 2006.

Atkinson, J. *Victorian Biography Reconsidered: A Study of Nineteenth-Century "Hidden" Lives*. Oxford, 2010.

Bowler, P. *The Invention of Progress: The Victorians and the Past*. Oxford, 1989.

Broughton, T. *Men of Letters, Writing Lives: Masculinity and Literary Auto/biography in the Late Victorian Period*. London, 1999.

Corbett, M.-J. *Representing Femininity: Middle-Class Subjectivity in Victorian and Edwardian Women's Autobiographies*. Oxford, 1992.

Cox, P. *Biography in Late Antiquity: The Quest for the Holy Man*. Berkeley, 1983.

Fleishman, A. *Figures of Autobiography: The Language of Self-Writing in Victorian and Modern Britain*. Berkeley, 1983.

Gagnier, R. *Subjectivities: A History of Self-Representation in Britain, 1832–1920*. Oxford, 1991.

Goldhill, S. *Who Needs Greek? Contests in the Cultural History of Hellenism*. Cambridge, 2002.

Homans, M. *Bearing the Word: Language and Female Experience in Nineteenth-Century Women's Writing*. Chicago, 1986.

Jones, H. *Revolution and Romanticism*. Cambridge, MA, 1974.

Larsen, T. *Contested Christianity: The Political and Social Contexts of Victorian Theology*. Waco, TX, 2004.

Lejeune, P. *On Autobiography*, trans. K. Leary. Minneapolis, 1989.

Levine, G. *The Boundaries of Fiction: Carlyle, Macaulay, Newman.* Princeton, NJ, 1968.

Marcus, L. *Auto/biographical Discourses.* Manchester, 1994.

Nussbaum, F. *The Autobiographical Subject.* Baltimore, 1989.

Olney, J. *Studies in Autobiography.* Oxford, 1988.

Olney J. *Autobiography: Essays Theoretical and Critical.* Princeton, NJ, 1980.

Pals, D. *The Victorian "Lives" of Jesus.* San Antonio, TX, 1982

Peterson, L. *Victorian Autobiography: The Tradition of Self-Interpretation.* New Haven, CT, 1986.

Saunders, M. *Self Impression: Life-Writing, Autobiografiction, and the Forms of Modern Literature.* Oxford, 2010.

Vincent, D. *Bread, Knowledge and Freedom: A Study of Nineteenth-Century Working Class Autobiography.* London, 1981.

Notes

On Keble, see K. Blair, *Form and Faith in Victorian Poetry and Religion* (Oxford, 2012). "Medicine divinely bestowed . . .": John Keble, *Lectures on Poetry* (Oxford, 1912), vol. 1, 22.

"The taste for poetry . . .": John Henry Newman, *Essays Critical and Historical* (London, 1873), vol. 1, 290–91, with e.g., D. deLaura, *Hebrew and Hellene in Victorian England: Newman, Arnold and Pater* (Austin, TX, 1969).

"Wordsworth unconsciously did . . .": William Hale White, *The Autobiography of Mark Rutherford* (London, 1881), 19.

"Instruction in all . . .": cited with excellent discussion by S. Gill, *Wordsworth and the Victorians* (Oxford, 2001).

"A medicine for my state of mind": John Stuart Mill, *Autobiography*, 7th ed. (London, 1882), 148.

"Preacher and prophet . . .": Charles Kingsley, letter to his wife in *Charles Kingsley, His Letters, and Memories of His Life*, ed. F. Kingsley (London, 1899), vol. 1, 96.

"There has been no biography . . .": R. Goodbrand, "A Suggestion for a New Kind of Biography," *Comparative Review* 14 (1870): 20.

U. von Möllendorf-Wilamowitz, Review of Georg Misch (1907) in *Kleine Schriften* (Berlin, 1972), vi, 123–24, well discussed by C. Guthenke, "'Lives' as Parameters: The Privileging of Ancient Lives as a Category of Research around 1900," in *Creative Lives: New Approaches to Ancient Intellectual Biography*, eds. R. Fletcher and J. Hanink (Cambridge, forthcoming). In contrast to the nineteenth-century emphasis on the self, the possibility of family intellectual biography is now being tested: see, e.g., D. Coen, *Vienna in the Age of Uncertainty: Science, Liberalism and Private Life* (Chicago, 2007).

Historical moment: see R. Koselleck, *Futures Past: On the Semantics of Historical Time*, trans. K. Tribe (Cambridge, MA, 1985); R. Koselleck, *The Practice of Conceptual History: Timing History, Spacing Concepts*, trans. T. Presner et al.

(Stanford, CA, 2002); S. Bann, *The Clothing of Clio: A Study of the Representation of History in Nineteenth-Century Britain and France* (Cambridge, 1984); J. W. Burrow, *A Liberal Descent: Victorian Historians and the English Past* (Cambridge, 1981); P. Fritzsche, *Stranded in the Present: Modern Time and the Melancholy of History* (Cambridge, MA, 2004); and, with particular relevance to the third section of this book, T. Howard, *Religion and the Rise of Historicism: W. M. L. de Wette, Jacob Burckhardt, and the Theological Origins of Nineteenth-Century Historical Consciousness* (Cambridge, 2006).

Thomas Carlyle: see, e.g., A. LaValley, *Carlyle and the Idea of the Modern* (New Haven, CT, 1968); A. Du Quesne, *Carlyle* (London, 1982); J. Rosenberg, *Carlyle and the Burden of History* (Oxford, 1985); with the background of S. Collini, *Public Moralists: Political Thought and Intellectual Life in Britain, 1850–1930* (Oxford, 1991).

Plutarch: see S. Goldhill, *Who Needs Greek? Contests in the Cultural History of Hellenism* (Cambridge, 2002), 246–93.

Psychological development: see S. Shuttleworth and J. Taylor, *Embodied Selves: An Anthology of Psychological Texts, 1830–1890* (Oxford, 1998); S. Shuttleworth, *The Mind of the Child: Child Development in Literature, Science and Medicine, 1840–1900* (Oxford, 2010)—with extensive bibliography.

Henry Sidgwick: see Schultz, *Henry Sidgwick*.

Lives of Jesus: see D. Pals, *Victorian "Lives" of Jesus* (San Antonio, TX, 1980); on Mrs. Ward, see J. Sutherland, *Mrs Humphry Ward: Eminent Victorian, Pre-eminent Edwardian* (Oxford, 1990); on Seeley, see D. Wormell, *Sir John Seeley and the Uses of History* (Cambridge, 1980); on losing faith, see R. Wolff, *Gains and Losses: Novels of Faith and Doubt in Victorian England* (New York, 1977); T. Larsen, *Crisis of Doubt: Honest Faith in Nineteenth-Century Britain* (Oxford, 2006).

"Diet yourself on biography . . .": E. Bulwer Lytton, *The Caxtons* (London, 1875), 232–33.

"Pressures of secularization . . .": M. Saunders, *Self-Impression*, 16.

"In deference to . . .": W. Brock, *A Biographical Sketch of Sir Henry Havelock, K.C.B.* (London, 1864), vii. For the publishing figures and contrast between Brock and Dickens, see Atkinson, *Victorian Biography*, 16. Tosh, *A Man's Place*, 174–75, notes how biographies of Havelock became less domestic as the century progressed.

Alfred Lord Tennyson, "Havelock." See also P. Brantlinger, *Rule of Darkness: British Literature and Imperialism, 1830–1914* (Ithaca, NY, 1988); B. Deane, *Masculinity and the New Imperialism: Rewriting Manhood in British Popular Literature, 1870–1914* (Cambridge, 2010).

On Macaulay, see J. Clive, *Thomas Babington Macaulay: The Shaping of the Historian* (London, 1973); C. Hall, *Macaulay and Son: Architects of Imperial Britain* (New Haven, CT, 2013).

"It is not a Life at all . . .": E. F. Benson, *As We Were*, 97.

"The true conception of biography . . .": E. Gosse, in *Encyclopaedia Britannica*, 11th ed. (Cambridge, 1911), vol. 3, 954; on Gosse, see A. Thwaite, *Edmund Gosse* (London, 1984).

P. De Man, "Autobiography as Defacement," *Modern Language Notes* 94 (1979): 919–30.

T. Carlyle, "Biography," in *English and Other Critical Essays* (London, 1915), vol. 1, 65–79.

"Reference and resemblance" is taken from the outstanding M. Saunders, *Self-Impression*, 141–42.

On William Hale White, see especially M. Saunders, *Self-Impression*, 110–24.

"We hardly know whether to call them fiction . . .": William Dean Howells, *Harper's* 72 (1886): 485–86, cited in Saunders, *Self-Impression*, 120.

"The story of my own life . . .": L. Stephen, "Biography," *National Review* 22 (1893): 179.

On Froude, see C. Brady, *James Anthony Froude: An Intellectual Biography of a Victorian Prophet* (Oxford, 2013); and for the scandal, see Broughton, *Men of Letters*, chaps. 3–5; for Oliphant's role, see D. Trela, "Margaret Oliphant, James Anthony Froude and the Carlyles' Reputation: Defending the Dead," *Victorian Periodicals Review* 29 (1996): 199–215.

"This is not a British statue . . .": M. Roberts, *The Private Life of Henry Maitland* (London, 1912), ix.

"Bitter, bad book . . .": Ford Madox Ford, "Literary Portraits—XXVIII: Mr Morley Roberts and *Time and Thomas Waring*," *Outlook* 33 (1914): 390–91.

"It was not his memory . . .": E. F. Benson, *Final Edition*, viii.

CHAPTER 7: TO WRITE A LIFE

Notes

"Read Haydon's Diary . . ." and other quotations on reading biographies: ACB, LXII, 35; on Farrar: ACB, LIV, 2; on Spencer: ACB, LIV, 4; on Scott: ACB, LVIII, 12.

"It is the answer . . .": ACB I, August 23, 1897.

Herbert Paul, *Stray Leaves* (London, 1906), 273. On Cory, see *Extracts from the Letters and Journals of William Cory*, ed. Francis Warre Cornish (Oxford, 1897); F. Compton Mackenzie, *William Cory: A Biography* (London, 1950). Reginald Viscount Esher, *Ionicus* (London, 1923). Benson's essay is the foreword to William Cory, *Ionica*, 3rd ed. (London, 1905). For a good background to such poems, see G. Nisbet, *Greek Epigram in Translation: J. A. Symonds, Oscar Wilde and the Invention of Desire, 1805–1929* (Oxford, 2013).

"I really love W.J.": ACB, XIX, 95.

"I read a few pages . . ."; "I wonder why": cited and discussed by Newsome, *On the Edge of Paradise*, 80. "He hated all that was cold . . .": ACB, XIX, 95. "Was bursting with suppressed . . .": ACB, XIX, 95.

"I wish I could feel . . .": ACB, XLIII, end page. "Felt truly ashamed . . .": ACB, LXIII, 26; "I could not tell her of the shadow . . .": ACB, XLVII, 31.

"I am here . . .": A. C. Benson, *Upton Letters*, 174.

On Symonds, see Horatio Brown, *John Addington Symonds: A Biography*, 2 vols. (London, 1905); P. Grosskurth, *Memoirs of John Addington Symonds* (London, 1984); B. Schultz, *Henry Sidgwick: Eye of the Universe. An Intellectual Biography* (Cambridge, 2004), s.v. Symonds; J. Pemble, ed., *John Addington Symonds: Culture and the Demon Desire* (Basingstoke, 2000), especially B. Schultz, "Truth and Its Consequences: The Friendship of Symonds and Henry Sidgwick," 22–45; P. Robinson, *Gay Lives: Homosexual Autobiography from John Addington Symonds to Paul Monette* (Chicago, 1999); G. Nisbet, *Greek Epigram in Translation: J. A.*

Symonds, Oscar Wilde and the Invention of Desire, 1805–1929 (Oxford, 2013); M. Kaplan, *Sodom on the Thames: Sex, Love, and Scandal in Wilde Times* (Ithaca, NY, 2005); Linda Dowling, *Hellenism and Homosexuality in Victorian Oxford* (Ithaca, NY, 1994).

"It was rather a fiasco . . .": Lubbock, *The Diary of Arthur Christopher Benson*, 234.

"To bed . . .": ACB, CXXII, 38.

"If I were a great writer . . .": ACB, LXVIV, 48–49. On form, see K. Blair, *Form and Faith in Victorian Poetry and Religion* (Oxford, 2012).

On Stephen Reynolds, see Saunders, *Self-Impression*, 165–207—a fine study.

"A man . . .": Stephen Reynolds, "Autobiografiction," *Speaker* 15, no. 66 (1906): 28, 30.

"But isn't it almost indecent . . .": ACB, LXXV, 18.

"Either extracted . . .": A. C. Benson, *House of Quiet*, 99.

"I do not know if . . .": A. C. Benson, *The Upton Letters*, 196; on Farrar and Spencer, 259–69.

"Read old letters . . .": ACB, LXIV, 70; "A bound vol . . .": ACB, XXXIX, 18; "I found a bundle . . .": ACB, LXIV, 71; "I read Maggie's Letters . . .": ACB, CLX, 38.

"In spite of the fact that . . .": A. C. Benson, *The Trefoil*, 253.

"What awful depths . . .": A. C. Benson, *The Trefoil*, 249; "My father struggling . . .": 250; "I learned long after . . .": 157.

"For if her marriage . . .": E. F. Benson, *Mother*, 12; "little authentic . . .": E. F. Benson, *As We Were*, 64; "remote enough . . .": 61; "tenderly and exquisitely": 64.

"Personality . . . so dominant . . .": R. H. Benson, *Confessions of a Convert*, 6; "kind of despairing impatience": 11; "rather oppressive . . .": 12; "the appalling atmosphere . . .": 15; "I felt . . . as the roof were lifted . . .": 16.

"A life of her own": A. C. Benson, *Mary Benson*, 32; "they were not wholly happy . . .": 39; "she formed a very close . . .": 40; "she was in the frame of mind . . .": 51.

"Though they all . . .": E. F. Benson, *Final Edition*, 101–4.

CHAPTER 8: WOMEN IN LOVE

Cholmondeley, M. *Red Pottage*. London, 1899

Cholmondeley, M. *Prisoners (Fast Bound in Misery and Iron)*. London, 1906.

Cholmondeley. M. *Under One Roof, a Family Record*. London, 1918.

Lubbock, P. *Mary Cholmondeley: A Sketch from Memory*. London, 1928.

Oulton, C., and S. Schatz, eds. *Mary Cholmondeley Reconsidered*. London, 2010.

Oulton, C. *Let the Flowers Go: A Life of Mary Cholmondeley*. London 2009.

Peterson, L. *Becoming a Woman of Letters: Victorian Myths of Authorship, Facts of the Market*. Princeton, NJ, 2009, esp. 207–24.

Notes

"I dictated . . .": ACB, LXXXIX, 23; "dreadful mass . . .": ACB, CLIV, 44; "the
most curious . . .": ACB, LXVIII, 15–16.

"Now this is a very difficult . . .": ACB, XXIV, 75; "If the worst . . .": ACB, XXIV,
76; "I am uneasy . . .": ACB, XXV, 66; "Marriage would solve it . . .": ACB,
LXXXV, end paper.

"An exquisitely selfish . . .": E. F. Benson, *Final Edition*, 78; "Quite a high . . .": 78;
"grossly and intentionally . . .": 79.

"MB in private . . .": ACB, LXXX, 17.

"What sent me into a gloom . . .": ACB, LXXXV, 51; "a vicious, harsh . . .": ACB,
LXXXVI 61.

"The whole thing was a storm . . .": E. F. Benson, *Final Edition*, 79.

"Not at all": ACB, CLV, 32.

"I don't think any writer ever . . .": ACB, CLII, 12; "the gift passed . . .": P. Lubbock, *The Diary of Arthur Christopher Benson*, 278; "Churlish to go on . . .":
Newsome, *On the Edge of Paradise*, 323.

CHAPTER 9: GRAPHOMANIA

Notes

L. Davis in *Obsession: A History* (Chicago, 2008), especially 105–24, attempts to link
graphomania to the nineteenth-century obsession with obsession.

History of postal service: Kate Thomas, *Postal Pleasures: Sex, Scandal and Victorian
Letters* (Oxford, 2014).

"I have just woken . . .": ACB, CLXXX, May 18, 1925.

Part II: Being Queer

From the sprawling, vast and often brilliant bibliography on Victorian sexuality, here are some of the books that are especially relevant
for this section:

Bland, L. *Banishing the Beast: English Feminism and Sexual Morality,
1885–1914*. London, 1995.

Castle, T. *The Apparitional Lesbian: Female Homosexuality and Modern
Culture*. New York, 1993.

Cocks, H. *Nameless Offences: Homosexual Desire in the 19th Century*. London, 2003.

Cook, M. *London and the Culture of Homosexuality, 1885–1914*. Cambridge, 2003.

Dellamora, R. *Masculine Desire: the Sexual Politics of Victorian Aestheticism.* New York, 1990.

Dellamora, R. *Victorian Sexual Dissidence.* Chicago, 1999.

Doan, L. *Fashioning Sapphism: The Origins of a Modern Lesbian Culture.* New York, 2001.

Doan, L. *Disturbing Practices: History, Sexuality, and Women's Experience of the Great War.* Chicago, 2013.

Foldy, M. *The Trials of Oscar Wilde: Deviance, Morality, and Late Victorian Society.* New Haven, CT, 1997.

Foucault, M. *History of Sexuality*, vol. 1, trans. R. Hurley. New York, 1978.

Gay, P. *The Bourgeois Experience: Victoria to Freud.* London, 1983.

Gibson, I. *The Erotomaniac: The Secret Life of Henry Spencer Ashbee.* London, 2001.

Hall, L. *Sex, Gender and Social Change in England since 1880.* 2nd ed. Houndsmills, 2012.

Kaplan, M. *Sodom on the Thames: Sex, Love and Scandal in Wilde Times.* Ithaca, NY, 2005.

Katz, J. N. *Love Stories: Sex between Men Before Homosexuality.* Chicago, 2001.

Koven, S. *Slumming: Sexual and Social Politics in Victorian London.* Princeton, NJ, 2004.

McLaren, A. *The Trials of Masculinity: Policing Sexual Boundaries, 1870–1930.* Chicago, 1997.

Marcus, S. *Between Women: Friendship, Desire, and Marriage in Victorian England.* Princeton, NJ, 2007.

Marcus, S. *The Other Victorians: A Study of Sexuality and Pornography in Mid-Nineteenth-Century England.* New York, 1966.

Mason, M. *The Making of Victorian Sexuality, and the Making of Victorian Sexual Attitudes.* Oxford, 1994.

Medd, J. *Lesbian Scandal and the Culture of Modernism.* Cambridge, 2012.

Poovey, M. *Uneven Developments: The Ideological Work of Gender in Victorian Britain.* London, 1989.

Porter, R., and L. Hall. *The Facts of Life: The Creation of Sexual Knowledge in Britain, 1650–1950.* New Haven, CT, 1995.

Richardson, A. *Love and Eugenics in the Late Nineteenth Century: Rational Reproduction and the New Woman.* Oxford, 2003.

Robb, G. *Strangers: Homosexual Love in the Nineteenth Century.* New York, 2003.

Roberts, M. *Making English Morals: Voluntary Associations and Moral Reform in England, 1787–1886.* Cambridge, 2004.

Roden, F. *Same-Sex Desire in Victorian Religious Culture.* Basingstoke, 2002.

Rowbotham, S. *Edward Carpenter: A Life of Liberty and Love.* London, 2008.

Sedgwick, E. *Between Men: English Literature and Male Homosocial Desire.* New York, 1985.

Sedgwick, E. *Epistemology of the Closet.* Berkeley, 1994.

Terry, J. *An American Obsession: Science, Medicine and Homosexuality in Modern Society.* Chicago, 1999.

Tosh, M. *A Man's Place. Masculinity and the Middle-Class Home in Victorian England.* New Haven, CT, 1999.

Vicinus, M. *Intimate Friends: Women Who Loved Women, 1778–1928.* Chicago, 2004.

Waites, M. *The Age of Consent: Young People, Sexuality and Citizenship.* Basingstoke, 2005.

Walkowitz, J. *City of Dreadful Delight: Narratives of Sexual Danger in Late Victorian London.* Chicago, 1992.

Weeks, J. *Sex, Politics and Society; the Regulation of Sexuality since 1800.* London, 1989.

CHAPTER 10: WHAT'S IN A NAME?

Bland, L., and L. Doan, eds. *Sexology in Culture: Labelling Bodies and Desires.* Cambridge, 1998.

Notes

Daphnis and Chloe: see S. Goldhill, *Foucault's Virginity: Ancient Erotic Fiction and the History of Sexuality* (Cambridge, 1990).

My Secret Life: see Marcus, *Other Victorians*; Gibson, *Erotomaniac*; S. Goldhill, "The Imperialism of Historical Arrogance: Where Is the Past in the DSM's Idea of Sexuality?" *Archives of Sexual Behaviour* (2015).

Goldsworthy Lowes Dickinson: M. Proctor ed., *Autobiography, Goldsworthy Lowes Dickinson* (London, 1973); A. Crawford, *C. R. Ashbee: Architect, Designer, and Romantic Socialist* (New Haven, CT, 1985); on Carpenter, see Rowbotham, *Edward Carpenter*; L. Ghandi, *Affective Communities: Anti-Colonial Thought, Fin-de-siècle Radicalism, and the Politics of Friendship* (Durham, NC, 2006), 34–66.

Acton and the Contagious Diseases Act: W. Acton, *Prostitution, Considered in Its Moral, Social and Sanitary Aspects, in London and Other Large Cities: With Proposals for the Mitigation and Prevention of Its Attendant Evils* (London, 1857); W. Acton, *Practical Treatise on Diseases of the Urinary and Generative Organs* (London, 1851); also see P. Levine, *Prostitution, Race and Politics: Policing Venereal Disease in the British Empire* (London, 2003); E. Bristow, *Vice and Vigilance: Purity Movements in Britain since 1700* (Dublin, 1977); F. Mort, *Dangerous Sexualities: Medico-Moral Politics in England since 1830* (London, 1987); J. Walkowitz, *Prostitution and Victorian Society: Women, Class and the State* (Cambridge, 1980).

For Boulton and Park, and Cleveland street scandals, see Cook, *London*; K. Thomas, *Postal Pleasures: Sex, Scandal and Victorian Letters* (Oxford, 2012); Kaplan, *Sodom on the Thames*, with Cocks, *Nameless Offences;* and for more general legal questions of masculinity, and the even more surprising case of Augustine Hall, see McLaren, *Trials of Masculinity*, 37–130.

W. T. Stead "The Maiden Tribute of Babylon," *Pall Mall Gazette*, July 1885.

"He does not feel . . .": ACB, LXVII, 11.

"Mrs Craigie has sent me . . .": ACB, XLIX, 14–15.

"Saying that her view . . .": ACB, XLIX, 24.

"Pathologizing of sexuality": see Foucault, *History of Sexuality*; D. Halperin, *One Hundred Years of Homosexuality and Other Essays on Greek Love* (New York, 1990); Katz, *Love Stories*.

"And then came a further surprise . . .": ACB, LII, 27—Latinists will also wonder about a pun on *ilia*: groin, thighs.

"Your two breasts . . .": *Song of Songs* 4.5.

"My darkest hours . . .": ACB, XXXVIII, 65.

"So passionate in expression . . .": A. C. Benson, *Memoirs of Arthur Hamilton*, 24; "weak, but singularly attractive boy": Benson, 24; "truly chivalrous . . .": Benson, 23; "I can hardly picture . . .": Benson, 24; "The other's was an unworthy . . .": Benson, 24; "I do not wholly know . . .": Benson, 26.

On the dangers of discovery, as well as Cocks's *Nameless Offences*, see for the brutal 1820s, C. Upchurch, "Politics and the Reporting of Sex between Men in the 1820s," in *British Queer History: New Approaches and Perspectives*, ed. B. Lewis (Manchester, 2013), 17–38.

CHAPTER 11: THOUGH WHOLLY PURE AND GOOD

Notes

Foucault, *History of Sexuality*; Cocks, *Nameless Offences;* Dellamora, *Masculine Desire*; Kaplan, *Sodom of the Thames*; McLaren, *The Trials of Masculinity*.

"Talk of a Rabelaisian kind . . .": ACB, VII, 184–85.

"I can never think of Mason . . .": Newsome, *On the Edge of Paradise*, 26.

Greek Anthology: see Nisbet, *Greek Epigram in Reception*.

"But, oh dear me, my heart . . .": ACB, XXX, 121.

"Then there was the Arthur Mason adoration . . .": ACB, XXXIV, 131.

"I woke early . . .": ACB, XXIX, 73.

"Boys do not know . . .": ACB, LII, 64.

On beastliness, see T. Laqueur, *Solitary Sex: A Cultural History of Masturbation* (New York, 2003); J. Stengers and A. van Neck, *Masturbation: The History of a Great Terror*, trans. K. Hoffman (New York, 2001); T. Jeal, *Baden-Powell, Founder of the Boy Scouts* (New Haven, CT, 1989).

"Can one trust . . .": ACB, LIII, 11–12.

On Howard Sturgis, friend of Henry James and Edith Wharton, "most feminine" of Benson's friends (Lubbock, *Diary*, 157), whose long-term companion was known as the Babe, a nickname that appears in E. F. Benson's novels, especially *The Babe B.A.*, see S. Gunter and S. Jobe, eds., *Dearly Beloved: Henry James' Letters to Young Men* (Ann Arbor, MI, 2001), especially 115–21. Newsome, *On the Edge of Paradise*, 183–269, catalogs the loves of Benson with Leporello-like zeal.

"P.L. is making . . .": ACB, III, 279.

The story of O.: ACB, LIII, 25.

"I think my selfish nature . . .": ACB, CVIII, 22; "Free love": ACB, CVIII, 39–40; "But it <u>must</u> be very surprising . . .": ACB, CVIII, 44; "These are very odd . . .": ACB, CVIII, 59.

"The public fondling . . .": ACB, CVIII, 70.

"I feel that I c^d almost . . .": ACB, CXII, 10.

"Pretty, irreproachably dressed . . .": ACB, XXI, 22—*deliciae* is a standard term from Latin love poetry for the object of desire.

"There comes one of the most <u>intime</u> . . .": ACB, LXIV, 74.

"graceful, ardent, impetuous . . .": ACB, LXVIII, 67–68.

"I was reading some scraps . . .": ACB, LXXXII, 83; on Hugh Walpole, see R. Hart-Davis, *Hugh Walpole: A Biography* (London, 1985)—which to my mind underplays the importance to both Benson and Walpole of their relationship.

"Behaves as a son . . .": ACB, LXXXII, 83.

"A long and lover-like kiss . . .": Newsome, *On the Edge of Paradise*, 261.

"How attractive was the pagan . . .": E. F. Benson, *Colin* (London, 1923), 213–15.

"Almost innocent shamelessness": E. F. Benson, *As We Are*, 81.

On Capri and the role of the Mediterranean in the Victorian and Edwardian imagination, see J. Pemble, *The Mediterranean Passion: Victorians and Edwardians in the South* (Oxford, 1987).

"We spoke . . .": ACB, CLXXVIII, 8.

"We discussed the homo sexual . . .": ACB, CLXXIV, 27. Teresa de Lauretis's adoption of Irigaray's term "hommo-sexual," followed by many feminists since, would be a pertinent cross-reference here: see T. de Lauretis, "Sexual Indifference and Lesbian Representation," *Theatre Journal* 40 (1988): 155–77.

On the invention of heterosexuality, see L. Doan, "'A Peculiarly Obscure Subject': The Missing 'Case' of the Heterosexual," in *British Queer History: New Approaches and Perspectives*, ed. B. Lewis (Manchester, 2013), 87–108; and the fuller and more provocative, J. N. Katz, *The Invention of Heterosexuality* (Chicago, 2005).

"As long as he had a pretty boy . . .": ACB, CLXXV, 39; Sayle holding hands: ACB, CLXXV, 40; "I expect S. was a homo sexual person . . .": ACB, CLXXV, 40. "He goes about . . .": ACB, CXVI, October 16, 1910. On Sayle, see J. C. T. Oates, "Charles Edward Sayle," *Transactions of the Cambridge Bibliographical Society* VIII, no. 2 (1982): 236–69. Those familiar with Cambridge might like to know that he was the son of Robert Sayle, the founder of the city's best-known department store.

R. Barthes, *S/Z* (Paris, 1970).

"O.R. has a morbid predilection . . .": ACB, CXXXIV, 43.

"Naturally pagan . . .": ACB, CLIV, 21. On neo-paganism, see R. Hutton, *The Triumph of the Moon: A History of Modern Pagan Witchcraft* (Oxford, 2000); M. Louis, "Gods and Mysteries: The Revival of Paganism and the Remaking of Mythology through the Nineteenth Century," *Victorian Studies* 47 (2005): 329–61; and R. Ackerman, *The Myth and Ritual School: J. G. Frazer and the Cambridge Ritualists* (New York, 1991).

"Had a <u>woman's</u> soul . . .": ACB, CXXIV, 2–3.

"I wonder why . . .": ACB, CXXIV, 13.

"The reproductive instinct . . .": ACB, CXXIV, 34.

"Told me several things . . .": ACB, CXXXV, 7.

"I can imagine a man . . .": ACB, LXV, 19.

"I am pleased to recognize . . .": ACB, CLIX, 45.

"I don't think . . .": Newsome, *On the Edge of Paradise*, 194.

"If one can trust a person . . .": Newsome, *On the Edge of Paradise*, 216. On the luminescently beautiful George Mallory, who was deeply involved with the Bloomsbury Group—he had an affair with Lytton Strachey's brother, before marrying, and dying on Mount Everest—see P. and L. Gilman, *The Wildest Dream: The Biography of George Mallory* (London, 2000).

It is hard to name Arthur Benson's queerness . . . : Lee Edelman's statement that "queerness can never define an identity; it can only ever disturb one" has prompted an extensive theoretical discussion, well traced in Doan, *Disturbing Practices*, 1–96; theory, as Doan notes, need not be set in opposition to a historical narrative based on archival sources: with Benson's diary we have an extraordinary document that traces a long-term and shifting engagement with an incipient pathologizing of sexuality: it is a performance of what has taken a long time to theorize. See L. Edelman, *No Future: Queer Theory and the Death Drive* (Durham, NC, 2004), and for further discussion of Edelman and queer theory in general, see, e.g., L. Huffer, *Mad for Foucault: Rethinking the Foundations of Queer Theory* (New York, 2010); S. Herring, *Queering the Underworld: Slumming, Literature and the Undoing of Lesbian and Gay History* (Chicago, 2007).

CHAPTER 12: HE NEVER MARRIED

Davidoff, L., M. Doolittle, J. Fink, and K. Holden, eds. *The Family Story: Blood, Contract and Intimacy, 1830–1960*. London, 1999.

Davidoff, L., and C. Hall *Family Fortunes: Men and Women of the English Middle Class, 1780–1850*. London, 1987.

Griffin, B. *The Politics of Gender in Victorian Britain: Masculinity, Political Culture and the Struggle for Women's Rights.* Cambridge, 2012.

Hammerton, A. J. *Cruelty and Companionship: Conflict in Nineteenth-Century Married Life.* London, 1992.

Michie, H. *Victorian Honeymoons: Journeys to the Conjugal.* Cambridge, 2006.

Peterson, M. *Family, Love, and Work in the Lives of Victorian Gentlewomen.* Bloomington, IN, 1989.

Notes

"Mama told me today . . .": ACB, II, 217.

"Much happier than the old bachelor . . .": ACB, III, 32–33.

"She is the fifth or sixth . . .": Viscount Esher, *Ionicus*, 98.

"Odd that I should begin . . .": F. Compton Mackenzie, *William Cory*, 51.

"I always wanted . . .": F. Compton Mackenzie, *William Cory*, 96.

"Subdued by the consciousness . . .": F. Compton Mackenzie, *William Cory*, 98.

"The years roll back . . .": F. Compton Mackenzie, *William Cory*, 159.

On J. A. Symonds, see P. Grosskurth, *John Addington Symonds: A Biography* (London, 1964); J. Pemble, ed., *John Addington Symonds: Culture and the Demon Desire* (Cambridge, 2000); S. Brady, *Masculinity and Male Homosexuality in Britain, 1861–1913* (Houndsmills, 2005), 157–209. On Henry James and "The Author of *Beltraffio*," see L. Edel, *Henry James, Volume IV: The Treacherous Years, 1895–1901* (New York, 1969), 114–21; L. Person, "James' Homo-Aesthetics: Deploying Desire in the Tales of Writers and Artists," *Henry James Review* 14 (1993): 188–203; L. Monk, "A Terrible Beauty Is Born: Henry James, Aestheticism, and Homosexual Panic," in *Bodies of Writing, Bodies in Performance*, ed. T. Foster., E. Barry, and C. Siegel (New York, 1996), 247–65.

"The difference between Christian and pagan . . .": Henry James, "The Author of *Beltraffio*" (Boston, 1885), 50–51.

On C. R. Ashbee, see Crawford, *C. R. Ashbee*; S. Goldhill, *The Buried Life of Things: How Objects Made History in Nineteenth-Century Britain* (Cambridge, 2014), 113–37.

"Comradeship . . ." letter, September 2, 1897, cited in F. Ashbee, *Janet Ashbee: Love, Marriage, and the Arts and Crafts Movement* (Syracuse, NY, 2002), 25; and discussed in Crawford, *Ashbee*, 75.

"I don't like being so much alone . . .": ACB, LII, 41.

"Oddly enough . . .": ACB, CXXIX, 52.

"He has formed habits . . .": ACB, XXI, 48.

"But I do rather hanker . . .": ACB, LV, 64.

"Of course the obvious thing . . .": ACB, LXX, 77.

"The incident of sexual intercourse . . .": ACB, CXIII, 17.

"MB and Lucy . . .": ACB, CXXXVI, 40.

"MB introduced the personal . . .": ACB, CXXXII, 53.

Telemachus: *Odyssey* 23, 104–20.

"Said she wondered why . . .": ACB, CLXII, 38.

"A very sad letter from Miss A . . .": ACB, CLXV, 42.

"Why is one brought up . . .": ACB, CLXXV, 40.

On Edwin Arnold, Mona Caird, and the Marriage Question, see Richardson, *Love and Eugenics*, 179–214; H. Quilter, ed., *Is Marriage a Failure?* (London, 1888), 2; "We had a most pleasant chat . . .": G. and W. Grossmith, "The Diary of a Nobody," *Punch* (November 17, 1888): 233.

On the New Woman, see P. Marks, *Bicycles, Bangs, and Bloomers: The New Woman in the Popular Press* (Lexington, KY, 1990); S. Ledger, *The New Woman: Fiction and Feminism at the Fin de Siècle* (Manchester, 1997); T. Mangum, *Married, Middlebrow, and Militant: Sarah Grand and the New Woman Novel* (Ann Arbor, MI, 1998); C. Gourley, *Flappers and the New American Woman: Perceptions of Women from 1918 through the 1920s* (Minneapolis, 2008); G. Cunningham, *The New Woman and the Victorian Novel* (London, 1978); A. Heilman, *New Women Fictions: Women Writing First-Wave Feminism* (Basingstoke, 2000).

"Devout and serious . . .": A. C. Benson, *Mary Benson*, 21.

"Our first home . . .": BFP, 1, 71–80, letter from Mary Benson to Edward White Benson, 1872, Sunday before Christmas.

"Tossings, doubts . . .": BFP, 1/79, 28; "The letter . . .": BFP, 1/79, 30.

On Ethel Smyth, see Vicinus, *Intimate Friends*, s.v. Smyth, especially 126–34.

"If there is such a thing . . .": Ethel Smyth, *As Time Went On* (London, 1936), 139.

"But oh! How I lament . . .": A. C. Benson, *Edward White Benson*, 764.

"I have scarcely . . .": ACB, LXXVII, 37.

"Precious balms . . .": E. F. Benson, *Our Family Affairs*, 105.

"If her marriage was a mistake . . .": E. F. Benson, *Mother*, 12.

"Her married life . . .": A. C. Benson, *Mary Benson*, 116.

Honor Moore, *The Bishop's Daughter: A Memoir* (New York, 2008); my thanks to Carol Gilligan, who put me on to this.

"Wives, be loyal . . .": H. C. G. Moule, *Colossian Studies: Lessons in Faith and Holiness from St Paul's Epistle to the Colossians and Philemon* (London, 1898), 234. Moule, like Benson, went to Trinity, Cambridge, became a fellow, then a schoolmaster, and then entered the church, with a crucial period spent at Durham. Moule's bizarre retranslation is discussed in context in the excellent Griffin, *Politics of Gender*, 132, which is particularly good on the political background alluded to in this paragraph. For discussion that focuses more on class and violence in marriage, see Hammerton, *Cruelty and Companionship*, which builds well on J. Gillis, *For Better, for Worse: British Marriages, 1600 to the Present* (New York, 1985). Gay, *The Bourgeois Experience*, has important background on the domestic too.

"The Eighties saw . . .": C. R. Ashbee, *Grannie* (Oxford, 1936), 59. The typescript of this privately printed memorial of his mother, written for his daughters, with many unpublished photographs, is in King's College, Cambridge, Modern Archive Centre. Bizarrely, like the Bensons, he called his mother "the Little Mother."

"I toiled . . .": BFP, 1/71–80, May 29, 1898; "seems to think . . .": June 4, 1898.

"Lucy and I . . .": BFP, 1/71–80, August 31, 1882; "Finally talk . . .": September 1, 1882.

"High price": Vicinus, *Intimate Friends*, 95.

CHAPTER 13: ALL LONDON IS AGOG

Notes

On the legal issues here, see in particular Cocks, *Nameless Offences*; Brady, *Masculinity and Male Homosexuality*.

"All went to their rooms . . ." E. F. Benson, *Final Edition*, 15–16.

"Mother's intimacies . . ." E. F. Benson, *Final Edition*, 12–13.

"My mother . . ." E. F. Benson, *Mother*, 23.

"A new female type . . ." E. F. Benson, *As We Are*, 40.

"She formed a very close friendship . . .": A. C. Benson, *Mary Benson*, 40.

On the Maud Allan trial, see Medd, *Lesbian Scandal*, 27–75, to which my discussion is especially indebted: Bland and Doan, eds., *Sexology in Culture*, 183–98; L. Doan, *Fashioning Sapphism*, 32–35; D. Cohler, *Citizen, Invert, Queer: Lesbianism and War in Early Twentieth-Century Britain* (Minneapolis, 2010). Interesting background stories in L. Cohen, *All We Know: Three Lives* (New York, 2012).

"Propagation of evils . . ." N. Billing, *Vigilante*, February 16, 1918, reprinted in *Verbatim Report of the Trial of Noel Pemberton Billing, M.P. on a Charge of Criminal Libel before Mr Justice Darling at the Central Criminal Court, Old Bailey*, ed. N. Pemberton Billing (London, 1918).

"You probably may have some idea . . .": *Verbatim Report*, 57.

"The Learned Counsel . . .": *Verbatim Report*, 57.

"There do exist . . .": *Verbatim Report*, 58.

"Clitoris is a Greek word . . .": *Verbatim Report*, 259.

"Are you aware . . .": *Verbatim Report*, 85.

"Intended the play . . .": *Verbatim Report*, 286.

"It is safe to say . . .": *Times*, June 5, 1918, 7.

On Winnington-Ingram, the standard biography, S. Carpenter, *Winnington-Ingram: The Biography of Arthur Foley Winnington-Ingram, Bishop of London 1901–1939* (London, 1949), should be read alongside the fine brief account in the *Oxford Dictionary of National Biography* by Jeremy Morris, which is much sharper on his politics.

"I am asking you . . .": *Hansard* 44 (March 9, 1921): 422, 423; "a most unnatural sin": 424.

On Macquisten, see Medd, *Lesbian Scandal*, 97–103.

"[In 1885] people found it difficult . . .": *Hansard*, 46 (August 4, 1921): 1802–3.

"The overwhelming majority . . .": *Hansard* [Lords] 14 (1921): 574.

"Simply to refer . . .": *Hansard* 46 (August 4, 1921): 1803.

"The study of the abnormal . . .": Havelock Ellis, *Studies in the Psychology of Sex, Volume II: Sexual Inversion* (London, 1927), 322; he is discussing Rudolf Virchow.

"Formerly it was assumed . . .": Edward Carpenter, *The Intermediate Sex* (London, 1912), 120, in his discussion of Ulrichs (on whom, see H. Kennedy, *Ulrichs: The Life and Works of Karl Heinrich Ulrichs, Pioneer of the Modern Gay Movement* [Boston, 1988]). On Carpenter, see S. Rowbotham, *Edward Carpenter: A Life of Liberty and Love* London, 2008; Ghandi *Affective Communities*; Katz *Love Stories*.

"To convince medical men . . .": cited and discussed in Doan, *Fashioning Sapphism*, 139.

"Practised now-a-days . . .": R. Krafft-Ebbing, *Psychopathia Sexualis*, 12th ed., trans. F. J. Rebman (New York, 1939), 396; on Krafft-Ebbing, see in particular H. Oosterhuis, *Stepchildren of Nature: Krafft-Ebbing, Psychiatry and the Making of Sexual Identity* (Chicago, 2000).

The response to Douglas is well discussed in Doan, *Fashioning Sapphism*.

"Provoked a storm of comment . . .": cited and discussed in Doan, *Fashioning Sapphism*, 114.

"At this moment . . .": V. Woolf, *Letters*, ed. N. Nicholson and J. Trautman (London, 1973), vol. III, 55.

Anne Lister, *I Know My Own Heart: The Diaries of Anne Lister, 1791–1840*, ed. H. Whitbread (London, 1992); Anne Lister, *No Priest but Love: Excerpts from the Diaries of Anne Lister, 1824–1826*, ed. H. Whitbread (New York, 1992). Anne Lister is discussed in Castle, *The Apparitional Lesbian*; Stephen Colclough, "'Do You Not Know the Quotation?' Reading Anne Lister, Anne Lister Reading," in *Sapphism in the Long Eighteenth Century*, ed. J. Beynon and C. Gonda (Farnham, 2010), 159–72.

"Sophisticated to an extent . . .": Vera Brittain, *Testament of Youth* (London, 2014), 501–2. On the effect of the war, see Doan, *Disturbing Practices*, 97–194.

"You must realize . . .": S. Hicks, *Difficulties: An Attempt to Help* (London, 1922), 262—a book I came across thanks to Medd, *Lesbian Scandal*, 111–14.

CHAPTER 14: CARNAL AFFECTIONS

Notes

"The many strange types . . .": Hicks, *Difficulties*, 260.

"A woman who seeks your wife . . .": Hicks, *Difficulties*, 260–61.

"She is the evil genius . . .": ACB, CXI, 6–7; "The fact really is . . .": ACB, CXIII, 98.

"Resented this intimacy . . .": E. F. Benson, *Final Edition*, 13.

"Because the Victorians saw . . .": Marcus, *Between Women*.

"How I liked him . . .": BFP, 1/79, Friday, March 17, [1898?], 16. The emotions and physicality here are markedly different from, e.g., Muriel Lester and Nellie Dowell as described in S. Koven, *The Match Girl and the Heiress* (Princeton, NJ, 2014).

Smyth, *As Time Went On . . .*, 38.

"Annie and I . . .": cited in Bolt, *As Good as God*, 84.

"Oh that sweet time . . .": BFP, 1/79, 22; "we went home . . .": BFP, 1/79, 22.

"Then I began to love . . .": BFP, 1/79, 29; "complete fascination": BFP, 1/79, 29.

"The restless desire . . .": BFP, 1/79, 38.

"Did you possess me . . .": BFP, 1/79, 28, January 4, 1881; "When one's heart . . .": January 14, 1881.

"Once more & and with shame . . .": BFP, 1/79, October 1, 1896. The best short discussion of this is in Vicinus, *Intimate Friends*, 88–98.

"Where people mistake . . .": V. Woolf, *Letters*, ed. N. Nicholson and J. Trautman (London, 1973), vol. IV, 200.

"These cures . . .": Smyth, *As Time Went On . . .*, 15–16.

"I have always claimed . . .": BFP, 3/38, Mary Benson to Ethel Smyth, September 8, 1889. Again, Vicinus, *Intimate Friends*, 135–41, is excellent on this relationship.
"<u>Don't tell Nellie</u> . . .": BFP, 3/38, October 26, 1889.
"Then there comes . . . <u>But</u>—and here we come . . .": BFP, 3/38, November 7, 1889.
"With great care . . .": BFP, 1/78, November 8, 1899. See E. F. Benson, *Mother*, 225–29.

CHAPTER 15: BE A MAN, MY BOY

Hall, D., ed. *Muscular Christianity: Embodying the Victorian Age.* Cambridge, 1994.

Newsome, D. *Godliness and Good Learning: Four Studies on a Victorian Ideal.* London, 1961.

Vance, N. *The Sinews of the Spirit: The Ideal of Christian Manliness in Victorian Literature and Religious Thought.* Cambridge, 1985.

Notes

On Kingsley, see F. Kingsley, ed., *Charles Kingsley*; U. Pope-Hennessy, *Canon Charles Kingsley: A Biography* (London, 1949); R. Martin, *The Dust of Combat: A Life of Charles Kingsley* (London, 1959); S. Chitty, *The Beast and the Monk: A Life of Charles Kingsley* (London, 1974); J. Klaver, *The Apostle of the Flesh: A Critical Life of Charles Kingsley* (Leiden, 2006)—the titles mark the shifts in interest in Kingsley over the last sixty years.
"Our men are too *peculiar*": A. R. Ashwell and R. G. Wilberforce, *Life of Samuel Wilberforce* (London, 1880–83): vol. II, 367–68, cited in O. Chadwick, *The Founding of Cuddesdon* (Oxford, 1954), 92–93.
"Foster a womanly defence . . .": cited in Chadwick, *Founding of Cuddesdon*, 93.
"Most vehement . . .": M. Kelly, *Froude: A Study of His Life and Character* (London, 1907), 38.
"You cannot understand . . .": cited in Chitty, *The Beast and the Monk*, 55–56.
"Darling, I must confess all . . .": cited in Chitty, *The Beast and the Monk*, 60.
"The races of Egypt . . .": C. Kingsley, *Hypatia* (London, 1904 [1853]), xiv.
On race, see from a vast bibliography (and particularly relevant here) C. Kidd, *The Forging of Races: Race and Scripture in the Protestant Atlantic World, 1600–2000* (Cambridge, 2006); I. Baucom, *Out of Place: Englishness, Empire and the Locations of Identity* (Princeton, NJ, 1999); R. Young, *Colonial Desire: Hybridity in Theory, Culture and Race* (London, 1995); A. McKlintock, *Imperial Leather: Race, Gender and Sexuality in the Colonial Contest* (London, 1995); George Stocking, *Victorian Anthropology* (New York, 1987); S. Qureshi, *Peoples on Parade: Exhibitions, Empire, and Anthropology in Nineteenth-Century Britain* (Chicago, 2011).
"Mere chaos . . .": Kingsley, *Hypatia*, 476.
On the public school, see J. Roach, *A History of Secondary Education in England, 1870–1902* (London, 1991); C. Stray, *Classics Transformed: Schools, Universities and Society in England, 1830–1960* (Oxford, 1998); J. A. Mangan, *Athleticism in*

the Victorian and Edwardian Public School: The Emergence and Consolidation of an Educational Ideology (Cambridge, 1981); J. A. Mangan, *The Games Ethic and Imperialism: Aspects of the Diffusion of an Ideal* (New York, 1986); J. Richards, *Happiest Days: The Public Schools in English Fiction* (Manchester, 1888); J. Chandos, *Boys Together: English Public Schools 1800–1864* (London, 1985); S. Rothblatt, *The Revolution of the Dons: Cambridge and Society in Victorian England* (Cambridge, 1968); Newsome, *Godliness and Good Learning*; Deane, *Masculinity and the New Imperialism*; J. Bristow, *Empire Boys: Adventures in a Man's World* (London, 1991); D. Randall, *Kipling's Imperial Boy: Adolescence and Cultural Hybridity* (Houndsmills, 2000).

"As to fighting . . .": T. Hughes, *Tom Brown's School Days* (London, 1857), 307–8.
"A man's body . . .": T. Hughes, *Tom Brown at Oxford* (London, 1869), 112–13.
"A poor, sentimental, snobbish romance . . .": ACB, CLIII, 31.
For Edward White Benson's educational relationship to Martin, see Newsome, *Godlinesss and Good Learning*.
"It seemed feminine . . .": ACB, LXII, 14.
"Indeed this afternoon . . .": ACB, LXXXII, 3.
"He has no love . . .": ACB, XCIII, 88.
Waldstein "is so tactless . . .": ACB, XLV, 62; "Does he really like games . . .": ACB, XLVI, 45.
Fred "understands women . . .": ACB, II, 184.
Reads Hugh's letters: ACB, CL, 17.
"For a time, shy . . ." and following quotations from E. F. Benson, *Mother*, 291–96.
"The men of the twenties . . .": Q. Crisp, *The Naked Civil Servant* (New York, 1983), 21.
"Of course, I think it would be <u>most</u> unadvisable . . .": letter of A. C. Benson to E. F. Benson, now in a private collection, cited in Masters, *E. F. Benson*, 213.

CHAPTER 16: "IT'S NOT UNUSUAL . . ."

Notes

"Despised herself for being so conventional . . .": T. Hardy, *Jude the Obscure* (New York, 1896), 230 (Part III, chap. 10). The relation to conventionality is, of course, a deep concern of this book.
"I don't think . . .": Newsome, *On the Edge of Paradise*, 194.

Part III: The God of Our Fathers

The bibliography on Victorian religion is as huge and sprawling as the bibliography on Victorian sexuality. Here, again, is a selection of the books that have been instrumental in forming the background of this section:

Bebbington, D. *Evangelicalism in Modern Britain: A History from the 1730s to the 1980s.* London, 1989.

Bentley, J. *Ritualism and Politics in Victorian Britain: The Attempt to Legislate for Belief.* Oxford, 1978.

Brooks, C. and A. Saint, eds. *The Victorian Church: Architecture and Society.* Manchester, 1995.

Brown, S. *Providence and Empire: Religion, Politics and Society in the United Kingdom, 1815–1914.* Harlow, 2008.

Chadwick, O. *The Victorian Church.* 2 vols. London, 1966.

Chadwick, O. *The Spirit of the Oxford Movement: Tractarian Essays.* Cambridge, 1990.

Gange, D., and M. Ledger-Lomas, eds. *Cities of God: Archaeology and the Bible in Nineteenth-Century Britain.* Cambridge, 2012.

Helmstedter, R., and R. Lightman, eds. *Victorian Faith in Crisis.* London, 1990.

Hilton, B. *The Age of Atonement: the Influence of Evangelicalism on Social and Economic Thought, 1795–1865.* Oxford, 1988.

Hinchcliff, P. *Benjamin Jowett and the Christian Religion.* Oxford, 1987.

Jay, E. *Faith and Doubt in Victorian Britain.* London, 1986.

Jones, T. *The Broad Church: A Biography of a Movement.* Lanham, MD, 2003.

King, B. *Newman and the Alexandrian Fathers: Shaping Doctrine in Nineteenth-Century England.* Oxford, 2009.

Larsen, T. *Contested Christianity: The Political and Social Context of Victorian Theology.* Waco, TX, 2004.

Larsen, T. *Crisis of Doubt: Honest Faith in Nineteenth-Century England.* Oxford, 2006.

Larsen, T. *A People of One Book: The Bible and the Victorians.* Oxford, 2011.

Machin, G. *Politics and the Churches in Great Britain, 1869–1921.* 2nd ed. Oxford, 1987.

Morris, J. *F. D. Maurice and the Crisis of Christian Authority.* Oxford, 2005.

Mullin, R. B. *Miracles and the Modern Religious Imagination.* New Haven, CT, 1996.

Nockles, P. *The Oxford Movement in Context: Anglican High Church-manship, 1760–1857*. Cambridge, 1994.

Parry, J. *Democracy and Religion: Gladstone and the Liberal Party, 1867–1875*. Cambridge, 1986.

Paz, G. *Popular Anti-Catholicism in Mid-Victorian Britain*. Stanford, CA, 1992.

Porter, A. *Religion versus Empire? British Protestant Missionaries and Overseas Expansion, 1700–1914*. Manchester, 2004.

Reed, J. *Glorious Battle: The Cultural Politics of Victorian Anglo-Catholicism*. Nashville, 1996.

Snell, K., and P. Ell. *Rival Jerusalems: The Geography of Victorian Religion*. Cambridge, 2000.

Stanley, B. *The Bible and the Flag: Protestant Missions and British Imperialism in the Nineteenth and Twentieth Centuries*. Leicester, 1990.

Thompson, D. *Cambridge Theology in the Nineteenth Century: Enquiry, Controversy, Truth*. Aldershot, 2008.

Thorne, S. *Congregational Missions and the Making of Imperial Culture in Nineteenth-Century England*. Stanford, CA, 1999.

Toon, P. *Evangelical Theology, 1833–1856: A Response to Tractarianism*. London, 1979.

Wheeler, M. *The Old Enemies: Catholic and Protestant in Nineteenth-Century English Culture*. Cambridge, 2006.

Yates, N. *Anglican Ritualism in Victorian Britain, 1830–1910*. Oxford, 1999.

Zachhuber, J. *Theology as Science in Nineteenth-Century Germany: From F. C. Baur to Ernst Troeltsch*. Oxford, 2013.

CHAPTER 17: IT WILL BE WORTH DYING

Jalland, P. *Death in the Victorian Family*. Oxford, 1999.

Lutz, D. *Relics of Death in Victorian Literature and Culture*. Cambridge, 2015.

Rowell, G. *Hell and the Victorians: A Study of the Nineteenth-Century Theological Controversies concerning Eternal Punishment and the Future Life*. Oxford, 1974.

Wheeler, M. *Death and the Future Life in Victorian Literature and Theology*, Cambridge, 1990.

Notes

Martin's death is discussed at length in Newsome, *Godliness and Good Learning*;
Edward White Benson's account is in Trinity College Library.

"But Martin's death . . .": A. C. Benson, *Edward White Benson*, 268.

"I need not here write . . .": A. C. Benson, *Edward White Benson*, 268–69.

On sin as a grand obsession of Victorian theology, see in particular Hilton, *Age of
Atonement*.

"Inconceivable . . .": Edward White Benson's diary cited in Newsome, *Godliness and Good Learning*, 191–92, and A. C. Benson, *Edward White Benson*, 444.
Archibald Tait, future archbishop of Canterbury and Lucy Tait's father, wrote
a 128-page account of the death of his five daughters from scarlet fever in 1856;
and his wife, Catharine, wrote a 139-page therapeutic diary, which she sent to
Mrs. Wordsworth, close friend to her and to Minnie Benson: see Jalland, *Death*,
128–42. See W. Benham, ed., *Catharine and Crauford Tait, Wife and Son of A. C.
Tait: A Memoir* (London, 1879) for Catharine's account.

"If anything ought . . .": A. C. Benson, *Edward White Benson*, 445.

"He with a sudden momentary look . . .": Edward White Benson's diary, cited in
Newsome, *Godliness and Good Learning*, 187–88.

"As surely as I see this paper . . .": A. C. Benson, *Edward White Benson*, 445.

"My dearest wife . . .": Edward White Benson's diary, cited in Newsome, *Godliness
and Good Learning* 188. On the Good Christian Death, see Jalland *Death in the
Victorian Family* 17–58.

"It takes all my confidence . . .": letter to Canon Crowfoot, cited in A. C. Benson,
Edward White Benson, 445.

"We are learning . . .": letter to Canon Wickenden, cited in A. C. Benson, *Edward
White Benson*, 445.

"I hope that I shall be able . . .": letter to Canon Crowfoot, cited in A. C. Benson,
Edward White Benson, 445.

"The mother's example": letter to Canon Wickenden, cited in A. C. Benson,
Edward White Benson, 445. Bishop Tait also thought his wife's fortitude greater
than his own: "Give me more of that genuine piety with which thou has blest
her," he prayed: Jalland, *Death*, 138.

"My dear wife is wonderfully 'kept . . .'": letter to Canon Westcott, cited in A. C.
Benson, *Edward White Benson*, 445.

"His mother's bearing . . .": Edward White Benson's diary, cited in E. F. Benson, *As
We Were*, 81.

"He is in perfect peace . . .": cited in Newsome, *Godliness and Good Learning*, 188.

"She had . . . a couple of hours . . .": E. F. Benson, *Our Family Affairs*, 75.

"Never . . . did . . . cease . . .": E. F. Benson, *Our Family Affairs*, 75.

CHAPTER 18: THE DEEPER SELF THAT CAN'T DECIDE

Helmstedter, R., and R. Lightman, eds. *Victorian Faith in Crisis.* London, 1990.

Jay, E. *Faith and Doubt in Victorian Britain.* London, 1986.

Larsen, T. *Crisis of Doubt: Honest Faith in Nineteenth-Century England.* Oxford, 2006.

Wolff, R. *Gains and Losses: Novels of Faith and Doubt in Victorian England.* New York, 1977.

Notes

"My human love . . .": BFP, 1/79, 32.
"And now I loved her . . ." BFP, 1/79, 32.
"So we went to Torquay . . .": BFP, 1/79, 32
"Is it not really the same sin . . .": BFP, 1/79, 25.
"Rouse, cleanse, fill . . .": BFP, 1/79, 20.
"I need <u>discipline</u> . . .": cited in Masters, *E. F. Benson*, 43.
"I have come to this . . .": Diary, June 10, 1876, BFP, 1/79, 35.
"An uneasy restlessness . . .": BFP, 1/79, 38.
"Oh <u>don't</u> I understand . . .": letter to Hugh, July 28, 1900, BFP, 3/73.
"I fancied most foolishly . . .": BFP, 1/79, 37.
"O Lor! Hugh, why . . .": letter to Hugh, January 5, 1899, BFP, 3/73.
"Make larger and slower . . .": letter to Hugh, January 16, 1900, BFP, 3/73.
"See the power . . .": A. C. Benson, *Edward White Benson*, 768.
"Later work was utterly different . . .": A. C. Benson, *Edward White Benson*, 769.

CHAPTER 19: OUR FATHER

Notes

"Talked about religion . . .": ACB, VI, 33.
On *In Memoriam* section 33, see J. Mays, "*In Memoriam*: An Aspect of Form," in *Tennyson, In Memoriam: A Casebook*, ed. J. Dixon Hunt (London, 1970), 259–89.
"I fancied that Christian mysteries . . .": F. D. Maurice, *Dialogues between a Clergyman and a Layman on Family Worship* (London, 1862), 182. Schleiermacher's *Christian Dialogue* is a fascinating prelude to these thoughts; for a full background and bibliography, see E. Newey, *Children of God: The Child as Source of Theological Anthropology* (Farnham, 2012).
"He had no idea . . .": ACB, LI, 51.
"You believe in a future life . . .": E. F. Benson, *Rex* (London, 1923), 161.
"How absolutely real . . .": E. F. Benson, *Rex*, 180.
"For the moment . . .": E. F. Benson, *Rex*, 205.
For Hugh's biography, see A. C. Benson, *Hugh*; Grayson, *Robert Hugh Benson*; Martindale, *The Life of Monsignor Robert Hugh Benson*—two volumes and most fully; Watt, *Robert Hugh Benson*. And autobiographically, see R. H. Benson, *Confessions of a Convert*.
"Was an official of a church . . .": R. H. Benson, *Confessions*, 92.
"Mutually exclusive . . .": R. H. Benson, *Confessions*, 93.
"Things that directly . . .": R. H. Benson, *Confessions*, 92.
"More and more . . .": R. H. Benson, *Confessions*, 93.

"Hugh did not find . . .": A. C. Benson, *Hugh*, 130.

"The Catholic believes . . .": A. C. Benson, *Hugh*, 130.

"Hugh was fretted . . .": A. C. Benson, *Hugh*, 131.

"He was identified . . .": R. H. Benson, *Confessions*, 70.

"A church that appeals . . .": R. H. Benson, *Confessions*, 94.

"Humility and singleness of motive . . .": R. H. Benson, *Confessions*, 102.

"Her system worked . . .": R. H. Benson, *Confessions*, 95–96.

"Simplicity itself . . .": R. H. Benson, *Confessions*, 97.

"Began to marvel . . .": R. H. Benson, *Confessions*, 117.

"To return from the Catholic Church . . .": R. H. Benson, *Confessions*, 142.

"If Hugh's father . . .": A. C. Benson, *Hugh*, 138.

"Your father's and your mother's son . . .": Martindale, *Monsignore Robert Hugh Benson*, vol. II, 245.

"I had the wonderful happiness . . .": Edward White Benson, *Diary*, Trinity College, Cambridge, cited in A. C. Benson, *Edward White Benson*, 580.

"His views I can only . . .": ACB, X, 15.

"We discussed with pain . . .": ACB, XVII, 24.

"The moment I get inside . . .": ACB, XXI, 64.

"Hiding really abominable . . .": ACB, XXVI, 67.

"Is like a child . . .": ACB, XXVIII, 39.

"I do feel that his absence . . .": ACB, XXXVIII, 68.

"The one thing Hugh wants . . .": ACB, XXXIV, 32.

"I cannot imagine . . .": E. F. Benson, *Our Family Affairs*, 330.

"As the death of Martin . . .": E. F. Benson, *Our Family Affairs*, 330.

"A soldier of the old fire-eating . . .": Watt, *Robert Hugh Benson*, 3.

"The painful thing . . .": ACB, LXXII, 21.

CHAPTER 20: SECRET HISTORY

Benkovitz, M. *Frederick Rolfe: Baron Corvo*. New York, 1977.

Corvo, Fr. Baron. *Stories Toto Told Me*. London, 1898.

Corvo, Fr. Baron. *In His Own Image*. London, 1924.

Corvo, Fr. Baron. *The Desire and the Pursuit of the Whole: A Romance of Modern Venice*, ed. A Symons. London, 1953.

Corvo, Fr. Baron. *The Venice Letters*, ed. C. Woolf. London, 1974.

Rolfe, Fr. *Hadrian the Seventh*. Harmondsworth, 1963.

Scoble, R. *Raven: The Turbulent World of Baron Corvo*. Devizes, 2013.

Scoble, R. *The Corvo Cult: The History of an Obsession*. London, 2014.

Symons, A. *The Quest for Corvo*. London, 1952.

Notes

"'Saw red' . . .": Watts, *Robert Hugh Benson*, 86.

"Say your prayers . . .": Watts, *Robert Hugh Benson*, 87.

"Exhaustingly charged . . .": Martindale, *Monsignor Robert Hugh Benson*, vol. II, 96. This friendship is given a Corvine perspective by B. Fothergill, "Rolfe and Benson: A Friendship's Downfall," in *Corvo, 1860–1960*, ed. C. Woolf and B. Sewell (Aylesford, 1961), 47–61.

"Father Benson had . . .": Vyvyan Holland, cited in Symons, *Quest for Corvo*, 173. For the sometimes shocking background to such a pursuit of the mystical, see A. Owen, *The Place of Enchantment: British Occultism and the Culture of the Modern* (Chicago, 2004), especially 186–220.

Benson's books were read by some precisely in their journey toward mysticism: see for the case of Muriel Lester, S. Koven, *The Match Girl and the Heiress* (Princeton, NJ, 2014), 212–13.

"Infernal exorcist . . .": ACB, LXIII, 63.

"A stuttering little Chrysostom . . .": Corvo, *Desire and the Pursuit*, 41. O. K. Parr, *Robert Hugh Benson: An Appreciation* (London, 1915), 35–36, claims that Hugh represented the collapse of the friendship in the guise of the collapse of the engagement between Enid and Nevill in Benson's novel *Initiation* (London, 1914). She further claims that High wrote to her to confirm this. If true, that he should have chosen to represent Corvo as a dangerous woman, is no doubt part of their complex intimacy.

"Must have been mad . . .": Grayson, *Robert Hugh Benson*, 94. A. C. Benson, *Hugh* 236–37.

"The man's a genius . . .": Watts, *Robert Hugh Benson*, 30.

On Benjamin Aelred Carlyle, see R. Kollar, "Anglo-Catholicism in the Church of England, 1895–1913: Abbot Aelred Carlyle and the Monks of Caldey Island," *Harvard Theological Review* 76 (1983): 205–24; R. Kollar, *Abbot Aelred Carlyle, Caldey Island, and the Anglo-Catholic Revival in England* (New York, 1995); and, in general, the seminal article of D. Hilliard, "Unenglish and Unmanly: Anglo-Catholicism and Homosexuality," *Victorian Studies* 25 (1982): 188–210. The cult of Corvo is discussed in a cultic manner by Scoble, *The Corvo Cult*.

"We had some dear talk . . .": Minnie Benson to Maggie Benson, BFP.

For some rare pictures of Hugh preaching and Hugh's funeral, see B. Warre Cornish, S. Leslie et al., *Memorials of Robert Hugh Benson* (London, 1915).

CHAPTER 21: WRITING THE HISTORY OF THE CHURCH

Chadwick, O. *Edward King: Bishop of Lincoln, 1885–1910.* Lincoln, 1968.

Church of England [E. W. Benson]. *Read and Others v. the Lord Bishop of Lincoln: Judgement Nov. 21, 1890.* London, 1894.

Russell, G. *Edward King: Sixtieth Bishop of Durham, a Memoir.* London, 1912.

Notes

"But how curious the change . . .": Edward White Benson, unpublished diaries, Trinity College, Sunday, March 8, 1891.

"I shall try to be . . .": Russell, *Edward King*, 86.

Victorian church-building: Brooks and Saint, *Victorian Church;* S. Goldhill, *The Buried Life of Things: How Objects Made History in Nineteenth-Century Britain* (Cambridge, 2014), 138–54; with A. Swenson, *The Rise of Heritage: Preserving the Past in France, Germany and England, 1789–1914* (Cambridge, 2013); J. White, *The Cambridge Movement: The Ecclesiologists and the Gothic Revival* (Cambridge, 1962); S. Tschudi-Madsen, *Restoration and Anti-Restoration: A Study in English Restoration Philosophy* (Oslo, 1976); M. Hunter, ed., *Preserving the Past: The Rise of Heritage in Modern Britain* (Stroud, 1996); D. Lowenthal, *The Heritage Crusade and the Spoils of History* (London, 1996).

"It is obvious . . .": G. Scott, *A Plea for the Faithful Restoration of Our Ancient Churches* (London, 1850), 54.

"Arisen from a great . . .": C. Barry, "The Position of Modern Architects in Respect of Architectural Restoration," *The Builder* 36 (1878): 127.

"Holy work . . .": *The Builder* 36 (1878): 1312.

"The exact parallel growth . . .": G. Wightwick, "On the Present Conditions and Prospects of Architecture in England," *Quarterly Papers on Architecture* 2 (1844): 10. On Wightwick, see R. Reid, "George Wightwick: A Thorn in the Side of the Ecclesiologists," in *'A Church as It Should Be': The Cambridge Camden Society and Its Influence*, ed. C. Webster and J. Elliott (Stamford, 2000), 239–57.

"We want *Protestant Churches* . . .": F. Close, *The Restoration of Churches Is the Restoration of Popery* (London, 1844), 17. On Close, see Goldhill, *Buried Life of Things*, 48–50.

On papal aggression, see Paz, *Popular Anti-Catholicism.*

On the Round Church, see Goldhill, *Buried Life of Things*, 45–51, building on White, *The Cambridge Movement;* and E. Rose, "The Stone Table in the Round Church and the Crisis of the Cambridge Camden Society," *Victorian Studies* 10 (1966): 119–44.

Public Worship Regulation Act: see Yates, *Anglican Ritualism;* Bentley, *Ritualism and Politics;* G. Graber, *Ritual Legislation in the Victorian Church of England: Antecedents and Passage of the Public Worship Regulation Act, 1874* (Lewiston, NY, 1993); D. Janes, *Victorian Reformation: The Fight over Idolatry in the Church of England, 1840–60* (Oxford, 2009).

On clergy jailed, see, e.g., M. Reynolds, *Martyr of Ritualism: Father Mackonochie of St Alban's Holburn* (London, 1965).

"Romish Tendencies . . .": J. Hanchard, *A Sketch of the Life of Bishop King: A Manual for Churchmen* (London, 1886); also cited in Russell, *Edward King*, 143–44.

"Happy, holy . . .": Chadwick, *Edward King*, 14.

"So ornate . . . the new mitre . . .": Chadwick, *Edward King*, 16, quoting the *Manchester Guardian* for 1886.

"His gentleness, his lovableness . . .": *Manchester Guardian*, May 7, 1889, quoted in Russell, *Edward King*, 171.

"It is evident that . . .": Russell, *Edward King*, 171.

"In advanced ritual . . .": A. C. Benson, *Edward White Benson*, 237.

"Now I own . . .": A. C. Benson, *Edward White Benson*, 251.

"It is most wretched . . .": A. C. Benson, *Edward White Benson*, 243.

"Was almost ashamed . . .": A. C. Benson, *Edward White Benson*, 237.

On John Kensit, see G. Machin, "The Last Victorian Anti-Ritualist Campaign, 1895–1906," *Victorian Studies* 25, no. 3 (1982): 277–302.

"First chasuble . . .": A. C. Benson, *Edward White Benson*, 124.
"The Church of England . . .": *Guardian* November 26, 1890, discussed in Bentley, *Ritualism and Politics*, 120.

CHAPTER 22: BUILDING HISTORY

Bremner, G. *Imperial Gothic: Religious Architecture and High Anglican Culture in the British Empire, c. 1840–1870*. New Haven, CT, 2013.

Harrison, M. *Victorian Stained Glass*. London, 1980.

Stubbs, W., et al. *The Cornish See and Cathedral: Historical and Architectural Notes*. London, 1889.

Swenerton, M. *Artisans and Architects: The Ruskinian Tradition in Architectural Thought*. Houndsmills, 1989.

Swenson, A. *The Rise of Heritage: Preserving the Past in France, Germany and England, 1789–1914*. Cambridge, 2013.

Swift, M. "Anglican Stained Glass in Cornwall and Its Social Context," *Journal of the Royal Institution of Cornwall* 19 (2009): 7–26.

Tschudi-Madsen, S. *Restoration and Anti-Restoration: A Study in English Restoration Philosophy*. Oslo, 1976.

Notes

"The one man . . .": A. C. Benson, *Edward White Benson*, 180.
On Pearson, see J. Quiney, *John Loughborough Pearson* (New Haven, CT, 1979).
On the Gothic Revival, see R. Hill, *God's Architect: Pugin and the Building of Romantic Britain* (London, 2007); K. Clark, *The Gothic Revival: An Essay in the History of Taste* (New York, 1962); White, *Cambridge Movement*.
"A splendid monument . . .": A. C. Benson, *Edward White Benson*, 692.
On Keble, see K. Blair, *Form and Faith in Victorian Poetry* (Oxford, 2012).
On F. D. Maurice, see Morris, *Maurice*.
On Martyn, see J. Martyn, *Henry Martyn, 1781–1812: Scholar and Missionary to India and Persia: A Biography*, Studies in the History of Missions 18 (Lewiston, NY, 1999); J. Sargent, *The Life and Letters of Henry Martyn* (London, 1819).
On Charles Simeon, see R. Harrison, "The Start and Stop of Simeon," in *King's College Chapel, 1515–2015: Art, Music and Religion in Cambridge*, ed. J.-M. Massing and N. Zeeman (Cambridge, 2014), 221–40.
On Samuel Walker, see K. Hylson-Smith, *Evangelicals in the Church of England, 1734–1984* (Edinburgh, 1989), s.v. Walker.
On A. P. Stanley, see J. Witheridge, *The Excellent Dr Stanley: The Life of Dean Stanley of Westminster* (Norwich, 2013), which replaces earlier biographies; also S. Goldhill, "What Has Alexandria to Do with Jerusalem? Writing the History of the Jews in the Nineteenth Century," *Historical Journal* 59 (2016): 125–51.
"He always recognized . . .": A. C. Benson, *Edward White Benson*, 470.

"Saint and martyr . . .": *Truro Cathedral Guide*, 14th ed. (1949), 12.
On Victorian historiography, see T. Koditschek, *Liberalism, Imperialism and the Historical Imagination: Nineteenth-Century Visions of a Greater Britain* (Cambridge, 2011); R. Koselleck, *Futures Past: On the Semantics of Historical Time*, trans. T. Presner, K. Behnke, and J. Welge (Stanford, CA, 2002); J. Burrow, *A Liberal Descent: Victorian Historians and the English Past* (Cambridge, 1981); P. Bowler, *The Invention of Progress: The Victorians and Their Past* (Oxford, 1989); B. Melman, *The Culture of History: English Uses of Their Past, 1800–1953* (Oxford, 2006); R. Mitchell, *Picturing the Past: English History in Text and Image, 1830–1870* (Oxford, 2000).
"Co-extensive with the nation . . .": A. C. Benson, *Edward White Benson*, 765.
"Many contemporary institutions . . .": A. C. Benson, *Edward White Benson*, 523–24.
"Seemed to be among us . . .": A. C. Benson, *Edward White Benson*, 2.
"The little particles . . .": A. C. Benson, *Edward White Benson*, 572.
"Full . . . of warnings . . .": A. C. Benson, *Edward White Benson*, 690.

CHAPTER 23: FORMS OF WORSHIP

Bentley, J. *Ritualism and Politics in Victorian Britain: The Attempt to Legislate for Belief.* Oxford, 1978.

Blair, K. *Form and Faith in Victorian Poetry and Religion.* Oxford, 2012.

Leighton, A. *On Form: Poetry, Aestheticism and the Legacy of a Word.* Oxford, 2007.

Notes

"If I were a great writer . . .": ACB, LXVIV, 48–49. Not for him great Tennyson's fear, "I dread the losing hold of form"; see Leighton, *On Form*, 63.
"I think in religious matters . . .": ACB, X, 5, December 23, 1901.
"Really strong anti-clerical feeling . . .": ACB, X, 5.
"Makes Englishmen sheepish": ACB, XLIX, 48.
"Being addressed straight to me . . .": ACB, XIV, 43.
"It is really monstrous . . .": ACB, XIV, 31.
"In the sight of the stars . . .": ACB, XIV, 22.
"Skipped chapel . . .": ACB, XV, 2.
"I close these troubled pages . . .": ACB, XV, 54.
"The only strength . . .": ACB, XXI, 69.
"We had an interesting talk . . .": ACB, LIV, 10.
"Religion, what is it? . . .": ACB, LXVIII, 67.
"I can hardly say I am a Xtian . . .": ACB, LXII, 101.
"If I could be sure . . .": ACB, LXVIII, 22.
"I was feeling the fire . . .": ACB, XCVIII, 4.
"I feel utterly and entirely deserted . . .": ACB, XCIX, 26.
"I do indeed desire . . .": ACB, CIV, 51.
"I do thank God . . .": Lubbock, *Diary*, 181.
"My principal interest . . .": ACB, CXXIII, 57.

"I think I am an almost pure agnostic . . .": ACB, CXXIX, 35.

"I wondered about the Resurrection . . .": ACB, CXXXVI, 37.

"Pusey seems to me . . .": ACB, CXXXI, 34.

"If Christ could come again . . .": ACB, CXXXI, 34.

"On the whole, I agree . . .": ACB, CLIX, 38.

"The best kind of Xtianity . . .": ACB, CXXXI, 46.

"Incomparable treasure . . .": A. C. Benson, *Along the Road* (London, 1913), 2.

"Tiny belfried church . . .": A. C. Benson, *Along the Road*, 3–4.

"What a mystery . . .": A. C. Benson, *Along the Road*, 4.

"A hazardous experiment . . .": A. C. Benson, *Along the Road*, 448–49.

"One of my own terrors . . .": A. C. Benson, *Along the Road*, 452.

"That concealment of affection . . .": A. C. Benson, *Along the Road*, 453.

"The old idea . . .": A. C. Benson, *Along the Road*, 454.

"Could there, to any impartial observer . . .": A. C. Benson, *From a College Window*, 240.

"Oh, that I knew . . .": A. C. Benson, *From a College Window*, 250.

"The brilliant sunrise": Olive Schreiner to S. C. Cronwright-Schreiner, May 8, 1908, in *The Letters of Olive Schreiner, 1876–1920*, ed. S. C. Cronwright-Schreiner (London, 1924), 279.

On Olive Schreiner, Amy Levy, and the one dominant perspective, see D. Nord, *Walking the Streets: Women, Representation, and the City* (Ithaca, NY, 1995); R. Livesey, *Socialism, Sex, and the Culture of Aestheticism in Britain, 1880–1914* (Oxford, 2007); S. Ledger and S. McCracken, eds., *Cultural Politics at the Fin de Siècle* (Cambridge, 1995); S. Ledger, *The New Woman*; A. Richardson, *Love and Eugenics*.

On the faddishness of Shaw and the reconstruction of Carpenter, see R. Livesey, *Socialism, Sex and the Culture of Aestheticism*, 102–31.

"A band of April-eyed young brothers . . .": E. F. Benson, *As We Were*, 312.

"But all the evening . . .": E. F. Benson, *As We Are*, 140.

CHAPTER 24: CAPTURING THE BENSONS

Szreter, S., and K. Fisher. *Sex before the Sexual Revolution: Intimate Life in England, 1918–1963*. London, 2010.

Note

"A man of single purpose . . .": Watt, *Robert Hugh Benson*, 192.

Acknowledgments

FRIENDS READ THIS MANUSCRIPT WITH ENCOURAGEMENT
and advice: John Henderson, Helen Morales, Catherine Conybeare.
I owe them much thanks, more than can be expressed here. I have
benefited for the last ten years from my colleagues in two research
projects at Cambridge, "Abandoning the Past in Victorian Britain,"
funded by the Leverhulme Trust, and "The Bible and Antiquity in
19th-Century Culture," funded by the European Research Council.
To the sixteen postdocs, three graduates, and eight senior colleagues
involved in these, much thanks for their continuing contributions to
my education, and, for this book, especial thanks to Gareth Atkins,
Michael Ledger Lomas, and Claire Pettitt. I have spent a good deal
of time researching for this book in the libraries of Magdalene College, Cambridge; Trinity College, Cambridge; and the Bodleian in
Oxford: thanks to all the librarians for making the hours possible
and pleasant.

12/16